Cover photo by Skip Moen

The Clock Tower, St. Mark's Square, Venice

GOD, TIME and the LIMITS of OMNISCIENCE

A Critical Study of Doctrinal Development

Skip Moen, D. Phil.

Oxford University

1979

revised for publication 2010

Dedication

This book is dedicated to the faithful readers of *Today's Word*. When I wrote this study many years ago, I never imagined that anyone would be interested in the conclusions. I was wrong. The persistent cry of these readers to print this work is the real motivation behind bringing it to the public.

Thank you.

A special "Thank you" must go to Rodney Baker of Adelaide who expended considerable effort to edit the manuscript and to Terry Watling of the Cayman Islands who meticulously corrected the dozens of typos.

Skip Moen
September 2010

Table of Contents

Introduction

More than three decades have passed since the original study contained in this book. Nothing in the subsequent research has overturned the development or the conclusions. In fact, further study of the radical differences between a theology based in Greek metaphysics and the experience of God elaborated in Hebrew thought has only served to strengthen the argument that omniscience and its many related doctrines exist as bastions of a worldview absent from the Bible.

Although I was not aware of the brilliant work of Abraham Heschel when I wrote this dissertation, I have subsequently come to love and admire his insights into the Hebraic mind. His chapter, "The Philosophy of Pathos," in *The Prophets*, is the most succinct exposition of my argument. Reading that chapter is a summary of the findings of this research, delivering a death-blow to the Greek presuppositions that support most contemporary Christian formulations of these doctrines. Heschel contends, and I have shown, that early Christian theological development does not flow from the Biblical encounter with God. It flows from pre-Socratic thinking about God. It results in a theology of abstraction and detachment, thoroughly contrasted from the intimate, engaged pathos of the God of Scripture. How Christian thought became so removed from its Biblical roots is yet another saga in the continuing story of ethnic and religious schism. All followers of YHWH have suffered in this tragic affair.

It is my hope that this work will offer more than an historical and logical exercise. Solving puzzles is not the goal. The goal is the revelation of a God who cares, a God who is completely involved in the history of men, a God who *feels* our pathos. Any theology that removes God's intimate connection with us is idolatry for such a god neither hears nor speaks nor empathizes with creation. Such a god is not the God of the Bible – and such a god cannot become the God of our theology without serious consequences.

Skip Moen
Montverde, 2010

"Who knows, God may yet turn and repent, and turn away from His fierce anger, so that we perish not?" Jonah 3:9

SECTION ONE

FROM CHANGE TO TIME

CHAPTER 1

THE THEOLOGICAL BACKGROUND OF IMMUTABILITY

Dealing with the impact of the idea of timelessness in theology is not a simple, straightforward task. Discussions of the meaning and implications of 'eternity' have gone on in the history of Christian doctrine for hundreds of years. In the process, the idea of timelessness has been elaborated within a matrix of other theological affirmations about the nature of God. Each element in this crisscross of thoughts has influenced the others. In order to isolate a single part of the complex, these overlaps must be uncovered. Even with the surgical technique of analysis required for such a task, the result will at best show an elaborated context rather than a single idea. With this in mind, it seems reasonable to begin the dissection with a treatment of several of the more substantial overlaps. In particular, we may see just how influential the development of timelessness was in the history of theology and how deeply rooted its own foundation is in Greek metaphysics if we begin by examining the connections between timelessness, immutability and impassibility. This indirect approach offers two immediate advantages. First, we can readily see some of the important context of timelessness. The precedent here is set by none other than Saint Thomas who claimed that God's eternity followed from His immutability. Secondly, treatment of doctrines in the contextual range surrounding timelessness will allow us to deal with areas which are more familiar to the believer (and perhaps ones which he would be more comfortable asserting). Only then can we gradually build a case for the re-examination of these doctrines.

Aquinas

In addition to the role they play as arguments for God's existence, the famous Five Ways of Thomas Aquinas have a major influence on the direction of the entire *Summa Theologiae*. The substance of these proofs is used to establish many of the divine attributes. They also determine the metaphysical categories for the analysis of divine being. For example, the first of the Five Ways (the argument for a prime mover based on the metaphysics of potentiality and actuality) is used in support of God's immutability, simplicity and perfection. Since Aquinas claims that God's eternity is a logical consequence of His immutability[1], an examination of the logic of God's eternity can begin with Aquinas' discussion of immutability. We shall discover that this leads us back to the first proof in the Five Ways which in turn leads to a commitment to certain underlying Greek concepts. More importantly, we shall find that an elaboration of these underlying metaphysical concepts brings forth a central idea about the nature of God - an idea which is so crucial and persuasive that it pervades the entire history of philosophical and theological thought about the divine.

In the opening discussion of immutability, Aquinas points out that he has already shown God to be the first being[2]. This reference to the first of the Five Ways demonstrates that the argument for immutability is based upon the same categories of motion (or change) as appear

---

[1] St. Thomas Aquinas, *Summa Theologiae,* Vol. 2 "Existence And Nature of God" (Ia. 2-11), trans. By Timothy McDermott (London: Blackfriars, 1964), pp. 135-139.

[2] Ibid., p 127.

in that proof. There he argues that any change in substance is an indicator of two things:[1]

1. the cause of that change must be another substance or entity
2. the potentiality for that change must have already been in the substance or entity changed.

Aquinas further argues that the causal condition necessary for the transition from a potential state to an actual state must be the introduction of influence by something already in the required actual state. If A is to change from potential state x to actual state y, it must be compatible with actual state y (i.e. it must have a y-state potentiality) and it must be affected by some other substance or entity B which is already in an actual state y. Only that which is actual can bring about the transition from potentiality to actuality. It is a contradiction in reason to imagine that a mere potentiality could, in and of itself, produce actual states of change in a substance. That a substance has potentiality is a description of its lack of some state, not of its hidden nature. Consequently, no mere possibility of some state, no lack of something, can be a sufficient condition for the actual production of a state. Aquinas concludes:

> For to cause change is to bring into being what was previously only able to be, and this can only be done by something that already is.[2]

As a consequence, Aquinas is able to assert that it is impossible that any substance should be in the same way and the same respect both moved and mover. "A thing in process of change cannot itself cause that same change; it cannot change itself."[3] The vast array of potentialities for a substance can only be reduced to any given set of

---

[1] Ibid. p. 13, 15.
[2] Ibid., p. 13.
[3] Ibid.

actualities for that substance through some already actualized substance.

This combination of potential and actual states appears to generate an infinite regress of state transitions. But Aquinas argues that this cannot be so, for if there were an infinite regress of necessary actualized states to account for the production of observable present change, no actual change could have ever occurred. For any change to occur there must always be a transition from potentiality to actuality. And such a transition always requires some prior actualized state. No matter how far back in the series of the causal chain one should look, that point would require an actualized state prior to the change. Thus, an infinite series of potential states could never produce the obvious changes which we observe unless one were to introduce at some point in the series an actualized state. And an infinite regress of actualized states seems rationally unsatisfying for in the final analysis each actual state of the regress could be explained by a previous actual state but the regress as a whole could never explain itself. Aquinas argues that the only satisfying explanation is the postulation of a first mover "who is moved by no other".[1]

The connection between this proof for the existence of God and the divine attribute of immutability is obvious. God is the prime mover in the causal chain. He puts the infinite regress to rest because He introduces the requisite actualized state necessary for the production of all other change. But this does not allow the generation of an infinite regress of actual states either for God is pure act, moved by no other. His explanation is to be found in Himself, not in some antecedent condition. Anything that changes does so because it had a potential which is

---

[1] St. Thomas Aquinas, *Basic Writings of Saint Thomas Aquinas*, Vol. One, edited and annotated by Anton C. Pegis (New York: Random House, 1945), p. 22.

actualized. But God, as pure act, must be fully and completely actualized. If He were not, He would have some mixture of potentiality and actuality and then the infinite regress could begin again with the question, "What prior state will allow God to actualize His potentiality?" God, as pure act, has no potentiality, i.e. He does not even have the possibility of change. Whatever God is, He is that in its fully actualized form. He transcends the movement from potentiality to actuality. Since whatever changes must pass from potential to actual, and God is without potential, it is logically impossible for God to change.[1]

If this were the only argument produced in support of immutability, any substantial criticism of the idea of God's unchangeableness in Thomistic theology would have to begin with a discussion of Aristotle's theory of change. Such critiques have occupied the efforts of philosophers and theologians in relation to the proofs for the existence of God.[2] But even though there has been considerable discussion over the success or failure of the Five Ways, we may welcome these criticisms without accepting that they thereby demolish the efforts of Aquinas. It may in fact be the case that the demonstrations of God's existence fail. But for our purposes it does not matter if they do. For we are presently interested in Aquinas' description of God's immutability no matter how that doctrine is supported. We wish to know what Aquinas meant when he said that God was unchangeable. In addition, by pressing Aquinas on the connection between immutability and other attributes of divinity, we can uncover much more fundamental reasons for affirming a doctrine of immutability – reasons which operate regardless of the failure of the Five Ways. Whether

---

[1] Cf. Aquinas, *Summa Theologiae*, Vol. 2, p. 127.

[2] Of the vast literature on the Thomistic proofs see especially Anthony Kenny, *The Five Ways: St. Thomas Aquinas' Proofs of God's Existence* (London: Routledge & Kegan Paul, 1969), pp. 6-33).

or not Aquinas is justified in establishing the doctrine by appealing to the categories of the Five Ways will be important later. Here it is crucial to clearly understand that logic of the doctrine and its relationship to other theological assertions. Let us turn to the other arguments used to establish this doctrine in order to see how they amplify the idea of a prime mover.

In the second argument for immutability, Aquinas reflects on a previous discussion of change and composition. He notes that everything which changes does so in respect of some aspect of its substance, i.e. part of it must remain the same and part of it change if we are to identify the change as a transition from one state of some particular thing to another state of that same thing. If the transition actually resulted in two instantly discontinuous, distinct entities without any intermediate stages, we would find it difficult to identify this as a change in a single substance. We would simply observe two entirely different entities in temporal succession. This would require alterations of the basic notion of change. According to Aquinas, this demonstrates that everything which passes though the transition from potentiality to actuality retains some aspects of its previous state while other aspects are altered. We say that a single substance has changed because we observe this composition of essence and accident. Aquinas concludes that everything which changes must be composite.

Since Aquinas has previously demonstrated that God is simple (not composed of parts), it follows that God's simplicity entails His immutability. The same categories of causality exhibited in the first of the Five Ways play an essential role in the arguments for God's simplicity. Briefly, Aquinas appeals to the discussion of transition from potentiality to actuality to support the claim that God has no body (the prime mover must be pure act without the inherent potentiality ascribable to bodies; God is the most noble of beings and corporeal beings are not as noble as spirits because bodies depend on spirits for their animation[1]), God is not composed of matter and form (matter has potentiality but God is pure act; God's activity as prime mover shows Him to be all form without matter[2]), God is to be identified with His own essence (there are no accidents in God as there are in all materiel entities[3]), and the essence of God is a necessary existent (but all composed things are contingent[4]). Once the idea of a prime mover is accepted, both immutability and simplicity understood within the categories provided by the Aristotelian theory of causality are straightforward logical extensions of the necessarily actualized and actualizing agent.

Aquinas develops one other implication of the first of the Five Ways in his third proof of immutability. He argues that whatever passes through transition from potentiality to actuality acquires, as an actual attributes, what was previously only a possible attribute. And this acquisition is to be seen as a real addition to that substance so that any full description of the substance after that change would include the previously unactualized possibility as a real predicate of the substance. But God is infinite and the infinite perfection of all being. As such He could not acquire anything new nor gain any previously unactualized characteristic. Aquinas understands infinite perfection as logically entailing absolute completeness. Thus, if God is infinitely perfect, He must be fully complete (in whatever predication is appropriate to Him) as He is. God could never gain any attribute or have predicated of Him any new condition for He must have and

---

[1] Aquinas, *Basic Writings*, Vol. One, p. 26.
[2] Ibid., pp. 27-28.
[3] Aquinas, *Summa Theologiae*, Vol. 2, pp. 29,31,39,41.
[4] Ibid., pp. 31,33,35.

always have had each of the appropriate divine attributes in its fully complete form.[1] The idea that there might be a fully complete description of God now which differed in some real way from a fully complete description at some previous time is absurd. God simply transcends such state descriptions in that He is and was and always will be what He is - the infinitely perfect necessary being.[2]

Having considered the arguments of Aquinas, we can clearly see their dependency on Aristotelian metaphysics. We might suspect that the theory of causality adopted from Aristotle is the most vulnerable part of the supporting framework of Thomistic theology. We have certainly seen that the causal categories of the first proof are found throughout the discussions of immutability and simplicity. As is widely acknowledged, the emergence of modern science has called in question the adequacy of these categories. But fruitful as such a critique might appear to be, I believe that there is a much more fundamental concept still to be unearthed from this metaphysical footing. While it does not lie as close to the surface as concepts like potentiality and actuality, it nevertheless is absolutely crucial for the development of a theology of God following Thomistic lines. The fact that modern day Thomists can deal with the basic attributes of God in the same manner as St. Thomas in spite of the domination of modern physics in the empirical world should make us wary of dismissing the whole Thomistic enterprise as outmoded Aristotelianism. Moreover, we must be particularly cautious when we consider that fact that even though "proofs" of God's existence have fallen on hard times both philosophically and theologically,

---

[1] Aquinas, *Summa Theologiae*, Vol. 2, p. 127.
[2] As we shall see, Aquinas holds this doctrine on the basis of a connection with timelessness, not infinite time (as might be implied in the language of this description).

theologians continue to assert many of the same attributes of divinity found in the *Summa*. This at least points to the possibility that the foundation of the continued theological attestation to the divine attributes lies not with the rather obvious causal categories of Aristotle but with something even deeper and more intuitive in our thinking about God. Therefore, we need to remove this outer layer and reveal the central core of this thought pattern by examining the history of these arguments- back in time from Aquinas to the Greeks. This can be accomplished by tracing the now concealed elements in the Thomistic arguments for immutability back to their sources. In the process, we shall consider the arguments found in Boethius, Anselm and Augustine before we explore the Greek heritage.

Boethius

     Finding sustained arguments for the divine attributes in the works of Boethius is not an easy task. *The Consolation of Philosophy*[1] does contain many arguments set in Socratic dialogue but these are intended to guide the reader toward the worship of God. They are not offered as careful, systematic elaborations of the doctrines of the Christian religion. Nevertheless, we may abstract several comments from the various *Theological Tractates*[2] and *The Consolation* which will give us a clear understanding of the meaning of these divine attributes in the work of Boethius.

     It will be helpful to give a rough summary of Boethius' description of the attributes which we wish to examine. On immutability, he says that divine substance is

---

[1] Boethius, *The Consolation of Philosophy*, trans. By S. J. Tester, Loeb Classical Library (Cambridge, Mass: Harvard University Press, 1973).

[2] Boethius, *The Theological Tractates*, trans. by H.F. Stewart, E. K. Rand and S. J. Tester, Loeb Classical Library (Cambridge, Mass: Harvard University Press, 1973).

without matter or motion[1], it is form without matter[2], it is one unity of essence and existence[3] "abiding, unmoved, and immovable" in eternity[4], and it abides "from eternity and unto eternity without any change."[5]

> For such is the form of the divine substance that it does not slip away into external things, nor does it receive anything external into itself but as Parmenides says of it:
>> Like the body of a sphere well-rounded on all sides, it turns the moving circle of the universe while it keeps itself unmoved.[6]

There is one rather lengthy development along the lines of Aquinas' argument for the prime mover in Book IV of *The Consolation*, although it would be misleading to suggest that it had the same consistent elaboration as the first of the Five Ways. In general, Boethius argues for divine being on the grounds that only such a being could keep the diversity of the universe from flying apart at the seams.[7] But in this particular passage he state that:

> The generation of all things, and the whole development of changeable natures, and whatever moves in any manner, are given their causes, order and forms from the stability of the divine mind. That mind, firmly placed in the citadel of its own simplicity of nature, established the manifold manner in which all things behave. And this manner, when it is contemplated in the utter purity of the divine intelligence, is called providence, . . .

---

[1] Boethius, *Tractates, De Trinitate,* p. 9.
[2] Ibid., p.11.
[3] Ibid.
[4] Ibid., p.23.
[5] Boethius, *Tractates, De Fide Catholica,* p. 57.
[6] Boethius, *Consolation,* Bk. III, Part XII, p. 307.
[7] Ibid., Bk. III, Part XII, p. 299.

For in the same way as a craftsman first conceives in his mind the form of the thing he is able to make and then puts the work into effect, . . just so God by providence disposes what is to be done in a single and unchanging way, . . .[1]

Turning to the discussion of simplicity, Boethius suggest that God has no accidents[2], no difference or plurality[3], is not composite[4], is by nature a unity of one[5] possessing existence as the nature of His being.[6] He states these descriptions as articles of faith. His demonstrations of their appropriateness are intertwined with the passages on God as the unmoved mover, God as the highest Good, as the Form of the Good[7] and the greatest conceivable being.[8] One instance where several of these affirmations are combined occurs in the poem at the end of Part IX of Book III of *The Consolation*.

O you who in perpetual order govern the universe,
Creator of heaven and earth, who bid time ever move,
And resting still, grant to all else;
Whom no external causes drove to make
Your work of following matter, but the form
Within yourself of the highest good, ungrudging; from a heavenly pattern
You draw out all things, and being yourself most fair,
A fair world in your mind you bear, and forming it
In the same likeness, bid it being perfect to complete itself
In perfect parts . . .[9]

---

[1] Ibid., Bk. IV, Part VI, pp. 357, 359.
[2] Boethius, *Tractates, De Trinitate*, p. 29.
[3] Ibid., p. 13.
[4] Boethius, *Tractates, Quomodo Substantiae*, p. 43.
[5] Boethius, *Consolation*, Bk. III, Part X, p. 281.
[6] Boethius, *Tractates, Quomodo Substantiae*, p. 43.
[7] Cf. Boethius, *Consolation*, Bk. III, Parts IX and X.
[8] Boethius, *Consolation*, Bk. III, Part IX, p. 277.
[9] Ibid., Bk. III, Part IX, pp. 271, 273.

With this collection in mind, what can be said about Boethius' treatment of the doctrine of immutability? He generally agrees with the formation of Aquinas in his description of God as the unmoved mover, pure form, uncomposed and a unity of essence and existence. That such descriptions are reiterated and justified in the work of Aquinas should not seem surprising since both of these theologians lean heavily upon similar Greek foundations. Because Boethius offers no well developed proofs for the doctrine of immutability of the order of those found in the *Summa*, we must ask if he contributes anything to the understanding of this doctrine rather than press him for some elaborate justification of the doctrine. In that regard, we notice that the connection between immutability and simplicity is quite apparent. It is because God possesses being and existence as a unity that He can have no accidents, and having no accidents, He is forever fixed in His nature and purposes. It is unnecessary for God to experience change as His understanding and actions are established in eternity which transcends the temporal order altogether.[1] In fact, the poem at the end of Book III, Part IX suggests that God even has some direct causal influence on time itself which He remains outside its transitions and implications.[2] Out of the simplicity of God's nature comes the generation of all things. Yet this simplicity knows no other pre-existent cause.[3] It is the unfolding of the form of the Good itself.[4] The connection between *timelessness* (timeless eternity) and immutability, impassibility and personhood will be treated in great detail later. It is enough

---

[1] Boethius, *Tractates, De Trinitate,* p. 23 in a parenthetical remark. Also compare the discussion of eternity in Book V, Parts III and VI.

[2] Boethius, *Consolation*, Bk. III, Part IX, p. 271. In particular consider the connection between time and motion in this passage.

[3] Notice the Aristotelian language of "You *draw out* all things".

[4] Cf. Boethius, *Consolation*, Bk. III, Parts IX and X.

at this point to recognize that Boethius spends more than two entire chapters of the fifth Book discussing this matter in connection with the problem of foreknowledge and free will. The importance which he gives to the notion of simplicity as a background to the doctrine of immutability points to another element in the theological context. That element is first alluded to in the quotation from Parmenides. In that passage, Boethius moves from divine substance without accidents or temporal contingencies to the unmoved mover. As he makes this transition, he employs the Parmenidean image of the sphere. This image is deliberately chosen for its connection with the Greek concept of perfection. And that concept has a powerful influence on the work of all of the early theologians.

Before examining the idea of perfection, however, it is important to treat the development of the divine attributes in two other early Christian thinkers - Anselm and Augustine. Since these two men draw heavily from Platonic concepts, any parallel ideas encountered in their discussions will enable us to strengthen our critique of the Greek foundation. Although we shall attempt to draw particularly on those passages dealing with the doctrines of immutability and simplicity, we must at the same time keep a watchful eye for connections with the idea of perfection. Ultimately the interconnected matrix of all of these concepts will provide the justification for speaking about God's unchangeableness as a foundation for timeless existence.

Anselm

When we turn our attention to the theology of St. Anselm, it would seem quite natural if we were to concern ourselves solely with a discussion of the famous proof in the *Proslogion.*[1] Anselm's development of the Ontological Argument has had a seminal place in discussion of the existence of God since its inception, and the debate over its validity rages as hotly today as it did with Gaunilo. Moreover, we certainly could find ample material there for analysis of the doctrine of perfection and rational completeness. However, for our purposes we are not so much interested in the logic of this famous piece of reasoning as in the picture of God which emerges from it. In order to give that picture the context it deserves, we must first turn to the arguments for God's existence in the *Monologion.*[2] For Anselm, these proofs of God's existence were not exercises in logical reasoning for the thinker's sake; rather, they were the development of rational analysis of the Christian faith for the believer. Anselm was convinced that reason could provide the ordered steps for the proofs of truths which faith already held with spiritual certainty. His treatment of the divine proofs and his understanding of the God who is revealed through then reflects this position. Anselm followed Augustine in his epistemological theory of the interrelation of faith and reason. But this debt to his predecessor was not limited to strictly epistemological matters. Augustine formed this theology in the network of Platonism and Anselm's proofs reflect this tradition as well. By turning to the proofs found in the *Monologion*, we shall be able to see what effect this combination had on his description of the nature of God.

Two distinct Arguments appear in the *Monologion*, the first from the comparative idea of goodness and the second from the existence of material objects. In both of these arguments a similar pattern emerges. Each proof presupposes that explanations of attributes and qualities in

---

[1] Anselm, *Anselm of Canterbury,* Vol. One, trans. by Jasper Hopkins and Herbert Richardson (London: SCM Press, 1974), pp. 89-112.
[2] Anselm, *Anselm of Canterbury*, Vol. One, pp. 3-86.

substances depend upon the existence of universals. This assumption is derived from the notion of participation developed in Plato's theory of the Forms. Anselm makes no attempt to justify this basic assumption. He merely employs it as part of his inheritance. When he constructs a proof of God's existence from the comparative term 'goodness', he relies on the premise that " . . . all other proofs are good through something other than what they are and that this alone is good through itself."[1] The same concept of participation is employed in the proof from existence.

> For whatever is exists either through something or through nothing. But it is not the case that anything exists through nothing . . . Thus, whatever is exists only through something.[2]

These arguments warrant belief in one thing which is good in itself and exists through itself. They are then combined to show that whatever exists through itself "exists most greatly of all".[3] And whatever exists most greatly of all is appropriately described as "supremely good, supremely great, the highest of all existing things".[4] Anselm deduces that whatever has ascribed to it the predicates 'supremely good', 'supremely great', and 'highest of all existing things' can only be a singular supreme being. "And this nature is the Supreme Good, the Supreme Greatness, the Supreme Being (*ens*), or Substance (*subsistens*) --- . . ."[5]

After establishing the category of predicate attributes of this Supreme Being, Anselm discusses the question, "What can and cannot be predicated of the

---

[1] Anselm, *Monologion*, p. 6.
[2] Ibid., p. 7.
[3] Anselm, *Monologion*, p. 8.
[4] Ibid.
[5] Ibid., p. 10.

Supreme Being substantively?"[1]   We might have entertained some suspicions about this question. If there is a Supreme Being, it is legitimate to inquire about its nature. But answers to such an inquiry could take two distinct and diverging paths. On the one hand, we could understand 'Supreme' as "the top of our own ladder", so to speak. In that case, we should have no trouble extrapolating predicates we normally use of human conditions. But the Supreme Being would then be no more than a super-man, although perhaps not tainted by the vices of certain historical examples of such supermen, e.g. the Greek gods. It is certain that Anselm did not entertain this understanding of the Christian God. He developed the second of the two paths. On that road, the Supreme Being must occupy a place of complete and absolute perfection, of highest logically possible value (although Anselm occasionally suggests that even this is not enough). In that case, no actual human predicate can truly describe the nature of God for whatever positive predicate is used, it will ultimately fall short because it remains only a human conception. Anselm makes this clear when he remarks:

> Thus, although the Supreme Nature can be spoken of relationally as supreme over all things or as greater than all things which it created (or spoken of relationally in some similar way), [these utterance] do not, it is obvious, designate its natural being.[2]

It is also obvious to Anselm that of those relational terms to point vaguely in the direction of divinity, only terms which are qualified as being "better to be than not to be"[3] may be appropriately applied to the Supreme Being. This qualification serves to guarantee that the Supreme Being

---

[1] Ibid., p. 22.

[2] Anselm, *Monologion,* p. 23.

[3] Ibid., p. 24.

will be spoken of as supremely good, true, just, powerful, wise, etc. but not as supremely evil, unjust, deceitful, or the like. In other words, even though our language as creaturely is too inferior to speak substantively of the Creator, what expressions we do use to point hesitantly in the direction of the Supreme Being can do so only if they are restricted to the noble or ethically superior qualities for "the Supreme Nature is supremely whatever good thing it is".[1]

Armed with this strong version of God's transcendence, Anselm comments on the divine attributes of simplicity, eternity and immutability. Because they belong to the group of predicates of the *via negativa*, these terms do not fall prey to the complaint that they are unworthy creaturely attempts to speak of the divine. Quite literally, they tell us what God is not. What we discover, according to Anselm, is that God is not composed, without beginning and end (in a quite special sense, as we shall see), and not mutable. Composition is an indicator of dependence for everything composite owes its existence to its parts. Because the Supreme Nature is totally independent, it must be simple.[2] That many different goods may be predicated of the supreme Nature does not indicate its composite being. On the contrary, ""All those goods must be one rather than many. Hence, any one of them is the same as all the others --- . . ."[3] And of God's eternity, Anselm says:

> . . . if the Supreme Nature were to have a beginning or an end it would not be true eternity - something which we have already uncontestably found it to be. Or again, let anyone who can, try to conceive of when it began to be true, or was ever not true, that something was going to exist. Or [let him try to

---

[1] Ibid., p. 26.
[2] Anselm, *Monologion*, pp. 26-27.
[3] Ibid., p. 27.

conceive of] when it will cease being true and will not be true
that something existed in the past. Now, if neither of these
things can be conceived, and if both statements can be true
only if there is truth, then it is impossible even to think that
truth has a beginning or an end . . . truth cannot be confined
by any beginning or end. Consequently, the same conclusion
with regard to the Supreme Nature, because the Supreme
Nature is the Supreme Truth.[1]

This is the third of three arguments of Chapter
Eighteen on eternity. It clearly shows Anselm's connection
between God and the idea of an ultimate (Platonic) Truth.
The other two arguments develop notions of causal
dependence for anything which has a beginning or end.[2]
Immutability is discussed in relation to the categories of
substance and accident. Since the supreme Nature is "in
every respect substantially identical with itself"[3], it can
never admit accidents of its nature which could cause any
change to itself. However, Anselm does allow that we may
speak of the supreme Nature as sometimes characterized by
predicates which seem to us to be accidental (e.g. Biblical
anthropomorphic expressions of God's feelings and
personality). But these characterizations are improperly
called accidents since the Supreme Being can "never in any
respect even accidentally [be] different from itself".[4]

Anselm makes two significant additions in the
Proslogion. The first can be treated rather quickly since it
obviously follows from the previous elaboration of
immutability. In Chapter Eight, he introduces the idea that
God is impassible.[5] This creates some difficulty for the
Christian believer's concept of God since that same God is
claimed to be merciful in His treatment of sinners.

---

[1] Anselm, *Monologion*, pp. 28-29.
[2] Ibid., pp. 27-28.
[3] Ibid., p. 40.
[4] Anselm, *Monologion*, p. 41.
[5] Anselm, *Proslogion*, pp. 97-98.

Anselm's remarks do not attempt to justify the attribute 'impassible'. Rather, they attempt to reconcile the apparent contradiction of the claim that God is both merciful and impassible. What he says by way of reconciliation will be treated later. That he recognizes impassibility to be a direct consequence of immutability has immediate importance. We see that the development of a theology of God which begins with a fundamental belief in a strong doctrine of transcendence can easily deduce immutability, impassibility and simplicity as consequences of the transcendental nature. This strong transcendence is nowhere more apparent in Anselm that in the second significant addition of the *Proslogion* - the Ontological Argument.[1]

We need not enter into the history of critical debate[2] over this proof in order to recognize that it views God in a truly unique fashion. The famous phrase of the argument indicates Anselm's belief that reason could vindicate the truth of the faith. God is "that than which a greater cannot be thought". As such, He is the one and only necessary being. But more than that, He exceeds whatever humble attribution we may ascribe to Him. As that than which none greater can be thought, He is absolutely perfect, lacking in His nature nothing good whatsoever.[3] Anselm's earlier treatment of the comparative attribute 'goodness' established the claim that "God is whatever it is better to be than not to be".[4] In this regard, Anselm considers it better

---

[1] Ibid., pp. 93-95.

[2] For a survey of the debate and the literature see John Hick, "Ontological Argument for the Existence of God," *Encyclopedia of Philosophy,* V, 538-542.

[3] Cf. *Monologion*, pp. 6-8; *Proslogion*, pp. 99, 104 and especially p. 74 where Anselm claims God is strictly ineffable, *greater* than can be thought.

[4] Anselm, *Proslogion*, p. 96.

to be "perceptive, omnipotent, merciful and impassible"[1] than not to be these characteristics. But the most important consequence of the description of God as that than which none greater can be thought is the connection with the treatment of time and space. The crucial passage indirectly claims that God is neither temporally nor spatially located and that these relations are strictly relations of imperfection.

> Now, anything which is at all in space or time is less great than that which is not at all subject to the law of space or time.[2]

This claim is critical to much of the later discussion of omniscience.

Augustine

Finally, we come to the works of Saint Augustine. Here we face a problem almost at the opposite end of the scale from Boethius. With Boethius we were confronted with a limited amount of material written primarily as deliberations by the believer for the worship of God. In Augustine, we face hundreds of pages of material covering every format from developed theological treatises to personal letters. Even so, several representative quotations will provide the general framework of Augustine's discussion of the divine attributes.

For Augustine, God is

---

[1] Ibid.
[2] Ibid., p. 102.

the origin of things and the source of their intelligibility, the
reason outside us and within us . . . It is God who carries
within Himself the entire truth-system, in Him the causes and
laws of being and thinking alike have their foundation; . . .[1]
A universal, eternal thought constitutes the norm for the being
and intelligible truth of things. This universal thought is God .
. .[2]

    This connection between the object of faith (God)
and the goal of reason (Truth) has already been
encountered in the work of Anselm. Anselm borrowed the
foundation from Augustine and it is in Augustine that the
full elaboration occurs. As in Anselm, recognition of this
foundation is important because of the impact it has on the
development of a theology of God. In particular,
Augustine draws the connection between God and Truth so
tightly that proving one is proving the other, worshipping
one is worshipping the other.
    Anyone familiar with Augustine will recognize this
doctrine of God and Truth to be a consequence of the deep
influence Neoplatonism had on his thinking. As early as
400 AD he openly acknowledged this debt.[3] In spite of the
fact that some argument could be made for his gradual
understanding that Neoplatonic philosophy and Christian
theology were more deeply divided than he originally
believed, Augustine owes much of his foundation and
framework to Neoplatonic categories. Yet he employed
these in a thoroughly theological way, consistent with his
belief that philosophy had a supportive role to play in the
complete understanding of the faith. With these points in

---

[1] Saint Augustine, *The Happy Life*, in *The Writings of Saint Augustine*,
trans. by Ludwig Schopp (New York: CIMA Publishing Co., 1948),
Vol. I, p. 16, an introductory remark by the editor, Ludwig Schopp.
[2] Ibid., p. 17.
[3] Cf. Augustine, *Confessions*, trans. by Vernon J. Bourke (New York:
Father of the Church, Inc. 1953), Bk. VII, Chapters 9 (pp. 176-180) and
20 (p. 190).

mind, it will be important to discriminate carefully between the philosophical background to any particular Augustinian doctrine and the theological use made of that background, for they are not always the same.

Turning our attention to the particular attributes of our study, we find that Augustine's understanding of God's nature is compatible with the theological treatments we have already reviewed.   In relation to the doctrine of immutability, he says that God is being in its truest form, i.e. "a nature which subsists in itself and is altogether changeless".[1] God's nature "remains always the same, is identical with itself throughout and cannot be corrupted or altered in any part, and . . . is not subject to time, nor different now from what it used to be."[2]

Under these descriptions, he calls God "perfect and immutable", and "so to speak, irreversible".[3] God exists as

> an eternal and changeless form which keeps such changeable things from loosing their existence and enables them to pass, as it were, through the phases of their temporal duration by the regularity of their movements and their separate and varied forms.   Such a form is neither circumscribed by place nor spread, as it were, through space; nor is it extended or changed in the course of time.[4]

---

[1] Augustine, *De Moribus Ecclesiae Catholicae Et De Moribus Manichaeorum (The Catholic and Manichaean Ways of Life)*, trans. by Ronald A. Gallagher and Idella J. Gallagher (Washington, D.C.: Catholic University of America Press, 1966), II, 1, 1 (p. 65).
[2] Ibid.
[3] Ibid., I, 13, 23 (p. 21).
[4] Augustine, *De Libero Arbitrio (The Free Choice Of The Will)* in *The Teacher, The Free Choice OF The Will, Grace And Free Will*, trans. by Robert P. Russell (Washington, D.C.: Catholic University of America Press, 1968), II, 16, 44 (pp. 153-154).

Immutability is the consequence of God's existence as unchangeable Truth[1], the form that gives being and existence to all other entities[2], the primary condition for any transition in changeable substances[3]. Since God is Being in the highest sense, perfect and self-sufficient, He must be pure essence without accident[4]. Not only does He remain absolutely unchangeable", it is logically impossible that He ever could undergo change.[5]

With the same Aristotelian categories, Augustine speaks of God's simplicity as not composite, sufficient in itself, not subject to any change in substance or nature. We need not repeat the previous arguments in order to see how such a doctrine arises in conjunction with the claim that God absolutely cannot change. Augustine closely links considerations of time and temporality with these strong doctrines of immutability and simplicity. In several different works, when he summarizes these views on God's attributes, all of these factors play leading roles. For example, in *De Utilitate Credendi*, he lists the attributes as descriptive phrases. Among these he includes the propositions that God is not the author of evil, has never repented of any act, never deceives, is invisible, incorporeal and uncreated, cannot change in substance or nature and is "not troubled by any stormy disturbance of the soul".[6] Even clearer is the rational invocation of Book V of *De Trinitate*.

---

[1] Ibid., II, 12, 33 (p. 142).

[2] Ibid., II, 17, 46 (pp. 155-156).

[3] Ibid., II, 17, 45 (pp. 154-155).

[4] Augustine, *De Trinitate (The Trinity)*, trans. by Stephen McKenna (Washington, D.C.,: Catholic University of America Press, 1963), V, 2, 3 (p. 177) and V, 4, 5 (P. 179).

[5] Ibid.

[6] Augustine, *De Utilitate Credendi (The Advantage of Believing)*, trans. by Luanne Meagher (New York: Fathers of the Church, Inc.,), 18, 36 (p. 441).

> Accordingly, let us think of God, if we are able, and insofar as we are able, in the following way: as good without quality, as great without quantity, as the Creator who lacks nothing, who rules but from no position, and who contains all things without external form, as being everywhere without limitation of space, as eternal without time, as making mutable things without any change in Himself, and as a Being without passion.[1]

Finally, a passage from *De Libero Arbitrio* demonstrates the strong connection with the idea of perfection.

> Anyone who does not believe that God is Almighty or absolutely unchangeable, or that He is the Creator of all things good, though surpassing them in excellence, or that He is also a most just Ruler of all that He has created, or that He has need of no other nature in creating, as if He were not sufficient unto Himself – such a one does not hold God in the highest esteem.[2]

As justification for these descriptions of God's nature, Augustine primarily employs an argument from his theory of knowledge. It is true that some occasional anticipation of the later Thomistic proofs do occur (e.g. when Augustine discuses change and concludes that everything that changes must be capable of receiving form, but since nothing can give form to itself, there must be an immutable and everlasting form giver who is God[3]). However, these arguments from observable elements in the world take a subordinate role to arguments concerning the powers and goals of reason. In fact, after a very lengthy discourse on the proof of God's existence from reason, Augustine makes the following typical remark:

---

[1] Augustine, *De Trinitate*, V, 1, 2 (p. 176).
[2] Augustine, *De Libero Arbitrio*, I, 2, 5 (pp. 75-76).
[3] Ibid., II, 17, 45 (pp. 154-155).

You granted that if I could prove that there was something above our minds, you would admit it was God, provided that there was still nothing higher. I agreed and stated that it would be enough for me to prove this point. For if there is anything more excellent, than this is God; if not, then truth itself is God.[1]

In spite of different approaches, the four theologians we have examined propose strikingly similar arguments for and understandings of the divine attributes. This unanimity may now be summarized under five basic themes in order to reveal the consistent underlying presuppositions of the arguments we have examined.

---

[1] Ibid., II, 15, 39 (p. 148).

CHAPTER 2

ARGUMENTS FOR IMMUTABILITY

The Five Themes

In both the Thomistic-Aristotelian and the Augustinian-Platonic developments, the doctrine of divine immutability is inextricably interwoven with the ideas of divine simplicity and perfection. While we have concentrated our exegetical efforts on the first two of these three, the idea of perfection has never been very far away from the discussion. In fact, as we elaborated the continuous themes which run through all four theologians, we found that the idea of perfection was very influential. Immutability is to be seen in relation to this context. We may summarize the various arguments encountered thus far in the following way:

> {1} Immutability is a consequence of God's infinity. To be infinite is to be absolutely complete. Nothing can be added to or taken away from absolute completeness. Since change always involves adding to or taking away, God cannot be subject to the categories of change.
>
> An important subset of this theme is the Thomistic development of potentiality and actuality. God as infinite is completely self-sufficient. In this sense, self-sufficiency does not relate to causal independence but to the idea that God can lack nothing essential to His nature; He is without potential. Since change always requires transition from potentiality to actuality, God as pure act cannot change.

{2} Immutability is a consequence of God's necessity. To assert that God is necessary is to say that He exists non-contingently. Anything that changes is contingent because the change must be accounted for in terms of temporally located state descriptions which are open to continuous revision. That is to say, no full explication of contingent existence is possible. But God's existence depends on nothing outside Himself. And this non-contingent existence means that a full explication of God is logically possible (at least for God). Thus, no temporal transition could have any effect on such an explication. And so we cannot assert that God could change.

{3} Immutability is a consequence of God's simplicity. Anything that changes does so through a transition of parts. A substance changes in some respect by an alteration in some part or parts of its nature. Identity is established through change by the constancy of parts which remain unaltered. But God's identity is a single unity identical with itself. That is to say, God's nature is undifferentiated, pure essence. Since only composite things have the parts necessary for change, anything which exists without composition cannot change. God exists without composition, therefore He cannot change.

{4} Immutability is a consequence of God's independence. This theme does not restate the ontological independence of God's necessary existence. What it draws attention to is God's role as the Creator. Since God both creates and sustains the world, His independence from it is an independence in kind, not in degree (in the presence or absence of creation, God is still God). Therefore, it would be demeaning to God's status as Creator to suggest that He was in any way dependent on the world. Anything which is an essential characteristic of the created order cannot be a characteristic of the Creator[1]. For the Creator is not subject to any of the limitations of His finite creation. Coming to be and passing away is most certainly an essential characteristic of the creation. Since coming to be (generation) and passing away (corruption) is the essence of change, change can only belong to the created order, not to God the Creator.

{5} Immutability is a consequence of God's nature as the True and the Good. God's nature is the ultimate source of all appearances in the created world. In particular, it is the perfect and total expression of the True and the Good. Whatever changes does so insofar as it participates in the ultimate Forms, but these Forms themselves have no need to change since they are the perfect and final expressions of essence as they are. God is the ultimate expression of the Forms. As Creator, He embodies every perfect essence. Just as absolute Goodness and ultimate Truth cannot change, so God cannot change.

These five themes are not intended to operate as independent and isolated arguments. Even a cursory reading will show that significant overlaps occur. What they do show is a condensation (and occasional modernization) of the continuity of arguments we have encountered from Aquinas to Augustine.

---

[1] It is, of course, trivially true that any necessary truth of existence applies to both God and His creation (e.g. whatever is, is what is and not something else). But it should be obvious that {4} attempts to capture the class of synthetically true predicates, not analytic (logically necessary) truths.

Infinity

There are two possible interpretations regarding the final role of the *via negativa* and they must not be confused. The first is to read doctrines that employ negative terms as claims about the applicability of our religious discourse to the *nature* of God. This is the approach adopted by Boethius and Augustine. Most modern Thomists see Aquinas in this camp. Here the use of a negative predicate really is an attempt to say something about what God is, conditioned by the limitations of *human* language in speaking about the *divine*. Therefore, the result is a positive theology although the route is somewhat in reverse. But the second approach is an attempt to deal not with the nature of God but with what can be *said* about God. It is a logical rather than an ontological thesis. A negative predicate is read as a claim about the logical status of religious language. Thus, *via negativa* statements are *not* statements about the nature of God but are statements about what we as finite beings must *say* that He is not. There is no imputed ontology. Under this interpretation, to say that God is eternal is not to say with Boethius that God is in His nature non-temporal but to say that we as finite must deny that God has any temporal categories (that God is beyond our categories of time). Immutability becomes the claim that God is beyond the categories of change. But this could not be understood as a claim that God cannot change if that means He is at rest (in opposition to change) for 'rest' is also a category of change. Any implication that God is at rest would entail that He is subject to the categories of change.

A similar argument would hold for other *via negativa* predicates. These interpretations can be attacked in two ways. The first approach leans toward mysticism. We might question the reasonableness of a theology that denies human language access to the divine but wishes to speak about the divine nature. This critique is clearly applicable to Boethius and Augustine and perhaps Anselm. But Saint Thomas is another story. Under the first interpretation, he will fare no better, but under the second interpretation, we must show either that he has the wrong categories (which would still leave positive theology vacuous) or that his logical denial is wrong, i.e. that the categories he denies are applicable to God *must in fact* be applied to God. We shall attempt to show that the very logic of the idea of a Biblical God cannot be rescued without application of the "finite" categories. We will examine the doctrines in terms of their ontological implications while making note of the logical categories they reveal. We will argue that both of these interpretations of the *via negativa* fail.

Let us examine each of the five themes put forth by Aquinas in greater detail. The first, that immutability is a consequence of God's infinity, asserts that the meaning of the term 'infinite' applied to God entails that He cannot change. What, then, is understood by the term 'infinite'? God's infinity is one of the predicates of the *via negativa*. The emphasis of these predicates is not to say what God is in any direct manner but to say what it is that God is not (and *perhaps* with qualification to imply something about what God is). To say that God is infinite is to say that He is not limited in any way. When theologians discuss Man's condition as finite, they usually speak of this in terms of spatial restriction, temporal span and ontological dependence. A man can only be in one place at one time. He is born at some specific time, lives for some specific duration and dies at some specific time. And his life is not of his own making. He is dependent on many other things for his very being, not least of which (assert theologians) is the sustaining power of God. In addition, Man is restricted in his abilities. He cannot do everything. He does not know everything. And he is far less morally good than he knows he ought to be. Man is ontologically, physically, epistemologically and morally limited. But God is infinite. Consequently, He is not limited in any of the ways which mark the limitations of finitude. God can do everything, does know everything, is not dependent in any way and expresses the perfect moral relation between what He is and what He ought to be.

Since God is unlimited, He is absolutely complete. To be without limits means to be fulfilled in every way. If God were to change, such a change would either have to add something to this unlimited existence or remove something from this unlimited existence. But obviously one cannot add anything to an unlimited existence. So if God were to change in such a way that something was added to His essence that could only mean that in the state prior to the change God was not unlimited in existence. This entails that prior to the change God was not God since He is by definition unlimited. Since an unlimited existence cannot lack anything, it is absurd to believe that anything could be added to God's nature. In like manner, if God were to change in such a way that something which He previously had was taken away from His nature, that would mean that God was no longer unlimited in existence. Change of a positive or negative sort is incompatible with the major premise that God is infinite. Since neither type of change is consistent with the assertion of God's infinity, it follows that God logically cannot change. *Per impossible*, if God were to change He would cease to be God.

Categories of actuality and potentiality are developments of a subset of the notion of God's infinity because they operate from the same definitions. If God is infinite, He is completely self-sufficient. Moreover, being infinite mean that God cannot have some quality as a mere potential, for even though it would be possible to say that God did not altogether lack such a quality (since He has it as a potential or latent possibility), this would entail that some possible change in God could actualize this potential and therefore add to the actual description of His infinite actual character. But God's infinity necessarily requires that He must be and have everything that He is. The conjunctive 'and' is not a conjunctive of two separate classes as though it could be read "that He must be (now) and/or have (at some time) . . ." It must be read as identifying two co-extensive and co-eternal classes. What God is He has and what He has He is. Therefore, argues Aquinas, since all change depends on the transition from potentiality to actuality for any substance which has the potentiality for change in the first place, God cannot be said to change nor is it logically possible that He is the kind of being who could change.

Necessity

The second summary theme speaks of God's necessity. This is perhaps the most difficult argument to follow in the literature we have examined. The reason for the difficulty does not lie in the paucity of sources. In fact, this argument receives a great deal of attention not only in the four theologians we have chosen but in continuing developments from these men. The real problem is the language itself. Talk of "necessary being" is itself problematical.[1] Given our present logical and ontological categories, we are not as comfortable with this particular expression as the church fathers were. As a result, most of the strength of the argument is lost in discussions of its semantics and the metaphysics of 'Being'. Rather than attempt to revitalize notions like 'necessary being', I have chosen to formulate the argument in the more

---

[1] Cf. Terence Penelhum, "Divine Necessity" in Basil Mitchell (ed.) *The Philosophy of Religion* (Oxford: Oxford University Press, 1971), pp. 179-190.

contemporary expressions of non-contingency. One might object that such a reformulation weakens the argument. But I find this unconvincing since the general theological character is certainly retained even in this form.

Some modern distinctions about the use of the term 'contingent' must be made immediately. 'Contingent' and 'necessary' are linked in at least two broad contexts. The first of these is the context of events. To say that an event is contingent is to say that it is merely possible, i.e. that it may or may not occur. To say that an event is necessary is to say that such an event must occur, i.e. that it is an instantiation in every possible world. The second context deals with proposition. A contingent proposition is usually treated as a proposition the truth of which may or may not be the case (the truth value is not determinable from elements of the proposition alone but depends on some additional statement or statements). A necessary proposition is a proposition for which the truth value can be determined solely on the basis of the information contained in the proposition. Such a proposition must be either always true (i.e. a tautology) or always false (i.e. a contradiction).[1] Obviously, characterizing these two classes of propositions in this way shows deep affinities with the notions of synthetic and analytic truths.[2] If that were not problem enough, difficulties determining the connections (if any) between necessary and contingent events and necessary and contingent propositions also exist. In spite of all of this, we may be on fairly safe ground when

---

[1] For reasons of space, we cannot elaborate these topics here. But as a general treatment, see D. W. Hamlyn, "Contingent and Necessary Statements," *Encyclopedia of Philosophy*, I, 198-205.

[2] I do not intend to rule out, by definition, the possibility of synthetic necessary truths. However, the notorious philosophical debate concerning the existence of such statements is beyond the scope of this study and the question is not germane to the present argument.

we assert that the initial meaning of the statement "God exists non-contingently", lies within the event context. That is to say, asserting God's necessity is asserting that the event of God's existence (if we may for the moment be allowed to call this an 'event') must be the case of its own internal logic. Obviously most events in our experience appear to be contingent. It is possible that they could not have occurred. In fact, it takes fairly little imagination to produce variations on the actual pattern of events in our experience - to imagine possible worlds which are logically coherent but do not contain as an actual instantiation some specified "ordinary" event. But the assertion of God's *necessary* (non-contingent) existence means that it would be logically inconceivable to imagine that such an event did not occur. Here is the setting of Anselm's famous proof (and an implied connection between the event context and the propositional context). If we consider the class of contingent events, we notice that as long as any particular substance is described contingently, its complete catalog of characteristics is under-determined. That is, any description of a contingently existing substance is always open to revision. As long as the descriptive history of that substance includes possible but as yet undetermined and uninstantiated states of affairs, any number of alternatives may yet occur.[1] No fully complete description can be given since either (1) the substance may turn out to have

---

[1] There is a fundamental assumption resident in this remark which needs to be acknowledged at this point although I will not defend its validity until much later. It is that there is such a thing as real contingency and that as a result, the future and the past are logically asymmetrical in certain crucial ways. Since contingent existence is temporal, this implies that such logical asymmetries are applicable to it. But the force of the traditional theology of God as a necessary being seems to suggest that these asymmetries do not apply to Him. This is primarily a result of the view that God's necessary existence is a timeless existence.

new properties not included in the present description, or (2) it may develop new properties later, or both (1) and (2). But the came cannot be said of a non-contingent existence. Non-contingent existence means that the existence in question logically must occur. And if it must occur, then its descriptive history is fixed, i.e. it is not open to various possibilities. All possibilities except the one actually instantiated are closed. Therefore, a full description of such a existence is logically possible. And such a full description could never alter since alteration would have to admit instantiations of other possibilities. If God exists non-contingently, He exists as the only possible (necessarily so) instantiation of that existence. As such, He is not subject to change.

Suggesting that the *initial* meaning of the statement, "God exists non-contingently", lies within the event context does not preclude us from recognizing certain connections which such a statement has within the propositional context. As we have already noted, the propositional context of this statement is directly connected with the event context in Anselm's ontological proof. In that Proof, Anselm attempts to demonstrate that the meaning of the propositional context implies a certain meaning within the event context. Anselm asserts that the completely rational definition of God necessarily implies that *actual* existence of God. A good deal of debate over this proof has concentrated on precisely this implication. Whether or not such a connection is in fact a valid one belongs to discussion of the Ontological Argument and is outside the scope of this study. Our interest lies in a different direction. Aside from noting that certain theological positions have, as a matter of record, tried to establish the connection between these two contexts, it is important to recognize that discussion about God's necessity implies a certain understanding of the term 'event'. In particular, to suggest that God's existence is an event is to suggest that the usual meaning of the term must be significantly qualified in order to be of use to the *via negativa* theologian. Usually 'event' is taken to have deep-rooted connections with temporal duration and temporal location. But we shall see that the theological tradition does not allow this sense of the term to be applied to God at all.[1] If the logic of 'event' entails temporality, the theology of the church fathers will have to give us arguments as to how assertions about God's non-contingent existence can be understood apart from any concept of event in a temporal framework. This problem looms in the background at the moment but it will come to the fore with vengeance when we press our analysis against the doctrine of God's eternity.

One other remark needs to be made on this second theme. That contingently existing substances are temporal has a great deal to do with the explanation of their open possibilities. It is as though the present moment of any contingently existing thing stands at the end of a funnel, leaving behind it the single strand of its actual history but embracing before it the innumerable possibilities of its future. On the other hand, non-contingent existence must be in the way that it is no matter where one takes a temporal slice to describe it, i.e. insofar as non-contingent existence has *any* relation to the temporal order, it can at best be described as forever the same. The connection between the permanence of God's nature, His eternity and attempts to understand theological affirmations of His plans and activities will become more important as we see the

---

[1] One might complain that I have no right to impose the modern distinction between events and propositions on Anselm and his tradition since he obviously did not think of God's existence as an event in the modern sense. But this complaint is unjustified precisely because the shift to modern terminology makes clear the underlying confusions and ambiguities of Anselm's argument and the *via negativa* tradition.

associations between immutability, timelessness and omniscience. [1]

Simplicity

To suggest that God is simple has a rather foreign sound these days. The metaphysical conceptions which ground this language are rooted in notions of essence and accident. Such conceptions are hardly popular ways of talking now. But they were crucial parts of the exposition of God's being in the Neoplatonic and Aristotelian developments of the early fathers. In that context, essence was divided into two classes - pure and undifferentiated on the one hand and composite and impure on the other. Identity through change was established in terms of essence. In order to answer the question, "How do I know that substance x at time t_1 is the same substance at time t_3 when some change has taken place in the interval t_2?", I must be able to identify the continuing essence of the substance in question. If I can identify a continuing essence through time, I will be able to report that some aspect (or accident) of the substance has changed. For example, let us imagine doing some Aristotelian physics under these categories. We identify a certain substance by observing that it melts as 70^0C., reacts with acid, has a specific gravity of 1.8 and is metallic. Later we notice that

---

[1] Does the thesis treat the fact that strong omniscience makes all existence non-contingent, i.e. the full determination of every existing thing is fixed, no possible alterations could exist since those alterations would make God's strong omniscience and infallibility false? But if that is the case, then how do we reconcile the preponderance of experience of temporal order and possible alterations with the notion that everything exists non-contingently? Furthermore, this would also contradict the doctrine that God does not need the creation to be God. In this dilemma, everything that is the case must be the case. Therefore, the creation was necessary, as is all the evil of the world, etc.

under ultraviolet light it changes from red to green. Is it still the same substance? After further tests we determine that all of the previous properties hold. We conclude that we are dealing with the same substance in both instances and that hose unchanged properties are attributable to its essence while color changes are merely accidental. Although this example is extremely simplistic (and fraught with other difficulties), it gives the general notion of essence and accident clearly enough for our purposes. How, then, is this sort of analysis applied to God? If God exists, He has an essence. This essence is either simple or composite. From the previous discussion of God's non-contingent existence, we know that whatever God is, He is that in a necessary way - He must be what He is. From the discussion of infinity, we know that the character of God's existence is an existence which can lack nothing. The conjunction of these two ideas is expressed in terms of essence by the phrase "pure and undifferentiated". God's essence is completely, actually, uniquely and necessarily what it is. In other words, God is simple for only a simple essence could be characterized in such a way. Any composite essence is made up of parts. While the combination of these parts themselves need not be identical with each other, the total conglomerate represents the whole essence of the substance. Therefore, composite essence is not pure and undifferentiated. We reasoned that a change in essence resulted in a change in identity. Any change which retained the essence of the substance undergoing change had to be a change in accident. And changes in accident can only occur in substances which are composite for only composite substances have an essence which is not pure and undifferentiated (which allows accidents). To put this another way, if God as pure and undifferentiated essence were to change, it could only mean that His essence as God would change, and He would cease to be God. If we suppose that God is composite (and this would be necessary if we were to suppose that God could change), we might be able to say that a change in God's accidents would not change His essence but we would then be forced to admit that He has accidents. And if we admitted this, we would reintroduce the problem discussed under the notion of God's infinity. In either case, if God changes He simply ceases to be the being we have defined as God. And the definition seems to be a compelling one. Therefore, the doctrine of simplicity entails the doctrine of immutability.

Worthy of Worship

The fourth theme of our summary diverges dramatically from the pattern of the first three. In preceding discussions, we dealt primarily with attributes of the *via negativa*. Each was shown to entail immutability by careful and consistent elaboration of the meanings of the terms involved. But the fourth theme is built on an altogether different foundation. In fact, one might be tempted to suggest that the first three operate on rational-logical grounds while the fourth operates on religious-experiential grounds. The dramatic difference of this theme is its development along the lines of worship. By asserting God's independence, this line of thought seeks not to show God's qualitative ontological difference from the rest of creation but to express God's status as the only one truly worthy of man's praise, adoration and worship. What it asserts is this: to recognize God as God is to recognize Him as Creator. And as Creator He stands on a different level from all of creation. Not only did God bring all that is into existence, He sustains it through His power and grace. Paul refers to this in a religious setting when he says, "In Him we live and move and have our being."[1]

---

[1] Acts 17:28a

Given this context, it would be demeaning to the character of God to suggest that He is tainted by any of the essential attributes of His creation. To intimate such a thing would be to lower God to the plane of the created and dependent order. A God who is most valued and most worthy of worship is not a God fashioned in the likeness of His own creation. At the very least that is taken to mean that God does not share in the rather obvious imperfections of creation. At most it implies that God is wholly other than His creation. Consequently, any characteristic which is inherently part of created being cannot be attributed to God the Creator. By any ordinary observation, nothing could be more characteristic of the created world than its generation and decay. Things come into being and pass from being. There is birth and there is death. These are the distinguishing marks of being created. If God is God, the *uncreated* being, He cannot be a god who comes into being and passes from being. Yet coming to be and passing away is the hallmark of change. Therefore, as God cannot be lowered to the position of His own creation by attributing created characteristics to Him, He must not be the sort of being who is subject to the vicissitudes of this created order. To be constantly worthy of worship and praise, God must be forever the same.[1]

---

[1] An interesting sidelight on the development of God's status as worthy of worship is the problem which arises concerning *any human* expression of God's nature. Anselm refers to this aspect of the problem of religious language in his comments on God's ineffability (*Monologion*, Chapter 65 and *Proslogion*, Chapters 15-17). It is a simple extension of the notion that God cannot be attributed any characteristic of finite creation to suggest that all human language *necessarily* falls short of true expression of the divine simply because it too belongs to the created order. Certainly some theologians have been willing to make this extension. But we must then seriously question what is to be made of all of the argument and explanation about God's nature. It may be religiously laudable to express God's majesty in such

Forms And Formed

The last of the five themes stands apart from the rest because of its particular metaphysical base. If any of the arguments owe their heritage to Plato, this one certainly does for it operates around the notions of timeless, unchanging ideals and the relation of participation. In this theme, God is seen as the ultimate Form of the Good and the True. Arguments begin by noting that the comparative terms 'good', 'better' and 'best' (or the equivalent expressions of degrees of truth) all assume some final standard of Good. In the Platonic sense, anything that was good in the world of appearance owed its predicate attribution to the fact that it "participated" in some way in this ultimate Good. Any change in the application of a term to some degree meant some change in the relation of the appearance to its ultimate Form, i.e. a new relation of participation. But the standard itself does not and cannot alter. The Form, as the final and complete expression of its essence, cannot change. Absolute Goodness and Absolute Truth could never be anything but what they always (timelessly) are. And since God is the ultimate expression of the Absolute, it is no more possible to say that God changes than it is to say that Absolute Truth does. This connection between the timeless Truth and the eternal God is extremely influential in the doctrine of omniscience, as we shall see.

---

high terms as to suggest that imperfect Man cannot even speak of the true God, but the end of that path must be utter silence. That is the way of the mystic (sometimes) but it is not the way of the history of Christian doctrine. It gives pause to the consideration that the *imago dei* may not be some combination of rationality, soul, or moral character but rather the very capacity for language itself. If the link between Man and God is sharing the capability of linguistic expression, then there is reason to believe that talking about God has validity because it is an expression of God's nature as found in human form.

Critical Remarks

At this point several general remarks can be made about the logical structure of all five themes. First, the development of immutability from infinity, necessity and simplicity proceeds along principally linguistic lines. Each of these assertions about God is elaborated in order to demonstrate necessary and sufficient conditions for immutability. Since the logical entailments appear to be valid given the initial assumptions about the meanings of the terms involved, any critique of the doctrine of immutability arising from these arguments will have to concern itself with reassessment of the terms 'infinite', 'necessary' and 'simple'. But here one must be very careful indeed. The history of Christian doctrine is replete with examples of reformulations of the basic attributes of God which failed because these reformulations had damaging consequences in other areas of the theological matrix. In this sense, theological development is like an intricately woven web. Some of the peripheral fibers can be altered without too much change in the entire structure. But a metamorphosis of any of the central core usually has disastrous consequences. The character and attributes of God stand at the heart of Christian belief and are therefore most likely to produce complete collapse of the system if they are altered in radical ways. In contrast, the last two themes present altogether different challenges. One deals with God as the object of religious worship. Perhaps more than any other, this argument finds itself at home in the Biblical setting. Critical efforts aimed at dislodging the notion of immutability from the foundation in worship will have to treat religious as well as philosophical areas. Here we must exercise caution about the distinction between recognizing the experience of the believer and reflecting upon that experience. The final theme perhaps presents the least difficulties for the modern critic. On the surface, it seems that undermining the Platonic metaphysics will overturn the argument. While this may be the case, there are reasons for choosing the steps carefully. Any attempts to replace the notion of participation in the Form of the Good and the True must still be able to deal with the obvious history of Christian discourse which speaks of God as the Truth or as Absolutely Good. Criticism must offer channels for alternative conceptions which retain the intuitions behind these descriptions. For if the critical task leaves us with only a negative assessment we are no closer to understanding the real nature of God than we were before the entire examination began.

Secondly, analysis of the five themes shows that the primary purpose behind the doctrine of immutability is to avoid applying to God the characteristics marking essential qualities of His creation. Assertions like the doctrines of God's self sufficiency, independence and necessity remove Him from the creaturely attributes of imperfection, dependence and contingency. God's infinity makes sure that He is not treated as limited. Expressing His nature in terms of the Forms seeks to raise Him to the highest level of truth and value. Two things appear from these efforts. The first is the thought that any god who did share the same characteristics as his creation would somehow necessarily share in its imperfections. The second is that reason demands that God be the greatest conceivable being. In fact, there is a significant tendency in all of these theologians to claim that God, in order to be God, must not only be the greatest that can be thought, He must be *greater* than can be thought. This tendency toward God's ineffability is that result of a commitment to Greek notions of the divine. In particular, it derives from the Greek conceptions of perfection, as we shall soon see.

We can summarize the intention behind these theological proposals in the following way: for God to be God, He must not share in any way the imperfections of reason and existence of His creatures. This summary statement is particularly significant because it highlights the central ideal of divine perfection. The stress on immutability is one of many attempts to secure God's transcendence. Simplicity, infinity, eternity and other doctrines are equally expressions of this transcendence. But the crucial model behind all of these predicates of the *via negativa* seems to be the model of perfection. The religious man recognizes only too well that he falls short of the mark. The philosopher struggles with the limitations of finitude. All of us experience the frustration which accompanies human reasoning. *But God is perfect!* He does not fall short (moral perfection), He has no limits (ontological perfection) and He knows without deficiency (epistemological perfection). Perfection demands that God be what we are not but only wish to be. If we review the metaphors (many long since dead) used by our four representatives, we find the following:

God is the most high
God is the most complete
God is immeasurable
God is most excellent
God lacks nothing

Most of these could be traced, I believe, to mathematical and geometrical foundations in Greek philosophy. The connections in some are quite obvious. All of these images are part of a very old tradition, a tradition much older than Aristotle and Plato. That tradition has already been encountered in a short quotation from Boethius. We must look much more carefully at that reference and its connection with the idea of perfection. But first we need to make some comments on the second doctrine of this section of the study, which, until this moment, we have rather ignored.

CHAPTER 3

IMPASSIBILITY: A THEOLOGICAL DILEMMA

Change and Feelings

There is good reason behind the silence concerning impassibility. According to the theological framework of our representative theologians, impassibility follows directly from the doctrine of God's unchangeableness. Therefore, if the justification of the doctrine of God's immutability in terms of His actions, thoughts and being can be uncovered, it is but a short and simple step to establish God's unchangeableness in terms of His emotions and experiences. It is patently obvious that the experience of passions is a transitory thing. No matter how lofty and admirable the feeling, it comes upon us at certain times and not at others. If anything in human personality is subject to change, it is certainly our emotional experience. But if God not only does not change but is logically incapable of change, then He most certainly transcends the experience of transitory emotions.

The Latin Base

Some idea of the development of such a doctrine as impassibility can be gathered from an analysis of the Greek and Latin roots which eventually contribute to the English term 'impassible'. The Latin root for this doctrine stems from the term *passio (patior)* which means "a suffering or enduring", "to bear, support, undergo, suffer, endure". Experiences which one must bear, endure or suffer are most certainly aspects of our created order. We often speak of suffering or enduring some feeling such as pain or depression. But it would hardly be in keeping with the order of the divine nature to suggest that God suffered pain or depression. In fact, for God to experience any emotion would imply that He had the potentiality of that emotional experience latent in His essence. And since we have already seen that this explanation would call into question the very being of God *qua God*, we must reject the idea that God has any latent potentiality for emotional experience. On the other hand, if we suggest that God experienced these emotions as actualities, we encounter the equally difficult problem of showing how language which describes God as constantly experiencing the variations of joy, peace, sorrow, anger, etc. could make any sense at all. What would it mean to experience pure and undifferentiated joy? How could 'joy' have meaning without any experience of sorrow? And how are we to reconcile the experience of this emotion and the possible experiences of other accompanying or contributing emotions with the idea that God never changes? The idea of continual and unabated experience of a single emotion seems to create a conflict in the logic of the use of emotional terms. Since the notion of God's essence has already been qualified by the expression "whatever it is better to be than not to be", we might expect that if we could ascribe emotional experiences to God, we would be limited to only those emotions which had some positive character. But it is immediately obvious that the distinction between "positive" and "negative" emotional states is highly arbitrary and that emotional states seem to require experience of their contraries if they are to be understood at all.[1]

---

[1] The theologian might object that it is only necessary that God recognize emotion in others, not that He experience it directly. But impassibility will not even allow vicarious experience. Nor is it helpful

The Greek Base

In these circumstances, the consensus of theological opinion followed the leading of Plato. Emotions themselves were things which were better not to have than to have. To see this development, we need to look at the Greek words behind the Latin *passio*. The Greek *pascho* (πασχω) means "to be affected by something from without" or "to have happen to oneself, to experience". It carries with it the idea of something done to one or something which comes about as a result of something happening to one. Thus, the Greek background for the Latin sense of "to suffer" is not the suffering associated with agony but the idea of being a passive recipient of some action. This is the passive form of the verb "to do or make". But the concept of God as pure actuality does not allow God's experiences to be expressed in the passive mood. God is the ultimate actor. He is always doing but nothing is ever *done to Him*. As the generator of all actions, His experiences are always in the active mood. To suggest that God could experience *pathos* (πασχω) would undermine the original thrust of the theological proposition that God is completely self sufficient and transcendent. *Pathos* suggests passive response. But God never merely responds. Since He is the first mover, He is always the originative actor in any change. God is always influencing but is never influenced. The ultimate initiative for any action always lies totally with God and not with men. In this Greek form, the doctrine of impassibility shows itself much more clearly as an extension of the idea of immutability. If immutability follows from the ideas of infinity, necessity and simplicity, then the expression that God is always the active agent, always in control and

---

to claim that the human Jesus allows God to recognize emotions. If Jesus is divine, the same difficulties apply to him in his divinity.

always the initiator is merely an extension of these ideas. It may not be entirely accidental that the context associated with the Greek word πασχω eventually found its way into the Latin *passio* and thereby took on dominating connotations of emotional experience. For Plato expressed the idea that the emotions are external to the self - that they are things which happen to you - and are not essential elements of the person. In addition, the Platonic ideal of rational superiority relegated emotional experience to the realm of undesirable but perhaps unavoidable distractions of finite, material existence. With this background, it is not surprising that early theologians embraced a doctrine of impassibility for the Christian God.

Conflicts

But the logical straightforwardness of such a doctrine is of little comfort to the believer and herein lies the difficulty. While it somehow seems less uncomfortable to accept the statements that God is the unmoved cause of existence, the unchanging and unchangeable transcendent Being, or the unalterable foundation and Truth of all creation, it is not so easy to embrace the consequence that God does not and cannot experience feelings. For one would expect that the believing community would have not a little difficulty living with the idea that God is not capable of experiencing the innermost concerns of His adopted children. More often than not, the believing community behaves in ways which totally ignore and even deny such a doctrine. The average believer may assert along with the theologian that God does not and cannot change but he continues to act in such a way that he implies God is receptive to, identifies with and shows empathy toward human expressions of sorrow, grief, joy, guilt, relief, hope and pain.

Reference to the difficulties encountered by the believer who accepts immutability and is then rationally constrained to accept impassability can be found in Augustine and Anselm. Augustine speaks of God as "a Being without passion" who "is not troubled by any stormy disturbance of the soul". Anselm asserted similar statements about God. But both men recognized that such statements seemed to stand in *utter contradiction* to the Christian teaching that God is merciful. How could a God who transcends all passions extend mercy (an expression of passionate involvement with the recipient) to suffering humanity? Some reconciliation of this difficulty was essential. And yet, it would be a denial of the entire Christian message to opt for the solution that the statements about God's mercy were merely primitive misunderstandings. Within this theological framework, mercifulness and unchangeableness are equally necessary attributes of the one, undivided God. Anselm's solution is instructive, not for the clarity it imparts but for the confusion it propagates.

> But how are You at once merciful and impassible? For if You are impassible You do not have any compassion; and if You have no compassion Your heart is not sorrowful from compassion with the sorrowful, which is what being merciful is. But if You are not merciful whence comes so much consolation for the sorrowful?
>
> How, then, are You merciful and not merciful, O Lord, unless it be that You are merciful in relation to us and not in relation to Yourself? In fact, You are merciful according to our way of looking at things and not according to Your way. For when You look upon us in our misery it is we who feel the effect of Your mercy, but You do not experience the feeling. Therefore You are both merciful because You save the sorrowful and pardon sinners against You; and You are not merciful because You do not experience any feeling of compassion for misery.[1]

---

[1] Anselm, *St. Anselm's Proslogion: With A Reply On Behalf Of The Fool By Gaunilo And The Author's Reply To Gaunilo*, trans. by M. J.

Anselm's proposal is admirable only in the respect that it attempts to retain both notions at once. Anselm sees that he is forced by logic to assert impassibility, but he also is sensitive to the heart of the believer which recognizes and trusts in God as the merciful Father. The thought that God is merciful from our perspective but not from His is consistent with a pattern of explanation generated by the *via negativa* tradition.[1] However, if we reduce talk about God's mercy to language about our own psychological states without any actual relation to the nature of God, we may create a situation which eventually leads to mysticism or religious delusion. That is to say, if talk about purportedly crucial attributes of the *Biblical* God turn out to be logically incompatible with the God of systematic theology, then we will be forced to provide some resolution to this conflict since we are apparently committed to both sides of the difficulty. To suggest that belief in God's mercy is really only a psychological statement of the believer's state of mind calls into question the basis of salvation for it seems to imply that there is no basis in God's nature for His action toward us. But claiming that the conflict is an irresolvable mystery does not help either for then the believer's understanding is in peril of falling into irrational proclamation.

The failure to produce a solution which is religiously satisfying and rationally consistent is quite illuminating in another way. That Anselm and others

---

Charlesworth (Oxford: Oxford University Press, 1965), Chapter VIII, P. 125.

[1] This pattern, which we shall later treat as the "two logics" explanation, is particularly significant in the problem associated with foreknowledge and free will. It requires that a single doctrine have both a divine logic and a human logic. See the full discussion of this problem in Chapter 9.

should find a reconciliation absolutely necessary yet so difficult to state indicates that there is something amiss in the formulations which force this situation upon the tradition. There seems to be little difficulty in elaborating the consequences of a doctrine of immutability in terms of God's existence and nature (although I shall argue later that such an assumption is radically mistaken). But when immutability forces the believer to acknowledge the additional consequence that God is necessarily untouched by human emotions, that God experiences no counterpart to our suffering and pain and that He cannot feel any form of compassion upon His creatures (even though we imagine that He does), something has gone wrong. More often than not it is just these sorts of feelings of comfort and acceptance which are integral elements of the believer's initial experience of God. These assertions are deeply-rooted in the Biblical narrative[1] and just as deeply a part of the life of practicing faith. In fact, it is difficult to understand how invocations to come into fellowship with God could have any persuasive effect at all if God is so removed from the human situation that He cannot share in any way in the lot that is ours. This interpretation of religious experience comes under direct attack when rational theology seems to assert that such experience is only relevant to our perspective - that God *qua God* is not the kind of being who ever could share our human condition.

Theological Explanation

I believe that what has happened to this theological endeavor fits the following pattern. A rational commitment is made to some particular presuppositions about the nature of God held as certain truth. From that commitment,

---

[1] Cf. Exodus 2:23-25.

various logical consequences follow. At first these are spelled out with internal consistency because they are rather removed from the actual religious experience of the believer. But continued elaboration which remains consistent with the presuppositions eventually touches base with that experience. At that point the rational commitment will either provide an understandable, workable explanation (which does not violate any of the canons of rationality held by the system) confirming the fundamental experience or it will not. If it does provide a reasonable explanation, the procedure will continue. Further consequences will be drawn as the circle grows wider and wider. Each encounter with additional information about religious belief or with actual instances of religious experience will be a new challenge to the system and particularly to the underlying presuppositions. But if rational commitment fails to give understanding of the religious experience, a second-order process must begin. Either the interpretation of the religious experience must be modified to be consistent with the logical consequences of the rational commitment, or the rational commitment will have to come under careful re-evaluation as to its explanatory power, adequacy, comprehensiveness and the like. The second-order process represents a crisis for those holding the system beliefs. It can be met by invoking an *ad hoc* modification (but then one must pay the price for loss of logical simplicity), by actually altering some element in the presuppositions (which may necessitate reconsideration at a new crisis point), by abandoning the presuppositions altogether (thereby opting to take up some new set), or by some less plausible maneuver (claiming that the crisis experience is delusory, for example).

The third of these possibilities produces radical alternation in theological understanding. The first two seek to retina some measure of the old way of seeing the nature of God but ask for a refocusing of the elements. In most cases, the encounter with irreconcilable situations does not produce alterations in the general theological system. But if the crisis reaches significant enough proportions to call into question the *entire* understanding of God which some rational commitment produces, then the path of theological revolution is open and the formative community puts itself in a state of flux.[1] I believe that the encounter between Thomistic-Augustinian theology (and any other theological expression which treats God under the same categories) and the explanation of the believer's relationship with a merciful Father is just the sort of case which could precipitate a theological revolution. On its own, it is not strong enough to force this situation. But when it is coupled with the implications which arise from analysis of the other *via negative* doctrines, I think that it can be demonstrated that a God who is immutable, simple, necessary and infinite is a God who is fundamentally incompatible with the Christian God who is personal. To force the doctrine of impassibility upon the believer simply because the logic of the theological system demands it is to sacrifice fundamental religious intuitions to an uncontrolled rationalism. What we see happening with this confrontation is the first glimpse (recognized by those who produced the systematic logical structure in the first place) that some fundamental constituent in the theological enterprise of making sense of experience has miscarried.

The foreshadowing of a complete revolution leaves us with an almost intractable dilemma for the *via negativa*.

---

[1] I wish to acknowledge the debt to Thomas S. Kuhn's *The Structure of Scientific Revolutions* (2d. ed; Chicago: University of Chicago Press, 1970). However, this acknowledgment is not to be taken as an endorsement of his position without qualification. While his views are particularly stimulating and suggestive, I question the implied relativism. See my article, "Paradigms, Language Games and Religious Belief," *Christian Scholar's Review*, 9 (June, 1979)

On the one hand, theological formulation must be true to its presupposition that a doctrine of God is possible as a consistent and rationally intelligible expression of the God of reason. The fundamental intuition that God is Truth applies to more than the moral realm. If God is the Creator and has created Man in His own image with rational capacities able to explore the workings of the creation and grasp some idea of the Creator, then the proposition that God is Truth seems to have ontological and epistemological implications as well. At least this was the conviction of the church fathers who we have examined. They believed that a natural theology was not only possible but necessary and that a true understanding of God would entail a true understanding of the method of knowledge and the being of things.[1] This seemed to be supported by the fact that God had given a revealed record to guide the endeavor.[2] Thus, a

---

[1] Some question about the compatibility of natural theology and the *via negativa* could be raised here. The fathers seemed to hold both systems as essentially consistent with each other. As we shall see, this arises from commitments to primarily Greek patterns of thought. We will argue that in some respects this combination is not consistent for the Greek thinkers and that it is logically incoherent when applied to the Christian God.

[2] Although we cannot discuss the issue of revelation here, the idea needs no justification as an historical element in Christian thinking. However, it should be mentioned that two major positions can be found on the implications of this record for a general systematic theology. The first, representative of the men we have considered, is that the Biblical record offers necessary further information for the enterprise of theology; that it clarifies and adds to the development of reasoning about God. But there is a consistent belief that Man can understand some of the things of God apart from this record. In opposition to this "natural" theology, the second view contends that without the record as such, no correct reasoning about the divine can ever occur. This latter position came into prominence more recently with the work of Karl Barth. Even though it represents a significant deviation in epistemology, the final product is much the same in relation to the catalog of the divine attributes. Since we are interested in these, the

commitment to the theological system means a commitment to the fundamental presupposition that there are no contradictions in God. To encounter an apparent impasse in the notions of mercy and unchangeableness means that the entire enterprise of rational theology is challenged. Reconciliation must be found. But it does little good to suggest confluence by the introduction of a technical "mystery". Only those doctrines which are considered so crucial to the faith that they could not be removed or ignored and so clear in presentation that they could not stand alternation are acceptable candidates for reconciliation by "mystery". Obviously, Anselm felt that the present case met those requirements. But we shall see that this "mystery" can be resolved when the categories which spawned it are subjected to rigorous criticism.

The situation with mystery is not uniquely a characteristic of the impassibility dilemma. The history of Christian doctrine asserts that the ideas of the humanity and divinity of Christ and the three persons of the Trinity are also theological mysteries. But the fact that the conflict between God's impassibility and His mercy should reach the proportions of struggle found in the class of doctrines where Christological and Trinitarian disputes are paradigms serves as an important reminder that this problem is no minor skirmish.

All in all, this short discussion of impassibility has not been without fruits. We have isolated the first indication of serious inconsistency between the theological metaphysics and the believer's interpretation of his experience of God. But we are not ready to evaluate this metaphysics which dominated Christianity for many centuries until we have reached the deepest recesses of its history. For that we must turn to the Greek heritage in an

---

two positions offer less problems than we originally might have anticipated.

effort to uncover the seminal ideas which produced the intuition that God does not and cannot change. And the theologians whom we have examined have provided us with the perfect starting point for such an examination. Not only are they each one steeped in the Greek mentality but they make specific reference to the Greek foundations which they depend upon. One could easily begin with the references in St. Thomas or with the explicit Neoplatonism of Augustine. But I have chosen a much less famous point of departure because this single reference indicates quite clearly a central tenet of the Greek idea of God which is ultimately responsible for the entire structure of the theological presentation of immutability.

CHAPTER 4

BACK TO THE PRESOCRATICS

Boethius' Debt

When Boethius discusses God's role as prime mover, he employs the Parmenidean image of the sphere. This connection points to the Greek tradition lying behind the development of immutability. In particular, it draws attention to the geometrical model resident in the Greek idea of perfection. Parmenides elaborates the idea of the sphere in discussions of the ultimate nature of reality.

> But, motionless within the limits of mighty bonds, it [reality] is without beginning or end, since coming into being and perishing have been driven far away, cast out by true belief. Abiding the same in the same place it rests by itself, and so abides firm where it is; for strong Necessity holds it firm within the bonds of the limit that keeps it back on every side, because it is not lawful that what is should be unlimited; for it is not in need – if it were, it would need all.

> But since there is a furthest limit, it is bounded on every side, like the bulk of a well-rounded sphere, from the centre equally balanced in every direction; for it needs must not be somewhat more here or somewhat more there. For neither is there that which is not, which might stop it from meeting its like, nor can what is be more here and less there than what is, since it is all inviolate; for being equal to itself on every side, it rests uniformly within its limits.[1]

---

[1] G. S. Kirk and J. E. Raven, *The Presocratic Philosophers: A Critical History With A Selection Of Texts* (Cambridge: Cambridge University Press, 1957), p. 276. Hereafter referred to as *Presocratics*.

It is immediately obvious that Boethius has taken his single line from this fragment out of context. While there are several thoughts in the Parmenidean passage which are compatible with Boethius' theology, it is clear that Parmenides is talking about Reality and the reality of Being and not about a god who is the cause of that reality. This is particularly apparent in the references to "limit". Parmenides specifically denies that what he is describing is unlimited.   Such a denial is certainly not applicable to Boethius' understanding of the Christian God.   Several other suggestions from Parmenides do parallel Boethius' concept of the divine.   We have encountered these in the emphasis placed on God's eternity ("without beginning or end"), immutability as the unmoved mover ("motionless", "abiding in the same place") and His independence or self sufficiency ("not in need").   But the specific claim of limitedness cannot be overlooked.   Why then should Boethius choose precisely this passage to express the nature of God?

Let us examine more closely the context of the quotation as it is found in Boethius. Boethius is discussing the divine nature. He notes that divine substance does not "slip away into external things nor does it receive anything external into itself". The need for this phrase arises from the distinction between the divine nature and the world. The separation between divinity and creation is simply an affirmation of the ontological distinction between God and His handiwork. God does not continue to be God because of some relation between Himself and His creation. His interaction with the world does not entail the slightest loss of His own essence on the one hand, nor does any action in the world affect the divine substance on the other hand. This is the context of "slip away" and "receive". Immediately thereafter follows the quotation from Parmenides. Boethius employs this Parmenidean idea to accomplish two things. The first is a summary remark on the nature of divine substance. Having shown that God's essence is not subject to change because of any activity of God or any action in the world, Boethius likens such an essence to the image of a sphere. For the Greeks, a sphere was the perfect geometrical figure. It was symmetrical in every direction, any line drawn around its surface was endless, rotation of the whole always presented the whole as though nothing had moved. The sphere was the figure of perfect completeness and mathematical and aesthetic simplicity. In this context, the Greeks associated such a figure with the divine. And it is precisely for these qualities that Boethius chooses the image. Drawn from the heritage of Greek devotion to the rational, it is the perfect representation of immutability and simplicity. In the Greek mind the sphere was a geometric and visual representation of unchanging, undifferentiated existence. For Boethius, it represents the principles of God's pure, uncomposed essence and His absolute unchangeableness. But Boethius has another purpose in mind for this image. While he uses it as a summary of the previous discussion, he also employs it as justification for another assertion about the divine being. For he immediately concludes that since any rotation of the sphere is indistinguishable from no rotation at all, this is grounds for supporting the idea of the unmoved mover. As far as we are able to tell, the sphere has not moved.[1] Boethius implies that God is the stationary force which causes all motion and which provides motion with its necessary frame of reference.

From this analysis, it is apparent that Boethius has two distinct applications in mind when he borrows the image of the sphere. The first is an attempt to express the

---

[1] W. Kneale, "Time and Eternity in Theology," *Proceedings of the Aristotelian Society*, 61 (1960-1961), 87-108, makes some interesting suggestions about the possible natural origin for the idea of movement without change in early Greek philosophy (see especially pp. 89-90).

idea of God's perfection.   The second is an attempt to justify the idea of the unmoved mover. Both of these are certainly within the context of the Parmenidean passage, but neither is applied to a god or gods by Parmenides. Since Boethius obviously felt that such an application was a legitimate procedure, we are entitled to ask what transition in the history of thought allowed the movement from the Greek notion of Reality to the idea of a Christian God. In other words, in order to complete the analysis of the impact of Greek philosophy on the *via negativa*, it is necessary to uncover the movement of thinking that allows the Christian theologian to appropriate assertions about Reality from the Greek perspective and ascribe them to a God outside that perspective.   Let us turn to the development of the concept of Reality in the Greeks and see what transition stages can be discovered.

Two Greek Themes

Following the hint from Boethius, we need to examine two themes in the Greek tradition: the idea of perfection and the argument for the unmoved mover. The first of these is a product of the drive for rational completeness in the realm of thought. That is to say, the Greek devotion to rational systems of explanation always strives toward the goal of complete axiomatic explanation. Perfection is understood in this sense. Western man has certainly inherited much of this tradition as seen in the unrelenting attempts in the history of thought to produce rational systems each part of which is a deductive consequence of previous parts or of apodictic axioms. One need only reflect on the impact of the model of pure mathematics or of Euclidean geometry to see this.   The previous discussion of the idea of rational consistency in natural theology is a typical example of the influence of this Greek heritage on the development of Christian beliefs. The second application of Boethius calls on a parallel but more obscure tradition. While the initial inception of the tradition may be more hidden than rational presuppositions like the idea of perfection, the final role of this parallel concern is just as influential in Western thought, especially in the development of natural science. The idea behind the unmoved mover is an attempt to work out a completely rational explanation for observed reality. In particular, it is an attempt to provide all of the links necessary to explain causation. The interface between these two themes is obvious: both demand fully rational, complete systems. But the first asks for a model of thought itself while the second calls for a model of the external world. The hope that reason would provide completely axiomatized systems for the realm of the mind and the material does not begin with Parmenides. In one form or another this emphasis can be found wherever and whenever Man asks why the world is the way that it is. But with the beginning of Greek philosophy, attempts to answer such questions took a decidedly rationalistic approach. In order to see that pattern finally influenced the conceptions of Christian theology, we must trace the development of these two themes in several seminal Greek thinkers. We will briefly sketch this development in some Presocratic philosophers and then comment on the final form of these ideas in Plato and Aristotle.

Anaximander and the Divine

In spite of the critical difficulties associated with the philosophy of Anaximander, he stands as a noteworthy example of the beginnings of these two themes in the rational context. In fact, the critical problems and disagreements surrounding him raise exactly the issues we wish to pursue. For even if no final consensus can be reached regarding the actual thought of Anaximander, his position undeniably presents the possibility of combining two central ideas in Greek philosophy, αρχη (*arche*) and απειρον (*aperion*). *Arche* is usually taken to mean beginning or source. That much is unproblematic. απειρον is understood to mean boundless, without limit or without definition. The debate is not so much about the individual meanings of these terms as it is about how they are related. There are at least two schools of thought on this matter which we may represent as the views of Jaeger and Burnet. Jaeger[1] (and most other scholars[2]) argues that the reference to Anaximander in Aristotle's *Physica* (203b6)[3] shows απειρον to be identified as αρχη (and, consequently, recognized as divine). This identification means that Anaximander saw the first principle, the beginning and the source of everything as the boundless and indefinite. While such an affirmation may seem of little consequence to modernity, it represents a major and radical development in intellectual history. This suggests that the real source and cause of the world is not one of the elements of the world-order but something altogether different; something which, unlike the world, is boundless. On the other hand, Burnet[4] contends that the relationship should be understood only as asserting that the απεριον is αρχη in the Peripatetic sense, i.e. απειρον is a material

---

[1] Werner Jaeger, *The Theology of the Early Greek Philosophers*, (Oxford: Oxford University Press, 1947). Hereafter referred to as *TEGP*.

[2] But see the criticism of H. F. Cherniss, "The Characteristics And Effects of Presocratic Philosophy," in *Studies In Presocratic Philosophy*, Vol. I, ed. David J. Furley and R. E. Allen (London: Routledge & Kegan Paul, 1970), PP. 6-11; and Francis M. Cornford, "The Invention Of Space," in Milic Capek (ed.), *The Concepts Of Space And Time: Their Structure and Their Development [Boston Studies In The Philosophy Of Science, Vol. XXII]* (Doordrecht: D. Reidel Publishing Co., 1976), pp. 3-16.

[3] Aristotle, *Physica*, in *The Works of Aristotle*, Vol. II, trans. by R. P. Hardie and R. K. Gaye (Oxford: Oxford University Press, 1930).

[4] John Burnet, *Early Greek Philosophy* (4th ed., London: Adam & Charles Black, 1930), p. 54 footnote 2.

principle of the same class as earth, fire, water and air. Thus the debate is really a clash over whether or not Anaximander was the first to use απειρον in a technical sense as an originative substance. Kirk and Raven suggest that it may be easier to resolve this debate by determining Anaximander's use of απειρον.[1] They make the following comment:

> Either το απειρον meant 'the spatially indefinite' and was implied to be indefinite in kind because it was not formally identified as fire, air, water or earth (to use Theophrastus' terms . . .); or Anaximander intended it to mean primarily 'that which is indefinite in kind', but naturally assumed it also to be of unlimited extent and duration – properties which, when expressed, would be expressed in terms of all-inclusiveness and divine immortality.[2]

What the precise argument for the proposal of το απειρον was is not crucial in our context. What is plain enough from the variation in Aristotle and Aetius is that Anaximander is described as introducing το απειρον on two different grounds. These are significant for our analysis of the Greek background of Christian theological traditions. One motivation behind the postulation of το απειρον as a first principle falls under the theme of natural explanation. Anaximander's first principle is an attempt to explain the observed natural order in terms of causal connections between elements in the order and deductions from reasoning about the order. In other words, the "boundless" was a first principle of natural causation. But this first principle also satisfied a second theme in Greek thinking. It was the postulation of a logically sound and rationally complete system. Anaximander's' principle aimed not only at providing a foundation for natural

---

[1] Kirk and Raven, *Presocratics*, pp. 107-108.
[2] Ibid., pp. 109-110.

causation but at providing that foundation as the fulfillment of a rational system of thought. There was not appeal to the transcendent mystery of some elusive working to the gods. Anaximander placed his cosmology squarely in the center of human reasoning and in doing so he attempted to combine explanation of natural causes with commitment to logical, axiomatic thought. If this analysis of Anaximander's motives is acceptable, some interesting features concerning connections between this Presocratic first principle and the Greek idea of the divine can be uncovered.

Kirk and Raven appear more cautious than Jaeger on the meaning and implications of απειρον, but even in their caution they support Jaeger in the observation that there was a natural connection between το απειρον and the Greek notion of the divine. Jaeger amplifies this when he suggests that the concept of the divine was transferred from the earliest Greek myths and made equivalent to the rational first principle. Jaeger feels that this transference has a very long history from the earliest Greek thinkers through Aristotle. The pattern usually establishes a first principle of Being on rational insights, notices that descriptions of the nature of this first principle parallel common attributes of the divine and makes an identification between these two. Such an argument establishes a perfect being from the reasoned hierarchy of the explanation of natural causes.[1] Jaeger believes that the philosophy of Anaximander is a prime example of this pattern. He says:

---

[1] Jaeger, *TEGP*, footnote pp. 203-206.

The Boundless is unborn and imperishable, all-encompassing and all-governing . . . , we are not surprised when Aristotle continues with the words, 'And this is the Divine, for it is immortal and indestructible, as Anaximander and most of the natural philosophers maintain.[1]

[The Divine] is introduced as an independent concept, essentially religious in character, and now identified with the rational principle, the Boundless.[2]

From passages like this it becomes clear that in using the concept of the Divine, pre-Socratic natural philosophy made a statement about the primary cause, since traditional religious thought traced everything that happened back to the gods (αιτιασθαι το θειον).[3]

This final thought of Jaeger is worth elaborating. It suggests that discussion by Presocratic natural philosophers of causal first principles was commonly associated with divinity because the heritage of Greek religious set a precedent for such an association. While this element is no doubt part of the explanation for the Presocratic use of divinity, I believe that we can uncover another central motive.

When the early Greek religious myths ascribed natural actions in the world to the ultimate efficacy of the gods, they did not necessarily intend to propose some rational theory of causality. More often than not, the introduction of the gods was simply a way of explaining such activity in terms that were most commonly observed to be associated with goal-oriented behavior, i.e. analogous with the purposes of human agents. But the history of philosophical pursuits breaks from this tradition. The earliest Greek philosophers attempted to develop rational

---

[1] Ibid., p. 31.
[2] Ibid.
[3] Ibid., footnote 44, p. 203.

theories of causal explanation *from within the natural order itself.* Feeble and ignorant as these attempts to produce a rational principle appear today, they were nevertheless radical approaches to the world in ancient times. For they were attempts to offer consistent and comprehensive explanation of the natural order and at the same time meet certain requirements about the nature of thought. Thus, concern for the production of a rational explanation of causality represents one side of the distinction we wish to make. This side, because it was connected with an explanation of causes, could quite innocently accommodate the previous tradition which accounted for the generation of things in terms of the gods. Here Jaeger's notion of transference is instructive. But the emphasis of the early Greeks was not only concerned with elements of the observable world. It was also involved with the notion of *completely rational* (axiomatic) explanation. In other words, the previous tradition of gods tinged with human frailties failed, not because the gods could no longer be invoked to explain occurrences of the everyday world, but because such gods were irreconcilable with the *rational* concept of the divine. So a second side of this development must be elaborated. It is the insistence that any explanation must strive toward rational perfection. Within the context of the Presocratics, we may distinguish these two themes as the equally important developments of the rational explanation of the natural order and the struggle toward rational perfection of thought.[1]

---

[1] We have mentioned the idea of rational perfection of thought many times but have not given it any prolonged explanation or definition. As the argument progresses (especially in Parmenides) more and more elements of this idea will become clear. Suffice it to say that it is really a goal or program rather than a single concept. It is the goal of producing a system of thought which accounts for every element of reality and every element of the system itself without any appeal to incompletely explainable terms. The closest example would be the

This is the context of Anaximander's introduction of το απειρον. If we read this term in the manner explained by Jaeger, we find that the suggestion is all the more startling since it implies that Anaximander even broke with previous attempts to explain the natural order in terms of its own *observable* elements when he proposed that the Boundless was not of the same class as air, water, earth and fire. The gods of the myths were left behind because rational insight demanded simpler, more concise, more complete answers that could be construed as axioms. In Greek thinking this meant balanced, symmetrical accounts. For the Greeks, an explanation that embraced these qualities reached the plane of perfection. And a first principle which embraced the Greek qualities of perfection once again made contact with the other element we are interested in—the concept of the divine.

Parmenides and Perfection

As we have seen, Jaeger draws attention to the relationship between the divine and the search for first principles by pointing to the tradition of the causal efficacy of the gods. Kirk and Raven simply suggest that it was typical of the Presocratics to ascribe divinity to anything which they reasoned to be immortal and of boundless power.[1] Such a suggestion certainly is consistent with the thought of Jaeger since it takes little reflection to see how parallel attributes might lead to identification. But what we

---

construction of a formal mathematics or geometry. As we shall see, this is a powerful influence in theology where God and His attributes are incorporated as ultimate explanations in the system. For God can provide not only the last step in the elaboration of perfect thought, He can also be used as the final step in the causal chain. These consequences are particularly important in the forthcoming analysis of the prime mover.

[1] Kirk and Raven, *Presocratics*, p. 116.

have also uncovered is the presence of another motive for discussing first principles in terms associated with divinity. Our discovery is not new. Jaeger himself indicates its place within the Presocratic tradition. But he does so only in terms of the discussion of Parmenides.

> What differentiates it [Parmenidean Reality] from our view is its perfect completeness, which is affirmed explicitly, and which is the very thing that would impress the Greek mind as something of a least divine rank, even if not as a personal God.[1]

Divinity is identified with the rational first principle not on the basis of any account of the moral or personal elements involved, but on the basis that the rational first principle meets the requirements of the perfection of thought. Indeed, one might legitimately wonder if moral and personal expressions of such a principle would not be major category mistakes.

Thus, causal first principles appear in the light of models of rational perfection. Models of rational perfection take on the role of causal first principles. The development of causal first principles leads to the theory of a prime mover. The development of rational perfection in thought leads to something akin to the Platonic Forms. But the mingling of these two trends meant that treatment of the idea of the divine became convoluted. This is nowhere more evident than in the Parmenidean theory of Being. When Boethius borrowed Parmenidean ideas to express his theology of God, he incorporated a unique combination of these two themes. This combination had radical effects on further theological development.

What, then, is the Parmenidean contribution to this development? Parmenides stands within the Presocratic

---

[1] Jaeger, *TEGP*, p. 108.

tradition as a consistent and significant continuation of the two themes we have uncovered. Reinhardt speaks of Parmenides as "the creator of the metaphysic of Being, which subsequently becomes in Plato and Aristotle an 'instrument for satisfying the longing for immortality and presence of the Divine in man'".[1] But Jaeger shows that this is not a new development. He says that this "rational style of thinking gives [the Presocratics] a new conception of the world which is deeply satisfying to their own religious sense".[2] In fact, Parmenides' philosophy can be seen as the logical culmination of one of the two emphases of the Presocratics – the quest for a model of perfect thought. This conclusion is supported by Jaeger's comments on attempts to handle the Parmenidean notion of Being as though it had the same function as αρχη.[3] If such attempts were convincing, we might be able to see the Parmenidean task as one of providing a more refined and perfected causal explanation for the natural world. But Jaeger rejects such attempts as inconsistent with the major division in Parmenides between the world of truth and the world of appearance. Citing the eighth fragment, Jaeger argues that the description of Being is a description of some "thing" wholly not of this world (a description similar in many ways, perhaps not coincidentally, with the Christian God as Wholly Other).

> He [Parmenides] thinks of his absolute neither as something that supports the facts of experience from beneath nor as their unmoved mover.[4]

---

[1] As cited in Jaeger, *TEGP*, p. 91.
[2] Jaeger, *TEPG*, p. 91.
[3] Ibid. ,pp. 105-107
[4] Ibid., p. 106.

This is the result of the uniquely Parmenidean ontology. Parmenides maintains no dualism of the world of Being and the world of becoming. For him, there is only one truth – the world of Being. The world of appearance (of becoming) is a world of error.

> True Being can have nothing in common with Not-Being. Neither can it be many. It must rather be one alone; for anything manifold is subject to change and motion, and this would be contrary to the persistence that is essential to the very nature of Being. Thus there are no οντα in the plural, but only a single ov. Of course, this conclusion does not agree with the evidence of the senses; but that means merely that the senses must be deceptive and need to be subjected to the strict scrutiny of the understanding (λογος).[1]

This is the context of the Parmenidean discussion of the sphere. We have already seen that the passage proposing that image deals with the concept of Ultimate Reality. But we still need to uncover the motive behind Parmenides' image. Why did Parmenides think it necessary to formulate such an inquiry about Ultimate Reality in the first place? Jaeger has provided a partial answer to that question. From his analysis we have learned that Parmenides' treatment of Being cannot be handled as a first principle of causation like αρχη. We have also seen that Parmenides maintains a very strong distinction between the truth of Ultimate Reality and the illusion of the world of appearance. The fragments leads us to see that this distinction is very important indeed. Parmenides attempts to develop one of the two lines of thought we recognized in Anaximander. He sets his goal to follow with logical consistency the quest for rational perfection in thought. In doing so he focuses the attention of thought on one of the central questions of Greek metaphysics: what is the real nature of Being? At

---

[1] Jaeger, *TEGP*, p. 102.

first sight, this seems to be in line with the general trend toward an explanation of the natural order. After all, it seems as though the question about the real nature of Being is just a variation of the search for explanation of the world in which we live. But this assumption is false. For this reading of Parmenidean Being places it in the context of αρχη and απειρον. And Jaeger is quick to point out that Parmenides is not like Aristotle.

> Parmenides is not like Aristotle: he does not think of the world as having two distinct aspects on an equal footing with each other – its aspect as something existent and its aspect as something moved. To Parmenides our world of Becoming is mere appearance; the world of Being is truth itself. He has no intention that his doctrine of the Existent should explain the natural world of multiplicity and motion.[1]

We can discover Parmenides' real motive by considering the consequences of a formalized rational system itself apart from any connection with the world of the natural order. Parmenides maintains an irreconcilable separation of the Way of Truth and the Way of Seeming because his reason demands it. When Parmenides introduces the distinction, he makes this clear.

> Come now, and I will tell thee—and do thou hearken and carry my word away—the only ways of enquiry that can be thought of [literally, that exist for thinking, *the old dative sense of the infinitive*]:[2]

This remark obviously sets the inquiry within the framework of Thought itself. Here we are not concerned with some apparent difficulty about the observable world. We are interested in analysis of only one thing: what can be

---

[1] Jaeger, *TEGP*, p. 106.
[2] Kirk and Raven, *Presocratics*, p. 269.

thought. Parmenides gives his answer to the interrogative form of this expression as the passage continues:

> . . . the only way, that it *is* and cannot not-be, is the path of Persuasion, for it attends upon Truth; the other, that it is-not and needs must not-be, that I tell thee is a path altogether unthinkable. For thou couldst not know that which is-not (that is impossible) nor utter it; for the same thing can be thought as can be [. . . *literally* the same thing exists for thinking and for being].[1]

He makes it plain that the only way for true thinking is the way of "it is". The contrast between the two ways is not a choice between competitive (or even plausible) possibilities. The contrast is a sharp logical one. Either one accepts the premises of reason and is therefore compelled to pursue the way of "it is", or one decides *against* reason to embrace the Way of Seeming. That it is a choice against reason follows from the fact that the underlying premise of the Way of Seeing is strictly "unthinkable". Mortal men certainly do embrace such a position, as Parmenides later asserts, but they do so by abandoning the constraints of logic. When Parmenides develops the structure of the argument in this setting, it is clear that his motive is to rigorously elucidate a logical deduction of the nature of Being from the fundamental premise that what can be thought (and can alone be thought) is "it is".[2]

---

[1] Kirk and Raven, *Presocratics*, p. 269.

[2] Unfortunately, determining the philosophical intention of Parmenides' use of the term εστι ("it is") is not at all as easy as determining the framework of his discussion of its application. Kirk and Raven remark that even the translation of the word is misleading since there is no clear distinction between the existential use and the predicative use of the verb (*Presocratics*, p. 269). In order to avoid this confusion, they suggest that the best reading might be "Either a thing is or it is not". But they go on to argue that Parmenides' attack on the possibility of

But Parmenides' concern with the proper object of thought is linked in very explicit ways with doctrines about the natural order. The assertion that the only possible thought is "it is" tells us something quite important about observed "reality". Parmenides simply claims that logic reveals that this "reality" is a complete illusion. Parmenides distinguished between the proper object of thought ("it is") and its complete contrast ("it is-not"). "What is-not" cannot be an object of thought because thought strictly cannot think what is not. But mortal men, in the Parmenidean scheme, do not suffer the delusions of the Way of Seeming only because they think that "to be and to be-not are the same, yet not the same . . ."[1] They believe the mistaken assumption that "what is" and "what is-not" are equally valid operators in the dialectic of

---

significant negative predication is possible only because Parmenides himself was confused about the two senses of the verb. That is to say, the expression 'it is' is itself ambiguous since it could be taken to mean that there is something which exists or it could simply mean that if there is something then it is in some way or another (it has some property or another). The first use of εστι implies that there actually is some existent, but the second use does not have this entailment. Kirk and Raven are right about the two senses of the term, but their objection to Parmenides does not seem to be as clear as it might be. The constructions which they employ in order to show that Parmenides does in fact fall prey to this confusion are themselves subject to criticisms along the same lines. It may be that Parmenides does not fare as badly as Kirk and Raven seem to think. However, discussion of this topic is too far afield for us to pursue here. Suffice it to say that at this point Parmenides is not so much interested in the "it is" as he is in the "it is-not". What he wishes to show is that on either reading of the crucial term, the thought is the same: the examination of not-Being (of negative predication) cannot provide knowledge and truth. Parmenides claims that thought cannot think what is-not and therefore truth, as the final goal of thought, cannot lie in what is-not. Truth must be the same for the object of thinking and the object of Being. This seems to be equally valid for either use of εστι.

[1] Kirk and Raven, *Presocratics*, p. 271.

change, i.e. that the concepts exhibit logically symmetrical relations and have similar existential properties. Reason, contrary to the observation of the senses, shows that such an analysis of existence must be an illusion.

> That which can be spoken and thought needs must be for it is possible for it, but not for nothing, to be; . . . [1]

> For never shall this be proved, that things that are not are; but do thou hold back thy thought from this way of enquiry, nor let custom, born of much experience, force thee to let wander along this road thy aimless eye, thy echoing ear or thy tongue; but do thou judge by reason the strife-encompassed proof that I have spoken.[2]

The argument is something like this. Reason unequivocally demonstrates that the object of thought must be what is. The senses, however, uncritically observe the constant coming-to-be and passing away of the elements of the natural world. Unenlightened man assumes that this marks the true existence of a dichotomy in Reality: what is and what is-not. But this reason firmly denies. Since "what is-not" cannot be thought, it cannot be an object of reason. Reason clearly shows that "what is-not" cannot be. "What is-not" is not *something* labeled 'what is-not'. It is nothing. It does not exist. So this part of the putative dialectic collapses. "What is-not" is just nothing at all. But this further entails that the other part of the dialectic must be radically re-evaluated in the light of the findings of reason. What remains is only "what is". And "what is" cannot not be. "What is" must necessarily be the case. Now this conclusion stands in utter contradiction to the observation of the senses. But that can only mean that it is the senses, not reason, which are illusory for the senses (which are

---

[1] Ibid., p. 270.
[2] Ibid. p, 271.

notoriously uncritical) must be subjected to logic and logic in this case stands as an irrefutable denial of the veracity of sensory experience.

With this argument it is clear that Parmenides is not offering a new or refined first principle of natural causation. Indeed, he considers the very idea to be a falsehood. Reality is "what is", and "what is" necessarily must be and necessarily must be completely unassociated with "what is-not". Thus, Parmenides' initial concentration on the theme of the rational perfection of thought has resulted in at least a negative finding for the evaluation of the second theme of Presocratic philosophy. Accordingly, we must deny any attempt to produce a causal first principle of the natural order as a foolhardy enterprise of sensory illusion. We must think purely the thought of "what is" if we are to understand the Truth. But reason is able to tell us more about "what is" than just that it is. And it is the rational deduction of the nature of "what is" that occupies the rest of the philosophy of Parmenides.

Boethius' Application

Parmenides' rational deduction of the nature of Ultimate Reality sets the stage for the return of the theology of Boethius for conclusions that Parmenides draws about the nature of Being appear perfectly applicable to the idea of the Christian God. Parmenides claims that the nature of Being must be uncreated and imperishable, complete and without end. He argues that this is the only possible rational description of "what is" since "what is" is always now and all at once. It is the undivided unity of Being which prohibits any suggestion that it should be differentiated by successive temporal location either in the past or the future. "What is" is eternally present. It cannot come to be nor can it ever cease to be. It can neither increase nor decrease. It is always exactly what it is, full and complete in itself. These statements of Parmenidean monism are famous in the history of philosophy and hardly need exposition here. But it is crucial to point out how similar they are to the statements which we have already seen in the theological tradition of the early fathers. This is not accidental. Parmenides concludes that Being is linked with the eternally true conception of thought (εστι) because of the unique logic of the expression, "The only way of thought is the way of 'it is'".[1] Kirk and Raven summarize the position as follows:

> . . . there cannot ever have been a time in the past, nor will there ever be a time in the future, when the statement εστι is anything but true. It follows, therefore, that past and future are alike meaningless, the only time is a perpetual present time, and Being must of necessity be both uncreated and imperishable.[2]

Not only is Being uncreated and imperishable, it is indivisible[3], motionless and finite.[4] With these conclusions, we return to Fragment 8 and the quotation of Boethius. It should be obvious that striking parallels exist between this analysis and the *via negativa*. Both sets of predicates speak of simplicity, indivisibility, eternity, incorporeality, ingenerability and immutability. But there is one major distinction, as we previously mentioned. Parmenides' concept of Being is finite and Boethius' God is infinite. There remain two questions to ask of Boethius' use of Parmenides. First, given this obvious difference,

---

[1] Cf. W. Kneale, "Time and Eternity," pp. 90-91 for suggestions on the connections between Parmenides' use of εστι and the timeless present of mathematical truths. Connections of this sort will have important consequences for our forthcoming analysis of time and change in Aristotle and Aquinas and for certain problems which are associated with the traditional doctrine of omniscience.

[2] Kirk and Raven, *Presocratics*, p. 274.

[3] Ibid., p. 275.

[4] Ibid., pp. 276-277.

was Boethius justified in borrowing the Parmenidean image and applying it to God?   Secondly, what motives could have prompted Boethius to use this Parmenidean image in the first place?

Several possible motives may be suggested for Boethius' use of this particular fragment. We can see how Boethius may have been struck by the existing similarities. In addition, Boethius did not share the exact project of Parmenides. Where Parmenides was anxious to produce a deduction of the characteristics of the nature of Being as the proper object of thought, Boethius was attempting to offer an ultimate explanation of the natural order. Thus the context of Boethius'' use of Parmenides is an argument for the unmoved mover. Parmenides' denial of the veracity of the senses set aside problems of causation as illusions. But Boethius' God was both the perfect Being in the realm of thought and the final ground of causation.   It was not difficult to find an ally in Parmenides insofar as he was able to clarify the nature of perfect Being. Boethius may have had some assistance in this particular application from Melissus of Samos who made an unconsciously brilliant accommodation of the work of Parmenides to Christian theology centuries before Boethius.

Melissus saw that Parmenides' description of Being as limited and the choice of the image of the sphere led to the ides that there must be *something* which limited the Parmenidean reality. Parmenides' assertion that Being is One would come under attack if "what is" is limited and everything limited is limited by something for then there must be something more than "what is". This problem introduced an "entity" which Parmenides explicitly denied—the Void. Melissus saw that if Being is limited, it must be limited by "what is-not", since Being is all that is. This meant that the Parmenidean contention that "what is-not" is unthinkable could fall prey to serious difficulties. Melissus solved this problem by tightening up the logic of the Parmenidean deduction. He reasoned that Parmenides' assertion that Being was limited or spheroid was "the last vestige of world-form which he [had] not succeeded in removing".[1] Melissus maintained the same unity of Being but drew the conclusion that Being must be infinite in both temporal and spatial contexts. His argument was simple. If "what is" is an indivisible unity, then it cannot be limited for any limit would imply that "what is" is part of a dichotomy with "what is-not".[2] Melissus made a similar application to the notion of eternity but, unlike Parmenides, he took 'eternal' to mean infinite extension into the past and future instead of an eternally enduring timeless present.

With this revision in the thought of Parmenides, the concept of Being takes on the same predicates as the God of the *via negativa*.[3] But if we examine the quotation in Boethius, we find a rather curious situation. Boethius cites exactly the Parmenidean passage which Melissus (and Boethius himself) would see as incompatible with the predicate 'infinite'. Since Boethius certainly did not believe that God was limited, it seems very odd indeed that he should employ the image of the sphere. For it is exactly this image which implies limitation. Why was Melissus so quick to see this difficulty in the thought of Parmenides when Boethius, with all the more reason to find the idea of limit unacceptable, embrace the image apparently without qualification? The answer lies in the distinction we previously made between the two trends in Presocratic philosophy. Parmenides and Melissus were interested in carrying forth the rational perfection of thought. In this effort they both denied the veridical character of the senses.

---

[1] Jaeger, *TEGP*, p. 106-107.

[2] Kirk and Raven, *Presocratics*, pp. 299-300.

[3] There are still some problems with the meaning of the term 'eternal'. As we shall see, considerations of time and change eventually forced theology to adopt a "timeless" view of this attribute.

They found no reason to provide a rational explanation of the world of natural causes.

But Parmenides left the thinker with a serious difficulty. If reason compels me to proclaim the truth of the immovable, simple, eternal, infinite (after Melissus) "it is", and at the same time to deny all of the sense experience to the contrary, how am I to account for the overwhelming preponderance of this world of error? In other words, while Parmenides gives an ultimately satisfying rationale for the object of pure thought, he does so at the expense of creating an absolute dichotomy between my thinking and my experience. And such a dichotomy treats one of the fundamental themes of the Presocratics and of Man in general (i.e. why is the world the way that it is?) most shockingly by denying that the theme needs to be or can be treated at all. Such a position must eventually collapse, perhaps not due to any lack of logical rigor but because Man lives in a world, real or imaginary, and he will continue to ask why it is as it is *even if* it is only an illusion. Parmenides' concept of an *illusory* world of the senses cannot find a foundation in his notion of ultimate Being. No answer can be given to the question, "Why is the world of appearance so overwhelming?" His concept of Being fails because it is an incomplete explanation not necessarily an inconsistent one.

But Boethius employed Parmenidean thinking as though it were part of the second trend of the Presocratics. That is to say, he used the Parmenidean image to argue for an ultimate explanation of the observable, sensory world. For Boethius, the image of the sphere was an image which had explanatory power in relation to the question. "Why is the world as it is?" He sees that the rotation of a sphere creates exactly the visual model of thought of an unmoved mover. The sphere moved without any change to itself or its appearance. Boethius' suggestion is something like this: imagine the nature of God to be like a perfect sphere. The perfect sphere shows absolute symmetry, balance and undifferentiated unity of substance. No movement of the sphere is ever detectable, no change ever seen. In like manner, God exists as the unmoved mover of the universe; perfect, complete, motionless as He moves everything else. Boethius picks this image because it helps him elucidate the reality of the unmoved mover. It provides a visual model for an answer to the question about the ultimate source of change. It allows Boethius to find an appropriate link between the search for the object of pure thought and the search for a rational first principle of causation. Boethius (*via* Aristotle) actually combines these two Presocratic themes in his treatment of this Parmenidean passage. On the one hand, he sees that the predicates of Parmenides' object of pure thought match the negative attributes assigned to God. On the other hand, he sees that the unmoved mover can be elaborated with the model of the sphere. God is the first principle of the realm of the sense and the proper object of the realm of thought.

Having uncovered Boethius' motive for the use of this image, we are also provided with the necessary information for its critique. For answering the question, "Was Boethius justified in borrowing the Parmenidean image and applying it to the Christian God?", can now be reformulated as follows: what are the consequences of attempting to apply these two traditions of the Presocratics to the person of the Christian God? An answer to this question need not deal exclusively with the particular representatives we have focused upon. We have already seen that the religious connotations and understanding of the Greeks encompass a field much larger than the philosophy of Parmenides. And it will soon become apparent that some combination of the themes of Presocratic philosophy is evident throughout the four representative theologians. Indeed, insofar as the same two questions of the Presocratics influence the work of Plato and Aristotle, the connection to Augustine, Anselm, Boethius and Aquinas is straightforward. Boethius has been taken as a paradigm case because of his explicit and controversial reference to the apex of one of these two Greek themes. But now we must turn to the continued development of these questions in the thought of Plato and Aristotle.

CHAPTER 5

THE GREEK GIANTS

It is perhaps unnecessary to point out the obvious connections between the seminal thinkers, Plato and Aristotle, and the work of Augustine and Aquinas. Whatever we might say about the dependence of our theologians on the work of these two Greek thinkers has surely already received the attentions of many scholars in and out of the circle of the church. It would be tedious and superficial to attempt to criticize such contributions. However, it may be possible to show the connections and alternations which occur between the themes of the Presocratics and the final outcome in the theology of the Christian God by making some very general remarks on the philosophical positions of these two men.

Plato On Time And Motion

Parmenides' analysis of the nature of Being set the stage for the work of the later Presocratics and for Plato. That is not to say that philosophical thought after Parmenides was not original or independent. It is only to say that the question of the relation between a rationally deduced model of the proper object of thought and the ultimate explanation of the world of natural causes occupied the efforts of most subsequent thinkers. Again and again the problem was now to reconcile the apparently sound reasoning of Parmenides regarding the attributes of pure Being with the obvious existence of change in the world of particular entities. Parmenides denied the possibility of change not on the grounds of some theory about the world but on the grounds of a theory about the foundations of thought. Plato attempted to meet this challenge by reformulating the theory of knowledge in such a way that both eternal (changeless) and temporal (changing) substance had real existence. That attempt was developed in the theory of the Forms and the doctrine of participation.

Any attempt to speak briefly about these concerns in the work of Plato will certainly appear either uninformed or over-simplified. Yet we do not need to enter into a fully developed critique of the theory of Forms. We need only to trace the outline of the connections between this theory, the Presocratic themes and the later Christian theology of God. Under these circumstances, only the most general appreciation of the theory of Forms is required to open the path of our investigation. It is immediately obvious that Plato's attempt to deal with the question set by Parmenides entailed the development of an entirely new ontology. As Gilbert Ryle point out,

> The Theory of Forms, as first fully developed in the *Phaedo* is a unified formulation of these several points [notions of definition, measurement, truth, conceptual certainties, knowledge and number], but it is also more than this. For Plato now proffers an ontology of concepts. A general idea or concept, according to this new doctrine, is immutable, timeless, one over many, intellectually apprehensible and capable of precise definition at the end of a piece of pure ratiocination *because it is an independently existing real thing or entity.*[1]

The Forms belong to the world of Being and as such they share the attributes of pure Being. But they also act as the models for the world of Becoming. The world of sense experience has a true reality. It is no Parmenidean illusion. But its reality is a mere copy of the world of Being. By

---

[1] Gilbert Ryle, "Plato," *Encyclopedia of Philosophy*, VI, 322.

participating in the Forms, the innumerable copies of true Being are able to exist in the world of Becoming. At the level of Becoming, things change. But changes in the world of Becoming are not reflections of similar changes in the world of Being. If a leaf in autumn changes from green to brown, that is no evidence that Green changes to Brown. The color Green will always be just what it is even though some temporal substance participating in that color undergoes a change to another color.

At least one major influence in the development of the theory of Forms was the certainty accompanying the truths of mathematics. Such truths do not and cannot come into being. While we may talk about discovering some mathematical truth, that does not carry the same implications as the notion of *inventing* a mathematical truth. Discovery implies that the truth was somehow already there. Finding it is simply a job of uncovering a timeless certainty. To invent something implies that one can bring it into being; that at one time it was not and now is. Plato used the timeless nature of mathematical truths as a model for his ontology of Forms. Forms exist timelessly and changelessly. They are perfect, complete and static. They operate like the axiomatic principles of an ontological geometry. While the world of Becoming experiences flux and transition, the world of Being remains the untouched ground of permanent Reality. This dual ontology allowed Plato to appropriate the Parmenidean rational deduction of the attributes of Being as a function of his notion of the Forms and simultaneously to make room for a full explanation of the changing reality of the world of Becoming. No denial of the sensory realm was necessary because the realm of the senses was subordinate to and given subsistence by the immutable Forms. On one level resided the timeless, immutable, complete nature of Being and on the other level the temporal, changing and dependent nature of beings. That truth was associated with the realm of the Forms was particularly significant for the development of a theology of God in Augustine. But there are some other pairs of opposition that stretch across this dual ontology which are equally significant. However, they did not receive full attention until Neoplatonism became a philosophical school of some force.

We must now make some remarks on the relationship between the nature of the Forms and the idea of the divine in the works of Plato. Trying to summarize Plato's use of the divine is extremely difficult. References to various aspects of his thought about the divine are spread throughout his work. Each piece is found in a different context and it is not obvious that the whole picture is consistent. Nevertheless, there are several important passages which we will examine as representative of his thinking. In the *Laws*, Book X[1], Plato entertains several questions on the existence, character and nature of the gods. His arguments that the gods are concerned with the activities in the world of both greater and lesser magnitude, that they are not subject to whims of character or the imperfections noticed in humanity and that they embody the superior and admirable human qualities with greater perfection are interesting but not essential to our present direction. It is true that these arguments set the stage for later applications of the Platonic tradition to Christian theology. Plato's idea of the gods expressed here is surprisingly similar to the nature and character of the Christian God. But the really important contribution of the discussion is the proposed relationship between the gods and the natural order.

Plato attempts to prove the existence of the gods from considerations of the idea of causation. In order to accomplish this end, he demonstrates the reasonableness of

---

[1] Plato, *Laws*, in *The Dialogues of Plato*, Vol. IV, trans. by B. Jowett (4th ed., Oxford: Oxford University Press, 1953), pp. 461-469.

the conclusion that "soul" precedes "body". The argument is as follows:[1] Either all things are at rest and nothing is in motion or some things are in motion and some are at rest. Observation clearly shows that the second of these alternatives is true. Descriptions of the motion of things lead to the question, "How and when are all of these things set in motion?" And this is answered by the proposal of a first principle. Since the first principle is the source of everything that is changing and in motion, it is the source of all that is generated (for generation is change). This first principle cannot itself be generated for that would require some preceding explanation. It must be a motion which moves other things but which is the source of its own motion. Its capacity for self-motion makes it superior to all other motions.[2] Since it is the motion responsible for the continued motions of other things, it must be the beginning of all motion. This self-motion is called "soul". Furthermore, since it precedes any generation of body, it must have all the attributes appropriate to the beginning and directing of all things. And these attributes clearly show "soul" to be divine.

This reconstruction of the argument in *Laws* is to some extent controversial. For one thing, the argument is full of references to other pieces of Plato's works which are simply left unexplained in this text (e.g. the notions of the ninth and tenth movements). For another, it is difficult to tell at times just what Plato's argument here seems to be. He takes several divergent strands and seems more inclined merely to assert his premises rather than defend them. Finally, even though Plato concludes that he has demonstrated the existence of the gods, he sets the discussion in the form of an hypothesis. He introduces the argument with, "Let us suppose that such-and-such", but he

---

[1] Plato, *Laws,* pp.461- 469.
[2] Cf. Plato, *Laws*, p. 463.

never returns to show that the supposition is well founded. Instead, he voices the conclusion as though it were no longer in any doubt at all. However, in spite of all of these difficulties, we notice that this passage gives significant foundation to the idea of a self-moved first principle of the natural generation of motion. If nothing else can be gained from this discussion, if the argument upon which it is based is faulty, this reference to an unmoved mover is alone important enough to warrant our attention. For it is plain that Plato wished to assert the divinity of such a first principle, and moreover, wished to associate this first principle with the functional role of the gods.

We need only mention a few additional points to complete the background found in Plato. Some of these will not become important in a critical context for a good while but they belong to this part of the history and should be introduced at this juncture. The first remark to be made deals with Plato's discussion of time and change in the *Timaeus*.[1] Plato argues that there is a distinction to be made between Being residing in eternity and Becoming characterized by temporality. He suggests that this which is created is necessarily corporeal, visible and tangible.[2] Created substance is dependent. But the realm of the Creator is removed from these limitations. The Creator's body had no need of anything or defense from anyone, it is spherical which is suited to its motion (circular), "in every direction equidistant from the center, a body entire and perfect".[3] The important contrast between the world of generation and the world of immutable being is further supported by a statement about the difference between time and eternity. Plato suggests that time was created with the

---

[1] Plato, *Timaeus*, in *The Dialogues of Plato*, Vol. III, trans. by B. Jowett (4th ed., Oxford: Oxford University Press, 1953).
[2] Plato, *Timaeus*, 31b.
[3] Ibid., 33d-34b.

heavens but eternal being is not subject to applications of past and future.[1]

> . . . the truth is that 'is' alone is properly attributed to it [Being], and that 'was' and 'will be' are only spoken of becoming in time, for they are motions, but that which is immovably the same for ever cannot become older or younger by time, nor can it be said that it came into being in the past, or has come into being now, or will come into being in the future; . . . [2]

The connections between time, change and motion, and the consequent idea that there is no time where there is no motion (change) will be crucial later. Historically, it is little wonder that the *Timaeus* had great impact on the Neoplatonic church fathers for they saw here a beautiful elaboration of the God of theology.[3]

The second remark concerns the connection between change and perfection. Here we need only refer to an article that will become important later. It suggests that Plato's discussion of perfection in the *Republic* provides us with an argument that perfect being cannot change because any change is an indication of corruption.[4] There are important parallels between this argument and some passages of Aristotle which we will soon treat. Suffice it to

---

[1] Plato, *Timaeus*, 37e.

[2] Ibid., 38b. and see Kneale, "Time and Eternity", pp. 92-94.

[3] In this regard see the remark of Jowett in Plato, *Timaeus*, p. 631., and Philip Merlan, "Neoplatonism," *Encyclopedia of Philosophy*, V, 473-476.

[4] Norman Kretzmann, "Omniscience and Immutability," *Journal of Philosophy*, 63 (1966), 409-421 cites the *Republic*, II, 381b, as grounds for the argument that a perfect being incapable of change and of knowing everything is contradictory. Kretzmann argues that knowing everything entails knowing what time it is and knowing this entails change. Kretzmann concludes that there is no perfect being. This argument and its epistemological implication has considerable bearing on our forthcoming discussion of perfection and omniscience.

say that Plato seems to have provided a bridge for the transition from the Presocratic idea of perfection to the later elements of Christian theology.

To summarize these brief comments on Plato, we have seen that his theory of Forms incorporates many of the attributes of Being described by Parmenides. Yet Plato was not compelled to follow Parmenides in the denial of sensory experience. His ingenious marriage of the two realms allows him to continue to uphold the Greek model of the proper object of thought and at the same time deal with the problems posed by a world of change. Plato's Forms, as timeless, immutable, perfect models for the copies in the sensory world, allowed his dual ontology to account for change without sacrificing perfection and permanence. Human reason could deal with both of these realms—one a product of pure ratiocination, the other as the continued empirical investigation of real change. On the whole, this solution was easily adopted by Christian theologians. Deductions of attributes of God followed the pattern set by the Greeks as they searched for a formalized model of thought. Untouched by the concerns of natural sensory experience, the deduction could proceed as a purely rational exercise. The result was a God who was perfect in the Greek sense of the term. In relation to the specific work of Plato, the theory of Forms became a fundamental assumption of the theology of Augustine. God merely took the place of these Forms and with the addition of certain Neoplatonic elements, exercised His role in the rational explanation of the whole of reality in terms previously ascribed to the Greek divine principle. At the same time, the notion of participation allowed accounts of the chain of causation. The unity of the world of Being remained undisturbed even though it became the final step in the causal ladder. Plato's argument for the divinity of the first principle of natural motion added the needed support for a combination of both of the Presocratic themes. The God of Christian theology became a synthesis of the divine and perfect thought and the divine basis of natural motion.

Neoplatonism

The impact of Plato on the theology of Augustine was not a pure and undiluted stream. Elements of Platonism were incorporated in the revisionary philosophy of Plotinus, producing a school of thought known as Neoplatonism. This combination lies at the root of the theological formulations of Augustine and Boethius. In spite of the fact that many of the Neoplatonists were bitter enemies of Christianity, these theologians were able to transform Neoplatonic doctrines into support for Christian beliefs. The exact historical relationship of the various schools of Neoplatonic thought of the development of Christian theology is not important for this study. What is important is the treatment of the realms of Being and becoming. In this regard, there are several crucial distinctions between divine and mundane reality which must be emphasized.

The dualism of the Neoplatonic tradition could be characterized in terms of the following pairs of opposites:

Being	Becoming
Truth	Illusion
Certainty	Doubt
Perfection	Imperfection
Immutability	Change
Timelessness	Temporality
Spirit	Matter
Goodness	Evil
Unity (Simplicity)	Plurality (Composition)
One (Undifferentiated	Many (Differentiated)

Most of these pairs are dealt with in the philosophy of Plotinus. Within that tradition there is little doubt that the expression of attributes on the side of Being are treated as divine, although certainly not as though they belonged to a divine person. The descriptions of the world of Becoming are, on the other hand, treated as undesirable but inevitable consequences of the evolving emanations of Being. Regardless of the attitudes expressed by Plotinus toward this dualism, the impact on Christian thinking was the continued refinement of the idea of perfection in the nature of God and the consequent insistence upon a doctrine of imperfection in the "fallen" creation. Thus, the characteristics belonging to Being as an outcome of the Greek development of a model of the proper object of thought were associated with the nature of the Christian God, while the second member in each pair of opposites was ascribed to the fallen creation.[1] God, as the proper object of thought and worship, became Ultimate Truth, Certainty, Goodness, etc.

This transition from Greek expressions of perfection to Christian attributes of God received several important additions as a result of the thinking of the Neoplatonists. In particular, the two pairs (Spirit-Matter and Goodness-Evil) became crucial characteristics of the distinction between God and His creation. Following the implications of these pairs, the material world was seen as evil in itself. Material things were identified by their temporal existence and by their capacity for change. It was obvious that God could never share in any respect in the essential nature of this creation and this meant that none of the characteristics of the order of Becoming could be attributed to Him. Thus, God as the perfect Being was distinguished from the fallen creation by extending the attributes of His essence beyond

---

[1] See, for example, Boethius on divinity, corporeality and freedom in *Consolation*, Bk. V, Part II (p. 393).

the limits of their normal understandings in ordinary language. As an example, we may notice the effect this thinking had on the term 'eternal'. We would normally distinguish 'eternal' from 'temporal' by recognizing that temporality is associated with coming to be and passing away. Thus, we might conclude that 'eternal' could only be predicated of something that did not come to be or pass away. That is to say, temporal existence implies some specific duration. But eternal existence implies that the substance exists forever (meaning "is incapable of generation and immortal"). The first is a finite measure, the second is infinite. This understanding keeps both terms in the same category (periods of time). But the Neoplatonists' heritage (and the Presocratic background) makes this reading impossible. Under Neoplatonism, temporal duration, whether finite or infinite, implies a mark of the material, imperfect and evil creation.[1] It was important, therefore, to assert that God's eternity was categorically different than temporality. 'Eternal' was understood as timeless, without any possible temporal application or relation. This effectively removed God from the associated implications of imperfection and evil but it did so only at a very great price as we shall shortly see.

Aristotle and the Unmoved Mover

If the Platonic-Neoplatonic combination provided the deduction of the attributes of a perfect Being as an object of pure thought as well as an account of the subordinate reality of the world of change, what contribution was left for the Aristotelian background to add? To this question we may suggest a rather simple

---

[1] Part of this difficulty stems from the view that time and change are not existentially separable. This premise will receive full treatment in the critique of Aquinas' view of eternity.

answer: the refinement and re-examination of the connection between these two ontological realms. But even though that in fact may have been the final outcome of the contribution of Aristotle to Christian theology, it was certainly not what Aristotle intended to do. He was much more concerned with the problems of the natural order than Plato. Plato's suggestion that observable reality was a subordinate existence had given second-class status to the world of Becoming. Where Plato was interested in the development of an ontology from pure reason, Aristotle drew his insights from the realm of sensory experience. Aristotle's denial of the theory of Forms was an effort to expose the artificiality of the Platonic dualism. In this effort, Aristotle attempted to generate an answer to the question, "Why is the world the way that it is observed to be?" Aristotle hoped his answer would also treat the problems generated by reason's search for a proper object of thought. In other words, Aristotle reversed the Platonic approach by asking first for an explanation of the natural order and then working out consequences for Being instead of producing a rational deduction of the essential attributes of Being and then trying to correlate that deduction with some explanation of the world.

A brief summary of the difference between these approaches can be found in the comments of Kerferd.

> For Plato, knowledge, if it is to be knowledge, must be clear, certain, and not subject to change. It can have these characteristics only if they are also found in the objects known. The objects of knowledge must consequently be definable, real, and unchanging, and so they must be non-sensible and universal—in other words, the Forms. (It may be noted that even if the view is taken that this misrepresents Plato, it is unquestionably what Aristotle attributed to him.) Aristotle came to reject the transcendence of the Platonic Forms, but he retained the Platonic view of knowledge as

knowledge of the universal and of the real. His problem, then, was to find a way to giving reality and permanence to the universal without re-introducing the Platonic Forms. Second, Plato had regarded the Forms as the causes of things being or becoming what they are or became. The change in the status of the Forms required of Aristotle a new doctrine of causation and a new source or sources of change and motion. Third, when Aristotle attempted to systematize the various branches of knowledge on the basis of his changed or changing conceptions of universals and of causes, he was led step by step to make profound changes in the general pictures implied by Plato and by Plato's predecessors, the pre-Socratics. These changes were so vast that we are fully justified in regarding Aristotelianism as a philosophical innovation of the first importance.[1]

Since our concern with Aristotle lies in his contribution to the theme which eventually reaches St. Thomas as the doctrine of the unmoved mover, it will be instructive to pay close attention to another paragraph from Kerferd.

The Eleatic doctrine of being initiated by Parmenides seemed to make predication impossible by treating identity and being as the same and arguing that being excludes diversity, so that a thing cannot have any predicate attached to it which is different from itself. To this, Aristotle replied with the doctrine of *Categories*, distinguishing a number of different senses of being and so making possible a series of different subject-predicate relations. The same Eleatic doctrine of being also seemed to make change and movement impossible by arguing that that which is, always is, and that being cannot come into existence out of nonbeing. The pre-Socratics after Parmenides endeavored to keep change and movement by positing unchanging elements which combine or emerge or separate on varying principles. Plato in the *Phaedo* struck a death blow at such elements and principles as the sources of change by arguing that a thing can never change into its opposite without being itself destroyed. Thereafter there were

---

[1] G. B. Kerferd, "Aristotle," *Encyclopedia of Philosophy*, I, 154.

two predictable courses for physical theory to follow. The first was to seek reality in a substrate behind the elements, a substrate to which varying qualities could attach. This was the course taken by Aristotle. The other alternative was to seek reality in unchanging permanent qualities, the Platonic Forms, with a minimal "location" in which varying temporary projections and combinations of Forms could occur and so constitute the phenomenal world. This second view is the "Platonic" view, and it was the view toward which Plato himself usually tended.[1]

Aristotle's doctrine of the substrate eventually involves a discussion of the four causes (material, formal, efficient and final). But these are part of the analysis of natural change in the world order. They do not answer the question of the ultimate source of change or motion. In order to deal with that topic, it is important to notice that Aristotle borrows the concept from the Presocratic natural philosophers that nature possessed a source of motion within itself. This distinguished his position from Plato who held that the natural world was not in motion in itself. In the Platonic tradition, although *Nous* was seen as the primary cause of motion, motion was produced by *Nous* acting upon other things. Movement in the natural order was the *reflection* of this action. It was not generated by the copies themselves. Since Aristotle denied the ontological status of the Platonic Forms, he was bound to give explanation to the ultimate source of movement in terms of some principle *within* the natural order. We have already seen that the Thomistic versions of Aristotle's arguments about ultimate causes of motion lead directly to the postulation of some self-mover. Aristotle comes to this conclusion through his conception of the movement of living creatures. Once he established that living creatures move themselves and/or are moved by forces from without,

---

[1] Ibid., p. 156.

the natural question arose: What makes a living creature move itself?

Aristotle discusses this question in the *Physics*, Book VIII.   He notes that a necessary precondition of motion is the existence of things capable of motion.   And these things either must have had a beginning (before which they were not) or they must be eternal.   Everything that has a beginning must be caused by something else already in existence (in Aristotle's language - already in motion).[1]   There are two explanations for this fact.   Either the first movement of the series was once at rest and then moved (i.e. that things capable of motion existed but no motion took place) or motion is eternal.   That is to say, if we wish to inquire about the ultimate explanation of the causation of things which come into being (have beginnings), we must finally postulate either a first movement or we must conclude that motion is eternal.   But the explanation of a first movement is unsatisfactory.   Aristotle argues that a first movement which is at rest and then moves itself implies a prior change since rest is itself the absence of movement as a result of some change.   Something must be postulated to explain the "rest" in the first movement.   Therefore, any attempt to suppose that there is a first movement will only lead us to a rationally unsatisfying infinite regress of rest and the cause of rest.   And such a regress prohibits the initial postulation of the *first* movement.   Since this possibility is eliminated, motion must be eternal.

This argument for the eternality of motion can be supported with a more direct defense.   Time is eternal.[2]

---

[1] Aristotle, *Physica*, VIII, 251a.

[2] Aristotle's argument for the everlastingness of time depends on the ordered relations of the temporal sequence.   He suggests that since the present "now" can be ascribed to any point in time, and "now" always implies a moment "before" and a moment "after", then no first moment

There could be no time if there were no motion. Therefore, motion is eternal (everlasting).[1] Armed with this conclusion, Aristotle remarks that previous philosophers have given three different descriptions of the natural order: reality is completely at rest, completely in motion or partially in motion and partially at rest. Aristotle rejects the first two of these as incommensurate with ordinary experience of the physical world. In addition, he claims the first hypothesis is overturned by the fact that some things have beginnings. It is interesting that Aristotle takes an approach decidedly different from Plato when he looks to nature itself as the arbiter in these arguments. His regard for ordinary sense perception as a fundamental element in the search for ultimate explanation allows him to turn to nature as a source of a first principle of causation.[2] Aristotle's own view follows the third description. Of the

---

of time is conceivable. Thus, time is everlasting (Cf. *Physics*, VIII, 251b 15-30). This argument presented theological difficulties for Aquinas which led Aquinas to adopt the Platonic conception of timelessness in spite of the fact that he maintained the Aristotelian definition of time and change.

[1] " . . . how could there be any before or after at all if time were not, or time itself be if there were no motion? For surely if time is the numerical aspect of motion or is itself a movement, it follows that, if there has always been time, there must always have been movement." Aristotle, *The Physics*, trans., by Philip H. Wicksteed and Francis M. Cornford, Loeb Classical Library (Cambridge, Mass.: Harvard University Press, 1960), Vol. II, p. 277.

[2] Aristotle's rejection of the line of argument which disregards the physical world (or calls it illusory) is clear. "To maintain that all things are at rest, and to disregard sense-perception in an attempt to show the theory to be reasonable, would be an instance of intellectual weakness: it would call in question a whole system, not a particular detail: moreover, it would be an attack not only on the physicist but on almost all sciences and all received opinions, since motion plays a part in all of them." Aristotle, *Physica*, VIII, 253a. Also see G. E. R. Lloyd, *Early Greek Science: Thales to Aristotle* (London: Chatto & Windus, 1970), Chapter 8.

things that are in motion or are moved (*suffer* motion[1]),
some have motion accidentally and some essentially. Quite
briefly, essential motion (called "natural" motion) is motion
arising from the thing itself. Thus, living creatures are self-
moved and have natural motion. Unnatural motion is
motion caused by something else. A rock thrown through
the air has motion caused by the thrower, not by itself. Its
motion is unnatural and violent. But the conclusion of all
of these distinctions is the same. Natural motion is moved
by something (self) and unnatural motion is moved by
something (another). Therefore, "all things that are in
motion must be moved by something."[2]

How are we to explain the movement of natural
motion? Aristotle argues that natural motion must be
understood in terms of some more primary cause outside
itself. This cause is "that which causes motion in such a
manner that it is not merely the instrument of motion."[3] As
such, it must be moved. This arises from the Aristotelian
distinction between the three things accompanying every
movement: the moved, the movent[4], and the instrument of
motion. The moved must be in motion, although it need
not move anything else; and the movent which causes the
motion must itself be unmoved. These characteristics are
applicable to the larger question about the ultimate source
of natural motion. The living creature moves. It is the
moved in the sequence. It is moved through some
instrument (self or soul). But the cause of that movement is

---

[1] Note the use of the passive verb from here as discussed in the
background of the doctrine of immutability and impassibility.
[2] Aristotle, *Physica*, VIII, 256a.
[3] Ibid., 256b.
[4] The term 'movent' is used in the Ross collection (*Works of Aristotle*).
In modern language we might use 'mover' instead but 'mover' implies
agent (*person*) in a way that 'movent' does not. This difference is
crucial and it should be kept constantly in mind even though we will
use the more modern term in order to ease strain on the language.

itself unmoved. As an ultimate explanation, this leads immediately to an unmoved mover. But we should not assume that this unmoved mover is some personal agent in the same way that natural motion is the mark of living agents in the empirical world. What Aristotle proposes is a first *principle* of causation, not necessarily a first *agent* of causation. He argues that this unmoved mover must be foundational to both natural and unnatural motion since it is the final explanation for all coming to be and passing away. Moreover, this unmoved mover is indivisible, without potential, one and eternal.[1] It is indivisible on the grounds that anything which moves must have parts, some of which are in motion while others are not, but an unmoved mover cannot move and therefore could not have parts. It is without potential on the grounds that motion is transition from potentiality to actuality but an unmoved mover which cannot move must have no potentiality.[2] It is one on the grounds that assuming plurality offers no final difference in the ultimate explanation of causation (one still arrives at the postulation of an unmoved mover) and rational economy requires us not to postulate multiple explanations without reasonable differentiation in the result. It is eternal on the grounds that motion is eternal.[3]

---

[1] Aristotle, *Physica*, VIII, 259a-260a. Note that 'eternal' here is understood as "everlasting" in Aristotelian physics. Aristotle's concern with the natural order led him to postulate infinite time and everlasting motion. But he still had a notion of "timeless", as we shall see.

[2] Kretzmann, "Omniscience and Immutability," mentions Aristotle's argument for a perfect being (fully actualized) entails immutability. He cites the reference in the *Metaphysics* (XII, 9, 1074b26) which we will discuss shortly.

[3] It should be noted that Aristotle's notion of time is in many ways a direct result of his notion of space and motion. That there can be no time without motion is a thesis which grows out of a spatialization of time. In other words, time is such that movement from one point in space to another describes transition from one instant to another. There

With these arguments, Aristotle is able to elucidate the relationship between the things that are always in motion and the things that are at rest in the single explanation of the unmoved mover.

> -- why is it that instead of all things being either in motion or at rest, or some things being always in motion and the remainder always at rest, there are things that are sometimes in motion and sometimes not? The cause of this is now plain: it is because, while some things are moved by an eternal unmoved movent and are therefore always in motion, other things are moved by a movent that is in motion and changing, so that they too must change. But the unmoved movent, as had been said, since it remains permanently simple and unvarying and in the same state, will cause motion that is one and simple.[1]

Having argued from the natural order to the first principle of an unmoved mover and having deduced some of the attributes of the nature of that unmoved mover, Aristotle now comments on the kind of motion necessarily imparted by this mover. This particular section of the *Physics* is extremely interesting because it brings us back to the notion of the sphere. The motion imparted by the unmoved mover must be continuous and primary in respect to time. This sort of motion is the only possible type for eternal, perfected things.[2] Two basic types of motion can be distinguished: rectilinear and rotary. All other motions are combinations of these. Considered in its pure case, rectilinear motion cannot be single and continuous since it always involves movement from one place to another, some alteration in direction and some point of rest. Therefore, the only simple and complete motion is rotary

---

is a very ancient fallacy involved in this conceptualization which we will discuss in detail under the problem of foreknowledge.

[1] Aristotle, *Physica*, VIII, 260a.

[2] Ibid., VIII, 260a-261a.

for it is the only motion which does not begin and end. It always proceeds in the same direction, its end and beginning perfectly coinciding so that no definite start or finish can be determined. On these grounds, Aristotle remarks that motion over a circle is the "only perfect motion".[1] He concludes that this motion is exactly the kind required by the work of the earlier cosmologists.

Rotary motion is the sort of motion we previously mentioned in connection with the appeal of the Parmenidean image. Now we have seen that Aristotle, arguing from the theme concerned with rational explanation of the natural order, suggest models similar to or at least compatible with the result of the Parmenidean rational deduction of the proper object of thought. Aristotle certainly does not deny the reality of the senses. His concern is to explain that reality. But he concludes that the first principle of causation must be an unmoved mover that is everlasting, infinite, simple, necessary and perfect. This is in close harmony with the description of the nature of the object of thought, a description arrived at from the other theme traced through the Presocratics. It should come as little surprise that by the time the philosophy of Aristotle reached the Christian theologians, both of these themes were used to describe the concept of God. In the Platonic tradition, the model of rational perfection gave impetus to a formulation of an unmoved mover which acted as an ultimate explanation for the stability of the perfect reality and its subordinate changing reflection. In Aristotle, the argument began from the other side of the coin. Following the reasoning of the early cosmologists, Aristotle argued for an unmoved mover as the final ground of a real changing world. But the attributes ascribed to this unmoved mover were the same for both systems. The

---

[1] Ibid., VIII, 264b.

combination resulted in a picture of a first principle of causation which retained all of the essential predicates of the Greek notion of rational perfection. And those predicates were exactly the sorts of things which Greek philosophers and Christian theologians identified as the characteristics of the nature of divine Being.

CHAPTER 6

A CRITIQUE OF THE GREEK TRADITION

The Greek Themes

We have been following two lines of inquiry since we began an examination of the Presocratic contribution to Boethius' use of Parmenides. On the one hand, we found a trend in early Greek thinking which attempted to move from the sense experience of the world to some first principle which would explain that experience. On the other hand, we saw a continual and growing emphasis on the development of a model of the proper object of thought along the lines of rational perfection. Most importantly, we saw that the concept of divinity was closely associated with *both* of these themes. When the Greeks developed ideas of first principles of explanation of the generation and subsistence of things, these principles took over the role previously assigned to the gods. When attempts to produce rational models of the perfection of thought developed, the divine was involved in the very understanding of perfection. Affirmation of religious status accompanied the attributes of perfection. Unity, completeness, simplicity and necessity were indicators of the divine and holy.

Natural Theology

The impact of these two Presocratic themes on the Christian concept of God cannot be overestimated. Men like Aquinas, Augustine, Anselm and Boethius were just as concerned with the aforementioned fundamental questions as the Presocratics. And attempts to give an integrated answer to the questions about the ultimate cause of things and the ultimate nature of Being were just as much a part of the Christian system as they were a part of Greek metaphysics. But unlike Greek metaphysics, Christian theology was able to draw on an additional source of information in formulating its answers to these questions. That source was the Biblical revelation. In the final analysis, these early Christian thinkers were really trying to show that natural theology led to the God of Christian Scripture. But the natural theology they began with was infused with concepts of the Greeks. Christian theology sought the God of the Hebrews but it took its impetus from the thinkers of the Aegean.[1]

The addition of Scriptural revelation offered both advantages and disadvantages to this construction of natural theology. As an advantage, Scripture provided recognizable guidelines about the character of God. Christian theology did not have to work in the dark, so to speak, since the revelation clearly indicated certain central attributes about God which informed the direction of these developments. Foremost among these were statements about God's moral character, His absolute holy and perfect will and His concern for and interaction with His creation. The God of the Hebrew revelation was unmistakably the Creator and Sustainer of the natural order. And just as

---

[1] It should be noted that the Biblical account of time and eternity (and the implications which follow from it) is not clearly in line with any of the Greek tradition. In spite of the fact that early theologians seemed to believe otherwise, there is good evidence that notions of a *timeless* eternity and a *changeless* deity are not to be found in the Judeo-Christian Scriptures. We cannot pursue these textual arguments here. If they are correct, then theological issues will have to be decided on grounds much like the ones we are exploring. Cf. Oscar Cullmann, *Christ And Time: The Primitive Christian Conception Of Time And History*, trans. by Floyd Filson (Philadelphia: Westminster, 1964) and James Barr, *Biblical Words for Time* (revised ed., London: SCM Press, 1969).

importantly, He was the single object worthy of worship, highest contemplation and praise. Working with this revelation was like having a picture of the final puzzle in its complete form. Instead of attempting to fit together pieces from rational deductions of the nature of perfection and arguments about the foundation of natural causation without any preconceived idea of the final result, theologians knew in advance the end product of their efforts. They were only required to fill in the missing chains of argument. But even though this offered heretofore unknown advantages, it also created grave difficulties because it had the further consequence that the God resulting from the production of reasoning without reliance upon revelation must eventually be shown to be consistent with the God of revealed truth. Since Scripture was taken to be the final and unshakable standard, it was absolutely essential that the picture of God produced from philosophical and theological argument should be compatible (in fact, identical) with the Biblical account.[1] And this created an uneasy situation for theologians who took seriously the idea of a natural theology. For more often than not the two pictures of God did not seem to square with each other. We have already investigated one area (impassibility) where the conflict seemed obvious and logically irresolvable. The appeal to technical "mystery" in the face of such conflict was an attempt to save the foundation of the natural theology and at the same time preserve the truth of Scripture. But the same difficulties touched upon in the doctrine of impassibility continued to plague any theology which attempted to create a happy

---

[1] In the light of historical study, there is considerable controversy over the unity of the Biblical picture of God. Although we cannot explore that issue here, it is undoubtedly the case that the early fathers of the church considered the Scriptural view consistent (or at least it was their intention to render it consistent).

marriage between a Greek based metaphysics and the revelation of the Hebrew-Christian God. Since the Greek development was not saddled with an *a priori* revelatory framework, it could approach questions about Ultimate Reality without concern for functions of integration and identification with a pre-theoretical personal and divine being. Christian theologians were required to incorporate these elements and this requirement produced some extremely important doctrinal conglomerations. For the most part, the concept of God was governed by a commitment to the Greek idea of perfection and its implicit metaphysics. As we shall see, this left unresolved and unaccounted for certain central tenets of the being of the Hebrew-Christian God.

The concept of God logically consistent with Greek metaphysics is very closely related to the God of our representative theologians. We must say "very closely" because the match is not exact. We need to focus upon certain discrepancies in order to produce a critique of this Greek background. But in the meanwhile, it should be noted that the Greek tradition provides a *genuinely adequate base* for speaking of the nature of the divine as simple, infinite, necessary, eternal, immutable and perfect. In fact, the Greek idea of the attributes of the nature of Being could be described in exactly the same manner. The addition of the Greek theme of αρχη and απειρον would allow us to have all of the background necessary to ascribe to divine Being the position of the unmoved mover. A combination of these two trends seems to cover all of the essential attributes of the *via negativa* description as well as God's role as the pure act ultimately responsible for all change. Is it really the case that Greek metaphysics was just waiting for the Christian God to come along and provide it with the single unifying factor it sought? That question can only be answered after we have shown that these two concerns of Greek metaphysics are in fact reconcilable in a single concept whether it be a divine first principle or a divine personal agent.   Since the Greeks struggled at great length to demonstrate this in spite of the fact that they had no *a priori* commitments to a revealed corpus, we might wonder if such a compatibility is so easily accomplished.   Can we consistently combine the trend for ultimate explanation with the analysis of the notion of perfect Being?   Given the dependence of our representative theologians on the Greek tradition, we can formulate the same question within the Christian tradition as follows: Is the God of the *via negativa* (the God of pure Being) identical with the God who creates and sustains the natural order (the God of ultimate causal explanation – the unmoved mover)?

The Greek Synthesis

With these questions we can begin our critique in earnest.   In the first part of this study, we saw that the theologians of the early church argued for an understanding of the Christian God based on the predicates of the *via negativa*.   Each of these theologians believed that God represented the synthesis of issues concerning the nature of ultimate reality and the first cause of the natural order. Immutability, more than any other doctrine, brings into greatest relief the disparate elements which these early theologians sought to combine, for immutability is viewed as the logical consequence of the nature of God as infinite, simple and necessary and at the same time is taken as part of the rational link between God as the prime mover (the pure act) and the constant alteration of the natural order. If problems of logical compatibility are to be revealed in any specific doctrine, we would expect the doctrine of immutability to show these difficulties.   After all, immutability straightforwardly asserts that God *cannot* change. The real problem for such a doctrine is not how it is deduced from more fundamental intuitions about divine being but how a God who cannot change can be the author and sustainer of all change. It is nothing less than remarkable that theologians such as Aquinas were able to use arguments for God's fundamental role as the author and sustainer of all change to *support* a doctrine of immutability. We have also shown that the same problem existed in the Presocratic roots. Anaximander sought to combine both themes by postulating that the first principle (αρχη) was unbounded (απειρον). Parmenides refined the analysis by showing that a logically consistent deduction of the attributes of Ultimate Reality made explanation of the natural order impossible. Plato and Aristotle struggled to overcome the devastating conclusions of Parmenidean monism. Each proposed a solution which once again managed a marriage of the two themes. But the lurking doubts of Parmenides remain. Because most of the theologians of the early church were overwhelmingly influenced by the work of either Plato or Aristotle, the combination of these two Presocratic ideals found in the most significant representatives of Greek thought was transferred directly to expressions of Christian doctrine. If Plato and Aristotle had solved the Parmenidean problem, then we would be justified in building upon that solution. But Christian doctrine did not reckon with the fact that the solution found by the Greeks was worked out in a context which had no necessity to demonstrate its compatibility with any revealed material. And it is just this theological burden which caused the first tremor of discontent in the edifice of the *via negativa* metaphysics. That God is merciful was an undeniable truth of Scripture. That the experience of mercy was incompatible with the God of the metaphysics seemed inescapable.

Tracing the quotation of Boethius back through the Greek heritage, we discovered that Boethius cited precisely the man whose work called in question the marriage of rational perfection and causal explanation. Parmenides reasoned that pure Being could have no connection with the world constituted by the senses. If theologians were to overcome this problem, they had to show some connection between God as pure Being and God as ultimate cause. Boethius tried to draw this connection in terms of the image of the sphere. But he did this without taking account of two important considerations: the refinement of Melissus and the implications of his own theological position. When Melissus revised the attributes of pure Being to include "infinite" rather than "finite", he eliminated the possibility of viewing Ultimate Reality as analogous to a sphere. Boethius ignored this revision because he had already accepted the marriage of the two Presocratic themes *via Plato*. Thus, he saw the image of the sphere as a productive way of moving from rational deductions about God's nature to conclusions about God's role in the foundation of motion. But Boethius could only make this transition from Being to causing by disregarding the logic of Melissus' argument, for the image of the sphere was appropriate in the Parmenidean context only as long as the system was finite. In addition, Boethius could accomplish his goal only by systematically ignoring in his own theological tradition the same element in the nature of God. That he is able to use this image in spite of the claim of his own theology that God was infinite can only be explained if we recognize that the image served an entirely different purpose in Boethius' theological construction than it did in Parmenidean monism. For Parmenides had claimed that this image was a result of the logically consistent elaboration of the Greek idea of perfection. That claim of Parmenides has been shown to be wrong. The sphere implied finitude and finitude was rejected as inconsistent with the nature of the proper object of thought. The image was never intended as a link between the world of Being and the world of Becoming. But Boethius adopts the image for exactly this purpose. Using the image in this way can at best only be metaphorical. It is strictly logically inconsistent with the attributes of perfect Being. For these reasons, this metaphor cannot be appealed to as logical grounds for a line between the God of the *via negativa* and the God of the first cause. If this conclusion is correct it shows that any system which tries to correlate the attributes of perfect Being (under the Greek concept of 'perfect') with a first cause of motion must avoid reliance on visual metaphors like the sphere. Given the concluding remarks of Aristotle on this topic, it appears that the Greek synthesis has not yet been accomplished.

Tensions lie those arising from the use of this image are found throughout the Greek tradition. Plato attempts an uneasy alliance between the rational deduction and the explanation of motion by postulating a dual ontology. Aristotle denied this and tried to derive the attributes of rational perfection from reasoning which began with an explanation of natural causation. The Parmenidean pronouncement provided the impetus in each case for Parmenides had effectively cut off one of the pressing themes of Greek philosophy from the other. A valiant struggle emerged to reconstitute the harmony originally achieved by appeal to the mythological gods. On the one hand, the rational deduction upheld the commitment to thorough logical consistency and produced a proper object of thought described in terms similar to those of the *via negativa*. But it left the question, "Is any action a possibility for a God (god) characterized by such attributes?" On the other hand, attempts to work out an argument for God as the ultimate cause of the natural order supplied reason with a God of pure act but left open the question, "Is such a God (god) compatible with the attributes infinite, simple, timeless, immutable, etc.?" Parmenides answered the first of these questions in the negative thereby eliminating the second question altogether. Plato and Aristotle tried to reintroduce the second question by reformulating the arguments of Parmenides. The foundation which they established was adopted by Christian theologians and became the presupposition of their doctrinal beliefs. But even though Parmenides' philosophical position was superseded in the process, none of the theologians went back to the fundamental intuition of his thought in an attempt to answer in the Christian context the doubt which he raised. That intuition was of the basic discontinuity between the character of the rational deduction from thought alone and the production of an ultimate justification of causation in the natural order.

SECTION TWO

TIME AND PERSON

CHAPTER 7

THE DOCTRINE OF ETERNITY

Aquinas On Eternity

Aquinas examines the notions of time and eternity in six inter-related questions:[1]

{1} What is eternity?
{2} Is God eternal?
{3} Does eternity belong to God alone?
{4} Is eternity different from the aeon and time?
{5} What is the difference between the aeon and time?
{6} Is there only one aeon?

The development of the doctrine of God's eternal existence arises only after examination of immutability and simplicity because the notion of eternity follows logically from a fresh consideration of the previous discussion of the idea of motion. In other words, the examination of motion in terms of potentiality and actuality leads to the belief in God as the immovable foundation and source of all creation. God alone is the unmoved mover. Immutability is the doctrine which expresses God's absolute permanence in the structure of a universe of activity. Immutability is the *logical* guarantee that God will remain forever the same. The phrase "forever the same" implies some connection between the absence of any change in God and the idea of time. This is the basis of the reconsideration of time and eternity. The second treatment deals with the facet of change directed toward duration. For example, one

---

[1] Aquinas, *Summa Theologiae*, Vol. 2, p. 135.

114

might say, "This substance has changed It has altered from state *A* to state *B*." This would be a case of examining the first facet of motion. In the Thomistic tradition, we would employ categories of potentiality and actuality in this analysis. But one could also suggest, "This substance has changed. It is older." In this case, it does not seem necessary for an alteration in the physical structure of the substance to have occurred.[1] Here the form of transition is not in terms of activity but in terms of duration. The picture is one of "enduring through time" as though the transfer from one instant to the next implied some change. The passage of time is viewed as a mark of change. A *full description* of some substance must include its temporal and spatial relations, and an alteration in these relations seems to constitute a change. The difficulty with temporal relations is that they cannot be stopped. Passage is inevitable.

Since Aquinas has already argued that it is logically impossible for God to change, it is incumbent upon him to demonstrate exactly how God's relation to time avoids the notion of passage. Aquinas has shown that logic demands the postulation of a first cause. Governed by the concept of perfection, he argues that this first cause must be pure

---

[1] Aquinas may not have accepted this claim for he follows Aristotle in asserting that change must occur for there to be time. Where there is no change, there is no time. But this principle of Aristotle needs some alterations in order for it to be an adequate foundation for the identification of change. For example, it must be restricted from cases where change amounts to only a change in relation. It was Aquinas' intention that there are some things which are timeless, but he does not restrict these to God alone. The required alterations in Aristotle's principle have been treated in W. H. Newton-Smith, *The Structure of Time* (Routledge & Kegan Paul, 1980), Chapter 2, section 2. I wish to express my gratitude to Mr. Newton-Smith for allowing me to consult this work prior to its publication and for his helpful suggestions on certain topological problems concerning multiple time structures.

activity without potentiality. Therefore, no coming to be or passing away could ever be ascribed to the first cause. And since change always involves some potentiality, he asserts that the first cause cannot change. But with a little reflection we can see a problem here. While we might continue to maintain that no unactualized potentiality could exist in God, we must still recognize that God's role as a first cause seems to imply that He is part of the causal chain which is itself constantly changing. In addition, claims about God's *existence* seem to imply duration and that alone would be enough to warrant us believing that God changed. Worse yet, in this system change implies finitude and imperfection.

Aquinas is able to extricate himself from this difficulty by establishing an analysis of time on the basis of his previous examination of motion. He intends to show that just as the examination of motion illuminated the characteristics of God's permanence, so an examination of time will illuminate the characteristics of God's eternity. But we must recognize from the beginning that Aquinas *assumes* the opposition of pairs involved (motion and time *versus* permanence and eternity). That is not to suggest that Aquinas offers no argument for a distinction between time and eternity. Points 1 and 4 or article 10 of the *Summa* deal specifically with this distinction. But the distinction is made *only after* the term 'eternity' has been defined, and that definition is provided *via* the assumption that eternity stands in opposition to time. As we shall see, Aquinas felt it theologically necessary to make this assumption.

The relevant material is found in Question 10 of the *Summa*. Even a brief reading of the text makes the connection with the doctrine of immutability clear. Under the heading, "What is eternity?", St. Thomas lays down a definition of *time* which frames all further discussion.

> Just as we can only come to know simple things by way of
> composite ones, so we can only come to know eternity by way
> of time, which is merely the *numbering of before and after in
> change*. For in any change there is successiveness, one part
> coming after another, and by numbering the antecedent and
> consequent parts of change there arises the notion of time,
> which is simply this numberedness of before and after in
> change.[1]

This definition, drawn from Aristotle (*Physics*, IV, 11, 220a
and IV, 12, 221b), places the conceptualization of time
within the structure of substantival alteration. According to
the interpretation of Aquinas, the concept 'time' is nothing
more than the ordered sequence of intervals associated with
some alteration of substance. As such, time expresses a
short-hand way of indicating a certain type of
measurement. That measurement has no function apart
from what it measures. Since the measurement 'time' is
strictly limited to the measured reality 'change in
substance', any application or attempted application of the
concept to realities which are not subject to change is a
conceptual mistake. As a numbering of intervals associated
with change, the application concept 'time' is appropriate
only to cases where previous observational or conceptual
evidence indicates the possibility of alteration in substance.

Aquinas uses the limits imposed by this definition
to establish the meaning and scope of the concept
'eternity'. Again, he appeals to the groundwork in the
doctrine of immutability, noting that "something lacking
change and never varying its mode of existence will not
display a before and after."[2] From this he infers that
"awareness of invariability in something altogether free

---

[1] Aquinas, *Summa Theologiae*, Vol. 2, pp. 135-137.
[2] Ibid., p. 137.

from change produces the notion of eternity."[1] That is to say, things that logically cannot be described as measured by intervals remain unchangeably the same. While one can assign a beginning and an end to things that change, anything that remains unchangeably the same cannot have a beginning or be subject to descriptions of successiveness.

It comes as no surprise that Aquinas assigns to the concept 'eternity' exactly those characteristics which he has determined can only be applied to immutable being. Eternity is seen as the contrasting opposite of time. Since time is the successive numbering of change, eternity must not involve succession. Eternity not only has nothing to do with successiveness, it also has nothing to do with measure because all measurement implies intervals and intervals belong only to the temporal. Moreover, whatever is eternal cannot be associated with change for all change is a mark of the temporal. Eternity is characterized by two things: unending existence and instantaneous existence of the whole.[2]

What is interesting is that Aquinas has not given us a definition of the concept of eternity so much as he has defined the scope of application of the predicate 'eternal'. It is not the pure notion that concerns him. Rather, he is interested with the implications that the predicate 'eternal' has for an understanding of the existence of God. There is no attempt to deal directly with the relationship between time and eternity in terms of the crucial ideas of event, interval or antecedent and consequent change and cause, nor with the difficulties associated with the concept of 'existence'. The real direction of Aquinas' thought is an introduction of the existential application of the term to the divine. Thus he asserts that anything that is (exists) eternally is unending and instantaneous.

---

[1] Aquinas, *Summa Theologiae*, Vol. 2, p. 137.
[2] Ibid.

As a prologue to explanation of this claim, Aquinas raises several problems for the doctrine and then mounts a defense against them. While some of these objections seem almost irrelevant, several may help us uncover motives behind the form of the doctrine Aquinas tries to defend. Understanding these motives will open the way to understanding the two crucial phrases. Aquinas argues for the concept based on the definition of eternity given by Boethius. Each objection raises an issue that questions aspects of this definition. But in no case is the definition *as a whole* ever challenged.

Elements of this definition can be found in Anselm (*Proslogion*, Chapters XIX and XX), Augustine (*Confessions*, XI, 13) and even Plato (*Timaeus*, 38b5). Because the definition from Boethius is so crucial to the entire understanding of eternity in Aquinas, it is appropriate to cite the complete passage.

> Let us consider what eternity is. For this reveals to us both the nature and knowledge of God. Eternity, then, is the complete possession of eternal life all at once—a notion which becomes clearer from comparison with things temporal. For anything which lives in time moves as something present from the past to the future, and there is nothing established in time which can embrace the whole extent of its life without distinction. It does not yet grasp to-morrow, and it has already lost yesterday. And even in the life of to-day you do not live for a longer spell than in the transitory moment. That, then, which is subject to the condition of time, even though (as Aristotle said of the world) it has no beginning or end and its life extends through endless time, is still not such as may be rightly judged eternal. For, though its life be endless, it does not grasp and embrace the extent of it all at once (*totum simul*), but has some parts still to come . . . And so, if, following Plato, we wish to give things their right names, let us say that God is eternal, but the world everlasting . . . Thus if you reflect on the immediate confrontation by which God discerns all things, you will judge that it is not foreknowledge of something as future, but rather knowledge of a never failing present. For which reason it is set far above the lowly details of the world and sees all things as though in a prospect from the highest summit . . . Those future

events which proceed from free will God sees as present. In relation therefore to God's sight of them and under the condition of divine knowledge they are necessary; but considered in themselves they lose nothing of the absolute liberty of their own nature.[1]

The obvious connection between God's timelessness (as distinct from the everlasting temporality of the world) and omniscience will be a very important part of the next section of this study. That timelessness is used as a solution to the conflict between God's infallible knowledge of all true propositions and the free will of human agents makes the attempt to understand and critique the doctrine of divine eternity even more pressing. Both of these related issues, omniscience by direct intuition and foreknowledge (or knowledge) of human free acts in the future, will receive attention after we have examined the issues of time, change and eternity.

On the surface, objections 1 and 5 of point 1 seem almost pedestrian. They involve some quibbling remarks about the words 'unending' and 'whole'. The actual objections and replies are not particularly important here. But the context in which they treat the concept of eternity is very revealing. In both cases, the idea of eternity is assumed to be integrally connected with perfection and completion.

The first objection Aquinas wishes to meet in his defense is that the use of the term 'unending' is a negative and implies some defect. Aquinas claims that simple (non-composite) concepts are not necessarily defective in their essence even if they must be expressed in negatives. Rather, the use of a negative term results from the infirmity of the human mind which requires as a first step the understanding of composite things and then denies this

---

[1] translation by W. Kneale, "Time and Eternity in Theology", pp. 95-96 from Boethius, *Consolatione Philsosphiae*, V, 6

composition to those things which reason asserts to be simple. The problem seems to be one of negative predication. The objection implies that something which requires predication in order to be understood must be imperfect in some way. Behind this implication is the following argument: If my description of a given concept describes the concept perfectly (makes the essence of the concept known), it will be a description of the positive characteristics of the concept. That is, all of the predicates will be direct affirmations of what the concept really is. On the other hand, the explanation of a concept which proceeds by denying that the concept in question is something else seems only partially successful. It tells me what the concept is *not* but it does not tell me what the concept is. And if knowledge is only attained through understanding the true essence of the concept, then negative predication will never allow me to attain knowledge of that concept.[1] More importantly, a concept which *requires* explanation in terms of negative predication must, on these grounds, be essentially defective (imperfect) in some respect. Aquinas does not quarrel with this theory of predication and its epistemological consequences. He simply shifts the ground of the observed imperfection. He asserts that the imperfection noted in negative predication is not to be found in the essence of the concepts under discussion but rather to be found in the weakness of the human mind. Why does he choose to make a topological rather than an epistemological shift?

We can identify two possible motives for this choice. The first concerns Aquinas' belief about the power

---

[1] The similarities with Parmenides' problem are striking and not accidental. *Via negativa* formulations require a certain epistemological presupposition about the nature of knowledge and this presupposition is common to both men. This will become clearer in the critique of omniscience.

of the tradition established in the *via negativa*. The second concerns his belief about the character of the attributes of divine being. In regard to the *via negativa*, Aquinas followed the pattern which asserted that the negative predicates involved are not strictly attributes of the divine being but rather are indicators of the unlimited character of the divine expressed within the confines of human categories. Each predicate expressed the fact that God's nature surpasses the limits of the human understanding. Since the limits of positive attribution are the limits of human intellectual categories, describing a being who surpasses those human limits can only be accomplished by pointing to the human limits and negating them. But all of this operation depends on the prior assumption that God's nature (essence) is *strictly* supra-human even in its conceptualization. Aquinas' famous notion of analogical predication is a move which attempts to meet the obvious theological gap created by this assumption. But even he admitted that analogical predication could operate only where there was some univocal point.[1] And formulations of the *via negativa* quite clearly deny any univocal elements between the opposing pairs. It would be absurd to suggest that predicates of the *via negativa* were strictly equivocal but this seems to be the direction in which they lean. They cannot be affirmations. They are denials in the important sense that they refuse to allow any limitations to be placed upon the understanding of God's nature. And any being which is unlimited is (in both the Greek and Thomistic schemes) complete and perfect. How could a being which lacked nothing fail to be absolutely complete? Thus, the operation of the *via negativa* asserts the virtual uniqueness of the being in question.

---

[1] St. Thomas Aquinas, *Summa Theologiae*, Vol. 3, "Knowing And Naming God" (Ia. 12-13), trans. by Herbert McCabe (London: Blackfriars, 1964), question 13, pp. 47-97.

The result of this perspective makes it impossible to locate the apparent difficulty of negative predication in the essence of the concept itself. That is to say, the *via negativa* guarantees that the being in question is perfect, without defect and lacking nothing which its essence requires. Therefore, the objection that the employment of negative terms implies deficiency in the essence of the concept discussed must be rejected. Since the necessity of negative predication remains, Aquinas is compelled to shift the location of the deficiency to the limits of human understanding. This shift is further supported by the thesis that the *via negativa* results from an attempt to express something beyond the limits of human categories. In other contexts we could reasonably challenge this entire theory of predication. We will not pursue the argument here because for us the important feature is the relation between the definition of eternity and the doctrines of God's infinity and perfection. This relation is just as strong in the fifth objection.

Aquinas states the objection like this: "Moreover, wholeness is the same as perfection. Given that eternity is whole, then, it is redundant to add that it is perfect."[1] Since the objection already acknowledges the connection between eternity and perfection, Aquinas finds no quarrel with it. He remarks that Boethius uses both 'whole' and 'perfect' to meet two different misleading possibilities. 'Whole' combats the misconception that eternity is really just the collected aggregate of time. Thus Boethius says eternity is an instantaneous whole (whether or not this expression makes sense will have to be discussed. If it is taken to be some sort of "all at once complete" picture, it certainly does *not* bear resemblance to the idea of the total collection of temporal moments, but it still involves temporal

---

[1] Aquinas, *Summa Theologiae*, Vol. 2, p. 135.

categories). Aquinas' second remark makes an interesting addition. He says that Boethius uses the word 'perfect' not for repeated emphasis but to counteract the conception that eternity contains any parts made up of temporal instants. That is to say, when Boethius claims that eternity is perfect, he means to reiterate the conclusion that eternity is two things – whole and complete. In contrast, "time itself is successive, and . . . an instant of time is imperfect."[1] Aquinas' assertion that Boethius uses 'whole' to counteract the belief that eternity is aggregate time must be addressed to the first of these two propositions – the successiveness of time. That eternity is whole must mean that it is not successive. This fits our previous description of the "all at once complete" picture. But an "all at once complete" something could still consist of parts just like a jigsaw puzzle may be complete but have hundreds of tiny pieces. To prevent us from conceptualizing eternity in the fashion of a completed puzzle, Aquinas draws on another aspect of the idea of perfection. Perfection implies complete unity (without differentiation). But any temporal instant is in itself incomplete and distinct. It is either the before or the after moment of change. It is only a single, incomplete and distinct part of a larger whole. Yet eternity is perfect and undifferentiated. Since no collection of imperfect parts will ever produce perfection, eternity must be something other than the collection of imperfect temporal instants. Eternity can have no temporal parts since temporality itself implies imperfection. This elaboration is consistent with the rebuttal Aquinas gives to the third objection that eternity is simple and should therefore not be called whole since whole implies parts. He replies that the wholeness of eternity is not due to its collection of parts but to its completeness. Eternity is defined as whole "because

---

[1] Aquinas, *Summa Theologiae*, Vol. 2, p.137.

nothing is lacking to it."[1] The connection with the Greek notion of perfection is obvious.

A Thomistic Definition

According to the definition of Boethius and the defense of Aquinas, eternity is characterized in the following manner:

> {1} Eternity is unending (it lacks both beginning and end) but this should not be understood to mean that it is some sort of duration (as we might characterize time by a line of ordered events)
>
> {2} Eternity is not successive nor is it the accumulation of successive instants. It cannot be viewed as having any parts nor is it the whole of any collected parts.
>
> {3} Eternity is not lacking in anything which would keep it from being complete (it is whole)
>
> {4} Accordingly, eternity has no connection with time as a whole (a total of successive instants) or with any temporal moment (one imperfect part of the temporal process)
>
> {5} Therefore, eternity cannot be an attribute of anything that changes.

We have touched on the suggestion raised by objection 2 of point 1 only in the most superficial way.[2] The reason for this is that the connection between eternity and eternal *life* raises some unusual problems which will be treated in our critique of the concept of divine person. What we have discovered is that each of the above characteristics turns on

---

[1] Aquinas, *Summa Theologiae*, Vol. 2, p. 135.

[2] The issue involved here is much more significant than merely a concern about the relation between divine life and human life. The Greek background of the *via negativa* predicates places them in a timeless but static realm. That does not appear to be even logically compatible with the concept of 'alive' or 'living'. As we shall see, this fundamental tension calls in question the entire *via negativa* tradition.

a denial of some ordinary conception of the idea of time. Even the initial observation that eternity is unending is stripped of its relation to ordinary concepts when the qualification is added that it is unending *without* succession. Thus far, at least, eternity seems to be a completely negative concept. It is not successive, it cannot be divided into parts, it cannot be related to change, it is *instantaneously* complete (an expression which seems necessarily *temporal*) and it has some supra-temporal kind of unending quality.

Examining the other articles under Question 10, we discover some amplification of these rather unusual claims. Article 2 makes the connection between eternity and immutability unmistakably clear. "The notion of eternity derives from unchangeableness in the same way that the notion of time derives from change."[1] From this Aquinas concludes that God alone has eternity proper (since God is immutable in the pure sense) and that God "is identical with his own eternity just as he is identical with his own nature."[2] Here Aquinas suggests that we humans come to grasp eternity by "grasping the idea of an abiding instant."[3] He has in mind the picture of some immutable moment which he says is the only way human beings can conceive of this concept. He affirms the identity of God and eternity but he denies that eternity can be described as any form of measurement, even measurement of the divine. Finally, Aquinas asserts that eternity "comprehends" past, present and future (the exact verb will be crucial in later discussions of omniscience).

In the third point of Article 3, Aquinas refers to the notion of a necessary truth. He concludes that necessary truths are eternal because they reside in the mind of God.

---

[1] Aquinas, *Summa Theologiae*, Vol. 2, pp. 139, 141.
[2] Ibid., p. 139.
[3] Ibid.

The connection with immutability seems to be justification for this claim.   A necessary truth remains forever identically the same.   But the notion of a necessary truth remaining forever (timelessly) the same raises an important distinction between uses of the word 'eternal' which have unsettling implications.[1]   We will have ample opportunity to consider the impact of this distinction when we criticize the entire picture of eternity which Aquinas offers.   For the moment, we need still consider the remaining elements of this picture provided by the fourth, fifth and sixth questions of this discussion.

Aquinas' fourth point raises the question we are concerned with as directly as one could expect – "Is eternity different from time?"   The objection he wishes to counter goes something like this:[2]

> Eternity and time are both measurements of duration. While they differ in the length of period they measure, they are related in that time is subsumed under the category eternity. Time is just a part of the span measured by eternity since time measures those things which have beginnings and ends while eternity stretches infinitely into the past and the future.

Aquinas supplies two other objections to his position under the same point.   The first suggests that since the "now" of time exists unchanged throughout time, and eternity has already been shown to exist unchangeably the same, the

---

[1] Aquinas does remark in places that 'eternity' sometimes means 'ages' (cf. *Summa Theologiae*, Ia. 10, 2) but this seems to affect only his interpretation of Scripture, not his philosophical theology.   His commitment to a creation *ex nihilo* and the Aristotelian connection between time and change caused him to rule out certain senses of 'eternal'.   For elaboration of these distinctions in Aristotle, see M. Kneale, "Eternity and Sempiternity," *Proceedings of the Aristotelian Society*, 69 (1968-1969), 223-238.

[2] Cf. Aquinas, *Summa Theologiae*, Vol. 2, p. 143.

two must be identical.[1]   Thus time and eternity are integrally related. The second argument proceeds from an Aristotelian point.   Quoting *Physics*, IV, 12, 221b28, Aquinas introduces a hierarchy of measurements.   The measure of the most fundamental change measures all changes as the measure of the most fundamental existence measures all existence.[2]   Since eternity measures divine existence which is the most fundamental existence, by order of the hierarchy, eternity must be the measure of all existence.   In particular, it must also measure finite existence (changing existence).   But finite existence is measured by time. So time must be part of eternity.   In spite of Aquinas' previous arguments concerning the uniqueness and simplicity of eternity, he realizes that he will have great difficulty making the concept apply consistently if he is not able to overcome these objections, for he has himself admitted that eternity includes a "flow of duration"[3] in the activity of the divine life and that it must be grasped in "the idea of an abiding instant".[4]

Even with these previous admissions, Aquinas is quite direct concerning the relation between time and eternity. "Time and eternity clearly differ".[5] What he understands by this claim is shown in his counter-arguments.   His first response attempts to meet the objection that time is really a subset of eternity. This, he claims, appears to be the case only because the argument is founded upon an accidental rather that an essential difference. That time has a beginning and an end is, according to Aquinas, merely a contingent fact. That eternity has neither beginning nor end is also contingent.

---

[1] Aquinas, *Summa Theologiae*, Vol. 2, p. 143.
[2] Aquinas, *Summa Theologiae*, Vol. 2, p. 145.
[3] Ibid., p. 137.
[4] Ibid., p 139.
[5] Ibid., p. 145.

For if we suppose that time has neither beginning nor end, a difference between time and eternity still remains. Eternity is an "instantaneous whole" measuring "abiding existence" while time is successive and measures change. Aquinas concludes that the objection would be valid if time and eternity were measures of the same type, but they are not.[1] In response to the other two objections, he admits that the "now" of time remains unchanged in its application to the present moment, but he argues that it takes on different forms. This alteration constitutes change. But eternity remains unchanged "both in substance and form".[2] Eternity cannot be equated with the "now" of time. Finally, eternity is the proper measurement of existence and time the proper measurement of change. But Aquinas asserts that "any existence which falls short of permanence in its existing and is subject to change, so will it fall short of eternity and be subjected to time".[3] Thus, changeable existence is measured by time but not by eternity.

      This final point is amplified in the discussion of the difference between time and aeon. Aquinas argues that eternity-aeon-time represents a continuum from absolute permanence (divine immutability) to complete changeableness (motion within the observed world). This

---

[1] Aquinas, *Summa Theologiae*, Vol. 2, p. 145. Aquinas holds this in opposition to Aristotle who believed eternity to be endless time. Aquinas' adoption of the Platonic notion of "timeless" eternity is fundamental to this argument. It was Aristotle's connection between time and change which forced this Platonic view on Aquinas.

[2] Ibid. p. 147.

[3] Ibid. Aquinas seems to have believed that his admission that eternity is a measurement was not damaging because it "measures" only divine (unchangeable) being. But strictly speaking, any admission of this sort undermines his position for he has previously claimed that all measurement is a mark of temporal, changing reality. Aquinas has fallen prey here to the temptation to say something positive about a *via negativa* predicate and the consequences are obvious.

continuum suggests that things which fall short of abiding existence do so in degrees. And the further they fall short of abiding existence, the more they are characterized by time and the less by eternity.[1] This seems to introduce some qualifications into the previous picture that eternity is totally and irrevocably distinct from time, i.e. not even of the same order. If eternity and time do in fact represent the two ends of a sliding scale, the absolute dichotomy between them is considerably weakened.

The Unity of Time

In the same text Aquinas discusses the unity of time. He argues that the:

> true ground of time's unity is therefore the unity of the most fundamental process in the world, by which—since it is the simplest—all mental processes are measured, as Aristotle says. Time is not only the measure of this process, but also an accident of it, and so receives unity from it. But time is merely a measure of other processes, and so is not diversified by their diversity, for one measure, when independently existent, can measure many things.[2]

It is difficult to determine exactly what Aquinas has in mind in this passage. The reference to Aristotle seems to be to the discussion of measure and unity in the *Metaphysics*. But the notion of "the most fundamental process in the world" is not at all clear in the Aristotelian context. Aristotle argues that measure is a function of quantity and quantity is reducible to unity. Thus, "'measure' means that by which each thing is primarily

---

[1] Aquinas, *Summa Theologiae*, Vol. 2, p. 149.
[2] Ibid., p. 153.

known, and the measure of each thing is a unit-- . . ."[1] He concludes that "the measure of number is most exact, for we posit the unity as in every way indivisible; . . ."[2] But these remarks do not seem particularly helpful in understanding the thrust of Aquinas' argument. If Aquinas is to be consistent with his previous description of the function of the measure of time, he must intend this passage to apply to motion or change. If this is true, then the fundamental process mentioned must be the general idea of motion (the transition from potentiality to actuality). This would certainly fit the description as the most fundamental process in the world. And it would show an obvious connection to the Aristotelian roots which viewed time as a "numbering of before and after". The indivisible unit of motion would be the isolated instant of time. If we were to assume that such a division of time were possible (that time ultimately could be conceived of as individual, indivisible units[3]), then the connection which Aquinas mentions might make sense. But that would only help us clear up the peripheral issue, "What did Aquinas mean when he referred this argument to Aristotle?" We will not as yet have touched the pivotal concern of the claim Aquinas wishes to make.

Looking at the immediate context of the argument, Aquinas' claim becomes even more confusing. He wishes to distinguish this statement of time's unity from three others. The first is a unity of numbers. Here he quotes Aristotle again (time is a numbering) but says that the unity

---

[1] Aristotle, *Metaphysics*, Books X-XIV, tans. By Hugh Tredennick, Loeb Classical Library (London: William Heinemann, 1947), p. 7.

[2] Aristotle, *Metaphysics*, Books X-XIV, tans. By Hugh Tredennick, Loeb Classical Library (London: William Heinemann, 1947), p. 7.

[3] One might consider the parallels in the Greeks (Zeno) and the resulting problems. This conception has a definite relationship to the spatialization of time.

of numbers alone is not sufficient to ground the temporal unity since "time is not a number abstracted from the things it numbers, but a numberedness existing in the things themselves . . ." [1] This suggests that the numbering of intervals is possible only because the idea of before and after is an essential element of the actual process of change. Time is not merely a convenient but abstract method of indicating these successions. It is rather a mathematical description of some *essential* aspect of finite substance itself. It is an essential characteristic of changeable beings. The second position Aquinas wishes to challenge derives the unity of time from eternity. This alternative argues that eternity is the source of all duration and since time is one measure of duration, time's unity is to be found in its ultimate source -- eternity. It should be fairly obvious that Aquinas finds this suggestion unsatisfactory. In his view, time is not to be subsumed under the category of eternity. He also rejects the possibility (the third position) that the unity of time is to be found in the unity of matter. But the stated reasons for his rejection of these last two alternatives are obscure. He says:

> Neither derivation seems adequate, however, for things that are one in source or in subject, especially when these are the distant source and subject, are not one simply speaking, but only one in certain respects. [2]

If we take this at face value, it seems to be easily overturned. After all, Aquinas seems to admit some sense of continuity between the distant source and the issue at hand (cf. "comprehended" and the continuum). And this is surely not consistent with his previous strong dichotomy

---

[1] Aquinas, *Summa Theologiae*, Vol. 2, p. 153.
[2] Ibid.

between time and eternity nor is it compatible with the claims made in the rejection of the first alternative. Aquinas must require individually complete and separate foundations for the unity of time and the unity of eternity. Otherwise, the "certain respects" which he admits would seem to be enough to establish a connection between the two.

We can certainly make a stronger case for the rejection of the second alternative out of the previous discussion Aquinas has given. But we are left with alternative three as a consequence of the apparent direction of the rebuttal to alternative one. Moreover, the founding of temporal measurement in the ultimate unity of matter seems to be in keeping with Aquinas' summary position on the true ground of time's measurement. For the fundamental process which he refers to must certainly be intimately connected with the idea of changeable matter. Aquinas is hesitant to accept the argument that time is founded upon the unity of matter simply because he does not wish to endorse a Greek concept of the material as co-eternal (on either interpretation) with the divine. Aquinas believes in creation *ex nihilo*. If he were to argue this alternative view of time's unity on the grounds that matter itself is derived and that the ultimate foundation of everything is the divine, immaterial, immutable Being, he could justifiably reject the alternative. But he could do so only by admitting a *significant and fundamental relation between* eternal, immaterial, immutable divinity and temporal, material and changeable substance. For then the measure of finite changing substance (time) would in fact be founded upon the infinite, eternal God. And it is just this sort of connection which Aquinas is apparently trying to avoid.

Upon reflection, we can see just how strange this line of argument has become. There is no question that Aquinas wishes to maintain a doctrine of immutability.

This follows from the *via negativa* presuppositions. And from immutability, Aquinas deduces the doctrine of eternity understood as timelessness. But Aquinas also wishes to support the notion of God as Creator and Sustainer for he sees God as the final synthesis of both Presocratic themes. In this role, God must be intimately connected with the world of change. And it is certainly appropriate for Aquinas to assert this connection if he wishes to uphold a doctrine of creation *ex nihilo*. For that is the paradigm case of God's interactions with the world. Yet Aquinas apparently denies any relationship between God's "activity" and the event order of the world on the grounds that such a relationship would destroy the logical dichotomy established in the doctrine of eternity. Here we encounter another example of disturbance in the theological matrix but this one will turn out to have logical ramifications of a much greater magnitude than the problem associated with the idea of impassibility. Since even now the tip of the iceberg shows through the water, we must ask what problematic context allows Aquinas to assert both creation *ex nihilo* and timeless eternity.

Now that we have begun the critique of the position put forward by Aquinas, we see Aquinas is caught between admitting a definite connection between divine, eternal, immutable Being and temporality or else accepting a doctrine of the co-eternal existence of the material world. Perhaps Aquinas would have fared better if he had not attempted to assert the unity of time at all. What motives lie behind such an assertion and why did Aquinas feel that statement of temporal unity had to be made?[1]

---

[1] Although it was not one of Aquinas' concerns, we may note that postulating the existence of co-eternal material will not really solve the problem created by the dichotomy. Parmenides saw this and denied the material. The Greek synthesis cannot be accomplished until his insight

The context of this discussion about the unity of time is an attempt to answer the question, "Is there only one aeon, as there is one time and one eternity?" This question alone makes clear Aquinas' motive. Time is the measure of all change. Suppose that there were two or more discontinuous temporal systems measuring change. Since they are discontinuous, they could be incommensurable.[1] It would then follow that some given change in the material world could be accounted for in different schemes. But that means that the very notion of change comes under attack for there is no reason to suppose that two discontinuous, incommensurable systems would attribute "before" and "after" to the same events in the same way. That is to say, events could not be put into an isomorphic correspondence between alternative systems. Under these circumstances, it would be impossible to speak of change as a fundamental process of the material world for the idea of change itself would be relative to the temporal system we wished to employ. Strictly speaking, what is an event in one scheme might fail to appear at all in the other scheme. Aquinas, however, is committed to the belief that the causal nexus of the material world (of all creation) can be traced back to a single unmoved mover and to a single creative "event". This means that every apparently discontinuous and incommensurable temporal scheme had in fact a common point in the first cause. Consequently, in

---

is given full consideration. But for Aquinas, the problem seems worse, for he cannot even begin the synthesis by postulating an eternal world.

[1] We must distinguish between comparison of *intervals* in two measurement systems and comparison of two measurement systems as *wholes*. The first relates individual points of one system to individual points of another. The second relates extended accounts (stories) of one scheme to accounts of another. Discontinuous systems could fail to be comparable in either or both ways. For further information on the logical coherence of such a possibility, see W. H. Newton-Smith, *The Structure of Time*, chapter 4.

the Thomistic view the adoption (or supposition) of radically different temporal measurement systems fails for any system can be reconciled with any other by tracing it back to the first principle and developing a correspondence from there. To suppose that there is in fact more than one temporal system (that time is not a unity) is to suppose either that there is more than one first cause in the material nexus or that change is infinitely regressive (that there is no first cause). According to Aquinas, both of these possibilities are self-contradictory. Moreover, each implies the denial of the Christian God *qua* Creator. Therefore, it is absolutely essential that Aquinas assert the unity of time. He cannot give up that unity without incurring a denial of the unique nature of the divine being.

But the inability to circumvent this difficulty by retraction leaves Aquinas open to critical attack. We have already indicated this line of criticism by pointing out the conflict generated by denying the first and third alternatives on the unity of time. One the one hand, Aquinas contends that time is a numbering "existing in the things themselves" and not an abstraction from the things numbered. But on the other hand, he denies that the unity of time can be established from the ultimate unity of matter. It is now clear why Aquinas wished to avoid the second of these possibilities, but in doing so he seems to have undercut his initial position. Certainly he does not allow the postulation of co-eternal matter, but he is then forced to assert that material existence arises not only *ex nihilo* but *ex non temporalibus*.

A Problem For Creation

Aquinas seems to have recognized this yet nevertheless embraced it. However, he appears not to have realized that this calls forth a general objection to his entire programme and to his strong dichotomy between time and eternity. Echoing Schleiermacher, we may state the objection like this:[1]

{1} God is either the cause (source) of the created order or He is not.

{2} If He is the cause of the created order, than at least one act of His existence can be given temporal location; namely, the act of establishing the material order.

{3} And if a single act of God can be given temporal location, then that act is compatible and correlated with the general scheme of temporal occurrence in the material world. (The creation of the material world is an act within the temporal scheme).

{4} Therefore, at least one act of God is appropriately located in the temporal process, i.e. it happened at *some* time.

{5} But if one act of divine being is locatable within the temporal process, than every other act of the divine Being can be correlated with the temporal process.

{6} Therefore, either God is timeless and is not the Creator or God is the Creator and is not timeless.

Actually, Schleiermacher developed this objection in its negative form and it is worth stating the negative features of this argument because they immediately call into question the dichotomy proposed by Aquinas. This version proceeds in the following manner:

{1} Imagine that God exists eternally and that this eternal existence is wholly and completely unrelated to the

---

[1] Friedrich Schleiermacher, *The Christian Faith*, trans. by H. R. Mackintosh and J. S. Stewart (2nd ed., Edinburgh: T. & T. Clark, 1956), paragraph 54, section I, p. 212. Also see the discussion in Nelson Pike, *God and Timelessness* (New York: Schocken Books, 1970), Chapter 6.

temporal order or the material world (God exists "outside" time).

{2} In order for this to be the case, there must be no *possibility* of relating any attribute or activity of God to the temporal process.

{3} Therefore, it is impossible that God could act in any way which might be given temporal location.

{4} But the act of creation has a temporal location (can be described in terms of "before" and "after").

{5} So it follows that a timeless God could not create.

We have applied this objection only to the idea of the original creation, but Schleiermacher saw that the same argument could just as easily be raised against any assertion of divine activity within the temporal process, in particular against claims of divine intervention and sustenance. Consequently, the scope of the objection is very powerful indeed. Aquinas' formulation of the unity of time coupled with his belief in the unique first cause leaves him in an almost intractable position. The position is only "almost" intractable because there remains one avenue of escape, as we shall see. But this exit is not without its own consequences. And those consequences will lead to even more frustrating problems for the idea of a timeless God.

The Beginning Of Time

What avenue could Aquinas choose which would allow passage around this present difficulty? The answer is directly proposed in Aquinas' commentary on Aristotle's *Physics*[1] and implicit in the Greek foundation of the

---

[1] Aquinas develops the argument as a consequence of his distinction between *real* and *imaginary* time. This distinction became necessary in order to disengage his theology from Aristotle's account that time was everlasting because the world was everlasting. Aquinas argues, "when we say that things were not eternally produced by God, we do not mean

Summa.[1] It is particularly related to the doctrine that time is a measure of change and change is an aspect of the world. Aquinas circumvents the present objection by maintaining that time "began" with the creation of the material world – that time was created along with change in substance. Therefore, any talk of temporal categories surrounding the creation "event" is strictly illegitimate. This is a denial that the creation of the material world is an event within the temporal scheme. If time begins with change in material substance, then it makes no sense to ask what happened *before* material substance existed. The concepts of 'before' and 'after' could not apply to an event which granted the very possibility of those concepts. God, in his no-temporal existence, could not be located within the temporal stream since His creative activity is not locatable by any application of 'before' or 'after'. His creation is not a change in substance; it is the very possibility of substance.

Even if we accept this solution as it stands (and we will find that it does not stand very well), we will be forced to adopt, as a consequence, a rather radical doctrine concerning Gods' continuing relation to His created order. While this radical doctrine does find a place within the

---

that an infinite time preceded in which God ceased from acting, and that after a determined time He began to act. Rather we mean that God produced time and things together in being after they were not." Aquinas, *Commentary on Aristotle's Physics*, trans. by Richard J. Blackwell, Richard J. Spath and W. Edmund Thirlkel (London: Routledge & Kegan Paul, 1963), p. 485. For the complete argument against Aristotle, see pages 485-487.

[1] The idea of the creation of time with the creation of the material world is explicitly proposed in Plato (*Timaeus*, 38b5). Cf. Kneale's comments ("Time and Eternity in Theology") on the transfer of this Platonic doctrine to Christian theology. Also compare Augustine, *City of God*, Books VIII-XVI, trans. by Gerald Walsh and Grace Monahan (Washington, DC: Catholic University of America Press, 1952), XI, 21, pp. 217-219.

history of Christian theology, it is certainly not one that would have been acceptable to Aquinas or the early church fathers. The proposed solution (putting the creation of time into the creation of the material world) speaks directly only of the initial creative act. It avoids the criticism that God must be temporally located in at least this act by suggesting that time begins with this act. God still maintains His no-temporal existence. But we have already noted that the argument against a non-temporal existence also calls into question the Christian doctrines of God's sustaining power and intervention. Since the present proposal deals only with the creation, these other important Christian doctrines remain significant counter-examples unless they too can be shown to be compatible with a non-temporal deity.

It appears that the only possible means of demonstrating such a compatibility must come through adoption of a deistic doctrine. This position allows God to remain in the isolation of non-temporality simply because it asserts that God has *no further action or interaction* with His creation after its inception. In other words, the deistic solution affirms the independent self-governing of the material world, on the one hand, and denies the possibility of divine intervention on the other. While such a position certainly rescues God from temporal location, it does so only at a tremendous price as far as Aquinas is concerned for it quite literally removes God from the world in every sense.

That Aquinas would find the deistic solution untenable goes without saying. But he would have rejected it on theological grounds in spite of the fact that he would then have had to face an unresolved difficulty concerning God's sustaining powers and interaction. The real question we must answer is this: Does the deistic solution really solve the problem of God and time? It should be clear enough that if the argument concerning the creation of time along with the creation of the material world collapses, so too will the need for adopting a deistic solution. Since the deistic position is only an *ad hoc* arrangement designed to relieve pressure created by the original proposal that time is created, it does not and cannot speak directly to the problem at hand. It is a second order concern and will only take precedence if the thesis of a creation of time is shown to be valid. Consequently, we may dismiss deistic considerations as a side-issue until we have shown that the idea of the creation of time cannot be avoided.

The difficulty we face is the logical compatibility of the doctrine of creation *ex nihilo* and the existence of a *no-temporal* God.[1] Creation of the material order seems to be temporally locatable. If it is an *act* of God (an event), then it happened at some time (regardless of how it happened or when it occurred, etc.). Yet God is, according to the *via negativa*, absolutely non-temporal, without any relation to time. Against this objection, Aquinas argues that time itself must be created. This solution is consistent with the commitment that he shows to the Aristotelian connection between time and change. Aquinas employs an argument something like this:

{1} Change is measured by time. Time is the measure of change.
{2} Wherever there is change, there must be time.
{3} Whenever there is time, there must be change.
{4} Therefore, where there is no change, there cannot be time; and when there is no time, there cannot be change.

---

[1] One might object that there is no reason, given the rise of modern science, to continue to believe in a doctrine of creation *ex nihilo*. I think that this objection is not well-grounded but it would make little difference to the problem here for it is clear that Schleiermacher's general argument eliminates any possibility of a non-temporal God creating anything at all. This would entail major problems for Christianity regardless of any particular doctrine concerning the first Creation.

Now the importance of the previous discussion of immutability can be seen. With that doctrine, theologians attempted to formalize the belief that God does not and cannot change. Under the influence of the Greeks, this changeless existence could only occur if it were not temporal. Since the presupposition of Aquinas' discussion of eternity is the doctrine of immutability, it is only reasonable that he should assert the creation of time with the creation of material substance. Prior to this creation, only God existed. And since God's existence is absolutely changeless, it provides nothing for the measurement 'time' to express. Consequently, time could only begin when something which had the possibility for change (and actually did change) existed. We might put it like this: In Aquinas' view, time could not have begun until there was an actual change in substance.[1] If our critique is to succeed in undermining the idea of the creation of time, it must attack the notion that time only occurs where there is change.

Time Without Change

Fortunately, this problem has had some recent and significant treatment in the development of tense logic. For our purposes, it is not necessary to enter into an elaboration of this area. We can understand the argument about time and change without pursuing the symbolic formulations of tense logic if we turn our attention to the remarks of J. R. Lucas in *A Treatise on Time and Space*.[2] Lucas cites an

---

[1] Notice that the first change cannot have a "before", creating an asymmetry which has several unusual problems of its own.

[2] J. R. Lucas, *A Treatise on Time and Space* (London: Methuen & Co., 1973), pp. 10-11.

argument of Isaac Barrow[1] who suggested that an initial
stationary state of the universe was possible (a stationary
state being one in which there is no change). If the thesis
that time is to be defined in terms of the occurrence of
change is true, then such a state would be logically
impossible, for it would logically exclude the existence of
any duration unmarked by actual change. But Lucas claims
that such a state is logically possible (i.e. it can be
conceived of without contradiction). His argument turns on
distinctions between the kind of propositions which can be
made in a situation where there is time without change and
in a situation where there is no time until there is change.
If time is defined in terms of change, it would be logically
impossible to have an initial changeless but temporal state
(it would be impossible to have *any* changeless, temporal
state but for this argument we need only consider this
particular state).   The question, "Can we produce an
entailment from the hypothesis that time has a beginning
which states that a stationary state is impossible?", should
be answered affirmatively.   What follows from the
hypothesis that time has a beginning? Lucas chooses one
conditional statement in particular; namely, "If it was the
case sometime that *p*, it was also the case sometime that it
was not ever the case that *q* was false." As he suggests, the
antecedent of this conditional will be false at that moment
of the beginning of time simply because it tries to assert
something about the past and there is, *ex hypothesi*, no past.
In this case, the entire conditional is true. Moreover, at any
later date the consequent can be made true by choosing that
same initial moment of time when there was no past. Thus,
if time has a beginning, this particular conditional
statement is always true. But the structure of this kind of
conditional is logically distinct from and not reducible to

---

[1] Isaac Barrow, *The Geometrical Lectures of Isaac Barrow*, trans. by J.
M Child (LaSalle, IL: Open Court, 1916), pp. 35-37.

the kind of propositions which can be made in a situation where either is an unspecified period of time without change. For the hypothesis of an initial stationary state is a much weaker one. The conditional statement which follows from the hypothesis that time had a beginning asserts that in every case, for any choice of q, the entire conditional is true. But the stationary state hypothesis does not allow us to make this claim. For example, we could choose a statement q, "Some of the stars were moving". Now this statement would be false in a stationary state since nothing whatsoever is moving. But the conditional statement which follows from the stronger claim that time has a beginning would imply that there was a time at which it was not ever false that "some of the stars were moving". And the hypothesis of a stationary state could not allow us to make this claim because without the assumption that time has a beginning we should only be able to assert that whatever statement we might make, its truth or falsity would remain constant in a state without change. That is to say, the falsity of the statement, "Some of the stars were moving", would be guaranteed to remain forever false as long as time went on without change. But that guarantee is not compatible with the implication of the conditional derived under the assumption that time has a beginning; namely, that there was a time when "Some of the stars are moving" was never false. The conclusion is this: time cannot be defined solely in terms of actual change.

A Debt To Aristotle

We can apply this analysis to the Thomistic position. Behind St. Thomas stood Aristotle and behind Aristotle the Presocratics. Aquinas draws from this heritage when he refers to Book IV of Aristotle's *Physics*. There Aristotle gives several arguments about the nature of time which are particularly influential. He notes that time cannot be movement *per se* since movement is characterized by being in something or someplace and by being either fast or slow and these are not applicable to time.[1] Nevertheless, time seems to be essentially related to movement in some way. He argues that time does not exist without change for our perception of time depends on our perception of change.[2] Time is something that belongs to movement and time and movement are always correlated with each other. Because "we apprehend time only when we have marked motion, marking it by 'before' and 'after'", we must conclude that "no time is *thought* to have elapsed when there is no motion."[3] This argument sets the stage for several other important assertions about the nature of time. Having shown to his satisfaction that time cannot exist without motion, Aristotle lays down the definition later adopted by Aquinas: "For time is just this—number of motion in respect of 'before' and 'after'".[4] The following passages collect Aristotle's thoughts about this definition:

A. It is clear, then, that time is 'number of movement in respect of before and after', and is continuous since it is an attribute of what is continuous.[5]

---

[1] Aristotle, *Physica*, IV, 10, 218b.

[2] Aristotle, *Physica*, IV, 10, 219a. Note the claim is an *epistemological* one.

[3] Ibid. (italics mine).

[4] Aristotle does allow that we can hypothesize existence without time (cf. Below, quotation C) but he does not allow that it makes sense to suggest time without existing *and* changing entities. In one sense, Aristotle could claim that we cannot conceive of time without change, i.e. we cannot imagine what it would be like to experience it because there is nothing to experience. But this does not show it to be logically impossible.

[5] Aristotle, *Physica*, IV, 10, 220a.

B. Not only do we measure the movement by the time, but also the time by the movement, because they define each other.[1]

C. A thing . . .will be affected by time, . . . time wastes things away . . .[2] . . . for we regard time in itself as destroying rather than producing, for what is counted in time is movement, and movement dislodges whatever it affects from its present state. From all this it is clear that things which exist eternally, as such, are not in time; for they are not embraced by time, nor is their duration measured by time. This is indicated by their not suffering anything under the action of time as though they were within its scope.[3]

D. It is clear then that it [time] must be in itself . . the condition of destruction rather   than coming into being (for change, in itself, makes things depart from their former condition), and only incidentally of coming into being, and of being.[4]

If we examine these statements in detail we see that Aristotle becomes more and more dogmatic about the connection between time and change as he progresses with the arguments. The pattern he present is this:

---

[1] Aristotle, *Physica*, IV, 10, 220b.

[2] Aristotle, *Physica*, IV, 10, 220a.

[3] Aristotle, *The Physics*, Vol. I, IV, 10, 221b. W. Kneale, "Time and Eternity in Theology", maintains that Aristotle rejected the timeless understanding of eternity for reasons similar to those behind his rejection of the Platonic forms. He claims that Aristotle held the weaker distinction between time and sempiternity. But this is not enough to account for some Aristotelian claims. Aristotle suggests that mathematical entities are eternal and he certainly cannot have meant that they *just happen* to always be the same (as omnitemporality-sempiternity would imply). This quotation clearly suggests that some things do *not exist in time*. Cf. Kneale, pp. 98, 102-103.

[4] Aristotle, *Physica*, IV, 10, 222b.

1. Time is not, strictly speaking, motion.
2. But time does not exist without motion.
3. Time belongs to motion.
4. Time and motion always correspond with each other.
5. Time is the number of motion.
6. Time does not occur where there is no motion.
7. Time is an attribute of motion.
8. Time defines motion (and motion defines time).

On the surface at least, there seem to be some internal inconsistencies between the propositions in this list. Aristotle begins by noting that time and motion are two distinct "things" and he ends by claiming that they are definitional equivalents. What process of thought allows him to pass from this distinction to an asserted equivalence? It is easy to see how the first few of the above statements are generated. Common sense indicates a correspondence between time and motion (change). Time without change is inconceivable, it appears, simply because there would be no way to determine that any time had elapsed. From our perspective, there is no difference between a time when nothing is happening and no time at all. It is this common sense view which Aristotle reflects in statements (2) through (6). On the other hand, common sense recognizes that time and change are conceptually different in spite of the tight connection between them. Time is the measure and change the measured.

But Aristotle asserts that of the two ideas, we never have one without the other, we never perceive one without the other and we cannot even imagine one without the other. Yet he wishes to maintain that they are distinct and different concepts. If these two concepts are mutually dependent in existence (occurrence), perception and conception, on what grounds are we able to assert that they are not identical? There are many examples of mutually dependent characteristics in existence and perception[1], but the difficulty arises with the third part of this claim. It is this sort of reasoning which leads Aristotle from statements (1) through (7) to statements (8) and (9). By drawing out the implications of the common sense view, he sees less and less distinction between the two concepts until finally he proposes that they are definitional equivalents.[2]

We have already shown that time without change is conceivable. What prevents Aristotle from entertaining this possibility is his confusion of the epistemological and ontological aspects of this relation. Because he adopts the implications of the common sense view that time could not be *known to us* without the presence of change, he asserts that time could not   *be at all* without the presence of change. But time without change is a *logical possibility*. And that it is logically possible is enough to demonstrate the inadequacy of the Aristotelian transition from the phenomenal subject to the ontological relation. This, however, raises a serious epistemological problem. The demonstration that time without change is a logical possibility does not refute what Aristotle was most concerned to show. It certainly seems that the knowing subject has no justification for asserting the passage of time in the absence of all change. Lucas makes some remarks on this problem:

---

[1] For example, consider molecular shift and shift in valence or electrical charge and electron excitation through a medium. Any specification of necessary and sufficient conditions for change will do. These only specify causally necessary but logically contingent situations. In Aristotle, the claim is stronger. We have shown the logical possibility of time without change but not the reverse (and for good reason). The relation is not symmetrical, as Aristotle believed.

[2] W. Kneale, "Time and Eternity in Theology," has shown that this strong connection between time and change is at least as early as Pythagoras. See pp. 90-92.

To prove the passage of time in the absence of change is as difficult as to prove the existence of objects in the absence of their being observed. But the skeptic is being unreasonably hard to satisfy. In any particular case, the report of the elapse of time experienced without there being any change so far as the person was concerned may be mistaken. Barrow himself lays emphasis on 'more perfect', and allows, with Aristotle and Lucretius, that a human mind may be unable to perceive the passage of time in the absence of external change. But not everyone need be mistaken. On some occasions, in particular, we are conscious of everything being still, and later, when our experience is put in question, we discover that , unknown to us, some change had been going on—that the Pleiades had moved behind the spreading elm. This is enough to vindicate our original experience as having been veridical and to reject gratuitous imputations of unreliability. We can affirm again that it is possible that every external thing we are conscious of is still, and then we are conscious of it as being still. It is only sometimes, to ward off the suggestion that our experience might have been illusory, that we need to refer to some subsequent discovery of there having been a change going on unnoticed while everything for us was motionless. The state of perfect tranquility is not only logically possible, but capable of being known by us individually, although epistemological difficulties prevent us proving to the skeptic the fact of our actually having had our calm hours. No contention can compel this conclusion, but only actual experience or the peaceful persuasion of the poets.[1]

Shoemaker and Newton-Smith have given some more general support to the "peaceful persuasion of the poets, with the following example.[2] Imagine a possible world inhabited by three different tribes. Although each tribe lives in a separate area, they have the ability to

---

[1] J. R. Lucas, *Treatise on Time and Space*, p. 13.
[2] Sydney Shoemaker, "Time Without Change," *Journal of Philosophy*, LXVI (June 19, 1969), 363-381; and W. H. Newton-Smith, *The Structure of Time*, Chapter 2. Newton-Smith offers a much improved example with considerations of possible objections concerning the acausality of time. I use Shoemaker's account for its simplicity.

communicate with and observe each other. The unusual thing about this world is that every third year the inhabitants of the first tribal area enter a state of suspended animation in which the entire area is instantaneously frozen into absolute changelessness. This state lasts for one year. The entire situation is repeated for the other tribal areas but with different cycles – the second tribe is frozen every fourth year and the third tribe every fifth year. This process goes on for sixty years. At the end of sixty years, we can see that any given tribe would have good reason to believe that something had happened to the other tribes at regular intervals and, on the reports of others, that they too had been frozen. But now that they can all communicate, they may discover that there is good reason to believe that in the sixtieth year all of them existed during a period of absolute changelessness; reasons which involve the previous observations, extrapolations, etc.

It is this evidence which makes the example reasonable. If we were to suppose that all three tribes experienced the state of suspended animation at the same time without previous cyclical alterations, no evidence could ever be convincing enough to give rise to the hypothesis of the actual stationary state, for then it would be no different than imagining that we experience such suspensions between our moments of consciousness – that for every moment of consciousness there are unspecified durations of suspended changelessness. The evidence for such a proposal is no more (or less) convincing than evidence for ideas like the continual momentary creation and destruction of all Being. As we shall see, certain key distinctions not recognized by Aristotle lie behind these epistemological problems.

In the face of these difficulties concerning the recognition of changeless states, we may feel that the claim to have shown the *logical* possibility of time without change is rather lame. But this logical possibility demonstrates that the notion of an immutable, non-temporal eternity cannot be supported from a connection between time and change. If time is even logically possible without change, then the idea that eternity differs from time because it is essentially changeless is false. It is no longer possible for Aquinas to assume that time belongs only to the realm of finite, changeable being.

From the passages cited in C and D above, we see that change always represented movement from what is toward what will be and this is a process of decay.[1] According to Aristotle, all temporal things move from some original state toward final deterioration. Certainly ordinary observation bears this out. Temporality implies change and change implies decay. When Aquinas accepted this implication, it became absolutely essential to remove God from the temporal order. God is perfect. As such, He could not lack anything that was necessary for His perfection. IF He were to change, He would either gain something He previously did not have or He would lose something He previously had. The Aristotelian implication supports the latter possibility. Either one makes perfection impossible. Perfect completeness could not be maintained in the presence of change. As long as time was a concomitant of this idea of change and completeness was the basis of perfection, there was no way of asserting that God could change without implying that God was not perfect. Following Aristotle, Aquinas reasoned that if God were temporal, He would necessarily lose His essential

---

[1] Aristotle's remark that time in itself is the condition of destruction rather than generation certainly accords with general observation, but it leaves some important correlations between change, growth, first cause and time unaccounted for. Aquinas seems to suggest that God's role as the unmoved mover can fill these gaps but that suggestion presumes that the important synthesis which the Greeks sought can be accomplished. The objections we are now exploring suggest that this presumption is mistaken.

perfection as all temporal things do. But the logical possibility of a stationary state allows us to separate the ideas of time and change. The Thomistic assumptions must be re-evaluated.

Time and Change

This conclusion is extremely important. It provides a critique of the Thomistic assumption and also forces us to reconsider the definition of time and the recognition of temporal passage. Let us first review the aforementioned epistemological problem: in the absence of all change, how could we know that some time has elapsed? The answer is straightforward – we could not know directly. Even Shoemaker's argument depends on indirect evidence. But this points out the interesting aspects of discussions of static states. There are moments when we wish to say that nothing was happening and we were still *conscious* of the passage of time. That is because we use the word 'change' in two senses. It can refer either to observable, external or physical alterations or it can refer to all of these *and* acts of consciousness.[1] This distinction leads to three possibilities for the epistemological relation between time and change. Two of these are consequences of direct experience.

1. The occurrence of physical change implies the passage of time.
2. The occurrence of mental activity implies the passage of time.

The third, based on the logical possibility of time without change, lies beyond direct evidence.

---

[1] I dismiss the possibility of using 'change' in the "McTaggartian" or "Cambridge" sense here for the same reasons mentioned in the literature. See Shoemaker, "Time Without Change," pp. 364-365 and 378-381; W. H. Newton-Smith, *The Structure of Time*, Chapter 2.

3. Indirect, non-experiential evidence derived from broader theoretical considerations may imply the passage of time.

While each of these is a sufficient condition, none is a necessary *and* sufficient condition for temporality.

An assertion that some time had elapsed could be based on any one of these three possibilities. Lack of physical change does not preclude evidence for temporal passage for I may still notice a change in my mental states or I may realize that I had existed for some duration (I have a memory trace). What is revealing about these two senses of the word 'change' is that the experience of internal time consciousness is *more primordial* than the recognition of external temporal succession. The difference between relations (1) and (2) is crucial. Aquinas blurs this distinction so that, on the one hand, he speaks as though eternity excludes all change (even mental ones), but on the other hand, he believes that God is a conscious being.

For Aristotle and Aquinas, time, motion and location stood together.[1] We have seen that ordinary reflection on states of the physical world leads quite naturally to this triad. But ordinary reflection requires the activity of a conscious subject – a knower. Thus the epistemological problem is generated. And the very statement of the problem leads us to see that primordial place of the knowing subject. "What direct evidence could we have for asserting that some time had elapsed in the absence of all change?" The answer – "None." – really says, "We, as knowing subjects, would have no way on our own of determining whether or not some time had elapsed

---

[1] Cf. The analysis of Bas. C. van Fraassen, *An Introduction to the Philosophy of Time and Space* (New York: Random House, 1970), pp. 11-20.

under those conditions." However, this merely leaves us in the neutral position of being unable to affirm or deny the elapse of time. It does not allow the refined Positivistic objection that since we have no *evidence* of the elapse of time either from external changes or changes in consciousness, we must conclude that no time *could have elapsed.* Even if the notion of change is widened to include both physical and mental states, we will still have reasonable ground to suggest the *possibility* of a temporal state of changelessness. Nevertheless, we must recognize that the reasonableness of this suggestion will have to be shown from more general considerations of the idea of evidence, and that the logical possibility of a static state does not affect the epistemological connection between time and change for the observer (so long as change includes both mental and physical occurrences). This distinction between the epistemological and ontological theses of our revised theory of time may be clearer if we pay some attention to an example which shows why the Positivist's objection fails.

Let us consider an analogy from the general theory of fields in physics. Imagine that we are asked to do some research to determine the exact effects of a certain field. At the initial stage we are given a definition of the field in terms of the charge on a test particle. Two interpretations of this definition are open to us. The first follows Positivistic understandings of hypotheticals by suggesting that where there is no test particle, there is no field. Thus, if the definition is true under this interpretation, we could conclude that the absence of a test particle made the presence of a field impossible. The second interpretation is rather more lenient toward hypothetical situations. It suggests that if there were a test particle, then there would be a field but it does not exclude the possibility of a field in the absence of a test particle. If we follow the first interpretation, we could have no reason for entertaining the existence of the field in the absence of the test particle. That is to say, we should have to rest content with the observational evidence we could gather from our experiments on the test particle and consider our work done. However, we have seen that this interpretation is not mandatory. It is still possible (conceptually, at least) that the field in question could exist without the test particle. We are therefore permitted to refine our definition of fields. We may discover that a fully integrated and rich theory of fields *requires* the description of fields *in the absence of the test particle.* In actual scientific practice, we find that field theory needs to be able to talk about fields without test particles because the introduction of a test particle alters the character of the field. Thus, if we depended exclusively upon the first interpretation of our initial definition, we should ultimately never have been able to account for the real nature of the field in question. Only by entertaining the hypothetical, "If there were a test particle, then there would be a field', will we be able to develop a full field theory. At the same time, we must recognize that if we are going to *observe* anything about fields, we will have to rely on the elements of the initial definition under the first interpretation. That is to say, epistemologically we must depend on the test particle's presence. But ontologically we must recognize the necessity of the existence of fields without test particles.

When we report these findings, our Positivist colleagues object that if we must rely on the inclusion of test particles in field theory in order to make *any scientific observations* about fields, we can have no evidence for suggesting the existence of fields without the presence of test particles. Here our appeal must be to the considerations of theory integration and explanatory power. We may admit that, observationally, we must include test particles. But such an admission does not damage the further claim that there are good reasons (though not, perhaps, physical evidence) for not accepting the initial definition. The logical possibility of a field without a test particle and the implications that such a situation has for further development of a general theory show that we are right to reject the restricted definition even if we are observationally bound to it.

The parallels between this example and the definition of time in terms of possible change may need some elaboration. We began with a definition of time which entailed the statement, "Where there is no change, there is no time". Such a consequence is similar to the Positivist's account of fields without test particles. In both cases we have shown the logical possibility of alternative states. Thus, the logical possibility of a stationary state is developed from the hypothetical, "If there is temporal duration, there could have been change", but not from the hypothetical "If there is temporal duration, there is change". Epistemologically, the knower is dependent upon those changes *actually* occurring to justify his observation of temporal passage in the same way that he must depend upon the introduction of a test particle to make observations about a field.

However, an objector might pose yet another difficulty. He might admit that further considerations about a general theory of fields give grounds for postulating the existence of fields without test particles. But that only means that the mere logical possibility of such a field is strengthened and supported because of the requirements of explanatory power and integration for the general theory. This results from the *need* to be able to talk about cases of fields without test particles. But this does not give license to suppose that every logically possible situation is a reality. What strength and support can be given for talking about cases of time without change? What considerations of a general theoretical nature justify the belief in such cases in spite of the epistemological difficulties?

Here the objector is suggesting that the theory of time is not well integrated and not rich enough to allow us to talk about anything interesting in cases where there is time without change. We may respond to this objection along two lines. First, we could disallow the objection. Given that similar arguments have been shown to fail in other cases, the onus of the proof rests upon the objector. Secondly, we can in fact meet the objection. We can supply cases where we would want to and *need* to talk about time without change as a part of a general and integrated theory. For example, we may find it necessary to talk about a stationary state as part of a description of change.[1] Or more importantly, we will need to talk about changeless time within the context of the metaphysical and theological developments of a new conception of God and temporality. While these considerations are not exactly parallel to the mathematics of fields without test particles, they are sufficiently rich and complex to show that an integrated theory of time will necessarily include talk of temporal passage in the absence of change.[2]

Consequences for Immutability

We have shown that the possibility of a temporally changeless state undermines the definition of time found in Aristotle and elaborated in Aquinas. In particular, we have seen that this logical possibility alone is sufficient to force the collapse of the doctrine of eternity interpreted as

---

[1] Cf. Shoemaker's example of the three tribes and Newton-Smith's elaboration of the connections of general topological considerations.

[2] Newton-Smith makes the point that plausible postulation of a temporal vacuum requires that "some improved account of events that actually did occur can be gained" (Newton-Smith, *The Structure of Time*, p. 67). The effort of this study is to demonstrate just such a point for the actual events of God's consciousness can be given improved explanation as a result of the reconsideration of time and change.

timelessness. But that does not mean that Aquinas will be forced to abandon the entire structure of the *via negativa*. For we have conceded as part of our attack that a changeless, although temporal, state is possible. What is to prevent Aquinas from salvaging the doctrine of immutability (which is fundamental to any connection between the *via negativa* and a God who acts) by reinterpreting exactly this changeless temporal state as the appropriate realm of God's existence? To overcome this possibility, we need to show that the *via negativa* theology cannot succeed even if it adopts the idea of a changeless but temporal God into its matrix.[1]

What would it mean to the structure of the *via negativa* to adopt the position that God's eternity was a temporal but changeless state? Such a reinterpretation would affect the network of the *via negativa* at two different levels. The idea of immutability involves two assertions. The first of these is that God never changes. The second is more fundamental. It is that God cannot (logically) change. At the first level, it would seem as though adoption of a temporal but changeless state would fulfill the requirements that God *does not* (as a matter of fact) change. By definition, any thing which existed in such a state would be immutable in this weak sense. But our previous remarks on redefining the idea of time show that such a condition could *only* produce a weak sense of immutability. Relative to the hypothetical definition of time, it would always be a necessary condition of such a

---

[1] It is possible, of course, for Aquinas to continue to maintain a strong distinction between time and eternity and still hold that there may be periods of changeless time. He could hold this position, however, only if he finally admitted that eternity is wholly other than time and that time cannot even be used as a basis for talking about eternity. This would be consistent with the Parmenidean strain in the *via negativa* but, as we shall see, it makes it impossible to believe that God is personal.

state that it was an event which was only *contingently* (i.e. could have been otherwise) changeless.[1] That is to say, when we redefined time under the open hypothetical, "If there is temporal duration, there could have been change", we were able to assert the possibility of a changeless state only on the condition that it could have been otherwise. Thus, the most that we could say about the character of God under this weak version of immutability is that during such a temporal state, God did not in fact change but that there was no *a priori* reason why He could not have changed. This is some consolation for proponents of a doctrine of immutability for initially there seems to be no reason why a weak thesis of immutability could not be extended indefinitely into the past and the future. It would then be appropriate to suggest that God never did and never will change.[2] But we shall see that further consideration prohibits even this minimal version of immutability. Before we pursue arguments to show that a weak thesis like this is incompatible with the Christian God, we must see what effect the redefined notion of time has on a strong thesis of immutability.

Unlike the weak thesis, the strong version does claim *a priori* grounds for asserting that God cannot change. This claim is supported by the more fundamental predicates of the *via negativa*; namely, infinity, simplicity, necessity and perfection. These predicates entail the claim

---

[1] Both 'necessary' and 'contingent' are notoriously ambiguous. The necessity of the present claim arises from the previous argument (i.e. the argument necessarily entails such-and-such). The contingency of the claim is in the event context (i.e. event *p* may or may not occur, it is not an instantiation in every possible world).

[2] An immediate problem, which we will not pursue, is that postulating God's infinite steady state requires that God not be in the same time frame that we are in (for our frame changes). But this means holding a belief in multiple time systems which are incommensurable. Cf. Above p. 128 for the consequences for a creative God.

that God logically cannot change, that God does not belong to the class of changeable beings (i.e. that it is self-contradictory to think of God as changing). The possibility of a temporally changeless state calls into question this entailment. Once the definitional equivalence between time and change is broken, the idea of a timeless God becomes suspect. The strong thesis of immutability can find no solace in the stationary state. Strong immutability requires a logical thesis which the temporal steady state cannot supply. The introduction of temporality, even at this marginal level, would vitiate all of the *via negativa* claims about temporality as a mark of the finite, and would, as a result, call in question the doctrines of infinity, simplicity, necessity and perfection. Infinity would need to be abandoned or reinterpreted in some limited context. Necessity could no longer be held since God's changelessness would be only an accidental feature of His existence. And since God would have the potential for change even if He never exercised it, the concept of God as pure act and undifferentiated essence would have to be replaced. Needless to say, the idea that God has a possibility for change would radically alter the theological and metaphysical concepts of perfection in the divine. It would no longer make sense to assert that if God changed He would no longer be God. The potential for change represented in the stationary state would be enough to entirely destroy the doctrine that perfection necessarily entails actual, absolute completion. Thus, it is clear that strong immutability could not countenance any suggestion that God might be temporal. If we are inclined to adopt the position that God remains changeless only because He exists in the temporal changeless state, we will have to pay the price of abandoning other *via negativa* predicates. Under these circumstances, it is little wonder that eternity was viewed as timelessness by Aquinas and other thinkers of this tradition.

The suggestion of a weak thesis of immutability came about as a result of noticing that God's existence in a temporal steady state could be indefinitely extended into the past and the future and would then give grounds for the assertion, "God never changes". This seemed to be some consolation for the loss of the logical necessity required for a stronger version of immutability. But in that earlier discussion, we argued that the knowing subject was dependent upon the actual occurrence of changes in order to identify the actual temporal passage. This is not to be confused with the claim that a temporal but changeless state might occur. It merely pointed out that it would be impossible for a knowing subject to identify such a state since, by definition, nothing whatsoever transpires in the steady state. But this distinction had a further consequence for the weak thesis of immutability. If immutability is grounded on the postulation that God's existence is a temporal but changeless state of *infinite* duration, it is grounded on the assumption that 'change' is understood in its widest sense embracing both physical and mental acts. And this entails that God, as a knowing subject, could not be conscious of His own existence in such a state since He could have neither direct nor indirect evidence for His existence.

God is a knowing subject according to every Christian theological system. The identification of temporal duration for any knower existing in that temporal span depends upon either direct or indirect evidence of actual change within the compass of the knowing subject. Even the identification of the static state required relations to actual changes and could only be accomplished *after* the static state was over. Something must change if the subject is to be able to recognize the passage of time, even if the change is only the minimal one of the end of a static state. We need not demand some alteration in the external world but we must at least have a mental change. And no

Christian theology has ever denied that God has mental processes – thoughts, at least. But if we try to support a weak thesis of immutability with the postulation of infinite temporal changelessness, we eliminate even the minimal requirements for identification of temporal passage. And since the doctrine of weak immutability is a doctrine about personal being, the elimination of the minimal requirements for the identification of temporal passage forces us to the conclusion that God could not be conscious of His own duration in an infinitely long changeless state.

It should also be apparent that the same criticism could be leveled against the strong thesis of immutability. Since strong immutability entails that eternity be regarded as timelessness and a timeless existence can, by definition, have no change, timeless existence for God must mean that God could not be self-conscious. This conclusion follows directly from the distinctions we made between the epistemological and ontological contexts of time *and* the assumption that all consciousness is temporal (endures through time). The second part of this statement had not been dealt with as yet and it will constitute the next chapter of this study. There we will attempt to show a logical entailment between consciousness and temporality.

Since Aristotle confused the epistemological and ontological contexts, he drew the conclusion that time could not occur where there was no change. He saw that the human subject could not identify temporal passage without change, but he did not consider the possibility of indirect evidence or the logical coherence of changeless time. Moreover, there was no reason for him to believe that the unmoved mover was conscious rather than an expression of the Greek first principle. When Aquinas adopted the Aristotelian unmoved mover, he specifically granted this principle the role of a personal God. Therefore, Aquinas had to face the question, "How can the unmoved mover (God) identify existence (or self-existence) in a changeless and timeless state?" Here the answer linked the doctrine of eternity with the attribute of omniscience. Briefly, the picture of God that the *via negativa* theology drew upon was something like this:

> God exists in timeless eternity. That means God exists as instantaneously whole and perfect. There is no need for God to be able to identify His own duration because He has no duration. The idea of duration belongs to temporality and God is absolutely distinct from temporality. In His existence as instantaneously whole and perfect, He is able to know instantaneously and perfectly everything. God neither gains knowledge nor loses it. By something like direct intuition, He knows timelessly that He *is* (timelessly).

This response seems to have escaped our criticism. It is true that it requires us to suppose that God knows in ways which are totally foreign to our won, but that would be consistent with the *via negativa*. The weak thesis of immutability fails because under its conditions the consciousness of the knowing subject depends on the identification of actual change. But the strong thesis seems insulated from such dependence. However, if we examine the logical compatibility of the strong view of immutability and the idea that God is a person, we shall discover that the thesis of a timeless God finally falls into hopeless linguistic confusion.

In our critique of time and change, we have arrived at the position that there is no good reason not to think of time as everlasting. But having no good reason *not to think* of time as everlasting is not quite the same as having good reason *to think* of time as everlasting. By reconsidering some central theological concepts, I believe we can show that there is also good reason to think that time is everlasting and that God is everlastingly temporal. In order to supply these positive reasons, we need to return to the two uses of the word 'change' and the idea of timeless existence.

The Senses of 'Timeless'

When we discussed the two senses of 'change', we suggested that expressions of the sort, "I've changed my mind", indicated passage of time even though no physical alteration need have occurred. In this regard, we noticed that even the thought of my own existence indicated duration. Can we imagine a case where it would be possible to say that X exists without implying duration? What are the temporal implications of the use of verbs like this and why do these verbs have the implications they do? In order to answer these questions we must return to a previous allusion to a distinction between two senses of the word 'timeless'. When we say that such-and-such a proposition is timeless we may mean either:

1. that it is meaningless to raise questions about temporality (and tensed expressions) in relation to this proposition, i.e. that it is *strictly timeless.*[1]

2. that the proposition expresses something true (false) on every occasion of its utterance, i.e. that it is *omnitemporally timeless.*

Let us carefully apply this distinction and see what results we can achieve when we take up the question of existence.

---

[1] Nicholas Rescher, "On The Logic Of Chronological Propositions," *Mind*, 75 (January, 1966), pp. 75-96, makes the distinction clear when he speaks of the "temporal equivocality of IS". He distinguishes four senses of IS: (1) the atemporal *is* that means is timelessly (Three is a prime number), (2) the *is* of the present that means is now (The sun is setting), (3) the omnitemporal *is* that means is always (Copper is a conductor), and (4) the transtemporal *is* that means is in the present period (The earth is a planet of the sun). Only (1) is strictly timeless. Cf. Rescher, pp. 75-76.

Strictly timeless propositions are those which entail that any question about their temporal relations turns out to be nonsensical. Here the paradigm cases are mathematical ones. Thus, the statement, "Four plus five is nine", is strictly timeless. It does not even make sense to ask questions about the proposition in relation to the passage of time (e.g. "When did four plus five become nine?" or "How long will four plus five be nine?"). On the other hand, statements which are omnitemporal do address themselves to questions of temporality but only insofar as they express what is always on every occasion true (false). For example, "Snow is white", is timelessly true in the omnitemporal sense because it says that on every occasion (every temporal occurrence) the statement is true but it still makes sense to ask of this statement things like, "How long has snow been white?" Expressions that are strictly timeless involve a claim of the inconceivability of temporal location or extension which expressions that are omnitemporally timeless show constant retention of their truth values in relation to any temporal utterance of the expression (i.e. they are freely repeatable without change in truth value but queries concerning their temporal relations are not nonsensical). Neither of these categories fit the ordinary expression of human existence. My existence is beyond doubt a temporally related event. It has both temporal location and extension. It also has, as a contingent fact, a beginning and an end. What should we say about the statement, "God exists"? Aquinas asks us to identify this as a strictly timeless statement, i.e. that it is nonsensical to raise questions about this statement in relation to time. Since this interpretation violates all the usual implications of 'exists' for personal beings, we must ask Aquinas to justify this special case.

With the mind of a Platonist, we might be able to consistently imagine the strictly timeless existence of some "real" entity on the order of the existence of the Forms.

But such an existence would be imaginable only if absolute immutability accompanied this order. Moreover, since changelessness alone could not guarantee that the existence in question was not nevertheless temporal (albeit in a static state), we must firmly maintain that strictly timeless existence cannot allow us even to raise questions which have *temporal relation possibilities,* nor predicate relations of such an existence which have an *implicit temporal framework.*[1] This sort of existence (if that is the correct word) may seem perfectly appropriate for certain abstract entities such as numbers and the Platonic Forms but very significant conceptual problems arise when this idea is applied to almost anything else and in particular to the existence of persons and a personal God.

---

[1] Cf. Genevieve Lloyd, "Time and Existence," *Philosophy*, 53 (April, 1978), 215-228.

CHAPTER 8

TIME AND PERSON

The Logic of Being a Person

There are two ways we might examine the idea of existence in relation to persons. The first deals with descriptions of the capacities of persons. Here it is useful to follow the argument produced by Coburn, Pike and others. Coburn says:

> Surely it is a necessary condition of anything's being a person that it should be capable (logically) of, among other things, doing at least some of the following: remembering, anticipating, reflecting, deliberating, deciding, intending, and acting intentionally.[1]

Once we grant that the concept of person must entail some of these activities and capacities, it follows that it necessarily implies temporality since some idea of duration and temporal location is necessary in order to make sense of the above capacities. For example, one could not remember without having previously experienced something to call to memory. Thus, remembering means *recalling the past* and that can only happen if the experiencing subject existed at some point which is now in the past. An entity without a past could not be said to remember. The same implications are true of the other capacities. Each one has some radical dependence on time.

---

[1] Robert Coburn, "Professor Malcolm on God," *Australasian Journal of Philosophy*, 41 (June, 1963), 155.

This analysis of the logic of personal capacities seems to destroy any hope of speaking of an essentially *timeless* person. But Aquinas might reply that God's existence as a person requires a special understanding of the activities and capacities associated with human beings. Suppose that he suggested that these capacities, when elevated to divine status, must be understood in some different (analogical?[1]) way. Could we mount any other evidence for the temporal basis of personhood which would counter even these efforts? Let us consider more carefully the general idea of personal existence in order to elaborate a criticism of the hypothesis of a timeless person.

---

[1] Our attempt to supply an additional avenue of support for the essential temporality of personal beings does not mean that we would be forced to accept a Thomistic doctrine of analogy if it were evoked to counter the argument of Coburn. I suspect that such a move on the part of the Thomist would be no more reasonable than other historical cases of analogical predication. And I see no reason to believe that analogical predication in relation to the attributes of personhood would escape from the criticisms one might raise against these historical cases. As we have indicated, the need for analogical predication stems from the original Thomistic commitment to the transcendence of the *via negativa*. It is a method hopeful of saying something about a God who is strictly speaking "wholly Other". Since the entire approach of the *via negativa* is under attack here, analogical predication will not escape the general criticism of this study. Moreover, Aquinas is clear that analogical predication can operate only where there is at least one univocal element between the two senses. And we have already questioned this possibility given the categories of the *via negativa*. Specifically, timelessness is so defined as to exclude any univocal points with temporality. If this is true, it seems difficult to understand how any *essentially timeless* expression of personal being could find a univocal point with temporal personal being. The conclusion is this: even if Aquinas could show univocal elements, our second line of attack will still call into question the *internal logic* of timeless person language. But there is little reason to believe that Aquinas could get this far since there is no warrant for believing univocal points exist.

Me and Mine

Christian theologians of traditional and non-traditional persuasion alike hold that God is personal. This quality of existence has been seen as the ontological distinctive which sets both God and Man apart from the rest of creation. The long history of the doctrine of the *Imago Dei* is the theological attempt to formulate precisely this similarity. What we need to show is that the qualifying difference "infinite, divine" person and "finite, human" person does not give logical grounds for postulating *timelessness* as a meaningful expression of divine personhood. From the human perspective, there is no doubt that personhood is temporal. I am the paradigm case of such an entity for I am the first and most readily accessible source of information about the entity 'person'. Those activities and capacities which are necessary elements of the concept of human person presuppose temporality. But they also presuppose a conscious possessor. I recognize them as *mine*. It is *my* remembering, *my* deciding, *my* anticipating, etc. which makes these behaviors uniquely personal. Thus, we are not inclined to ascribe 'personhood' to computers simply because they can recall information (remember), produce calculations (decide) or make projections (anticipate). In fact, that we retain a marked difference in the terms applied to the actions of human beings and computers even though these actions may be formally reduced, in one sense, to the same elements shows that even our language recognizes this fundamental constituent of personhood to be present in each of the behaviors mentioned.[1] Current philosophical debate on mind-brain theories is another indicator of the

---

[1] Cf. J. R. Lucas, *The Freedom Of The Will* (Oxford: Oxford University Press, 1970), p. 137.

tenacity of this unique relation of "mine-ness".[1] What we are really witnessing in this fundamental expression of personhood is the experience of self-awareness. Mental capacities and activities (as well as physical ones) are mine because I am aware of these capacities and activities arising from me and being sustained by me. The use of the expression 'I' indicates this unique experience for only a self-aware consciousness could genuinely express itself in the first person. 'I', 'me' and 'mine' are linguistic indicators of the underlying experience of personhood. And they are appropriate only of a being who logically has the capacity to recognize itself as an existing self.

It is important to point out a distinction here between the language used of and by the experiencing subject and the language used about the experiencing subject. As a knowing subject, I do not need to describe to myself my own experience as 'mine' nor does it make sense for me to denote myself to myself by using the pronoun 'I'. "In self-address ascriptive language can have no logical point."[2] But the unusual conditions governing self-address do not mean such denotation is always superfluous. Language about others or addressed to others is an entirely different matter. Reference to 'I', 'me' and 'mine' in intersubjective linguistic spheres marks the unique experiencing subject as an individual person. In the public language of the human community, such denotation

---

[1] Of several possible bibliographies on the subject, one could look at the selective catalogue in Kenneth Sayre and Frederick Crosson, eds., *The Modeling Of The Mind* (Nortre Dame: University of Nortre Dame Press, 1963), or R. C. Lindley and J. M. Shorter, "The Philosophy of Mind; A Bibliography, Part I: The Self" (published as a Study Aid by the Sub-Faculty of Philosophy, Oxford, 1977) which contains no less than 42 authors on the subject of artificial intelligence alone and 76 pages of bibliographical references in the general field.

[2] Peter Geach, *Mental Acts: Their Content And Their Objects* (London: Routledge & Kegan Paul, 1957), p. 120.

is paramount.   C. O. Evans draws a very important observation from this sort of distinction.   He notes that theories of the self are essentially divided between those interested in accounting for the identification of persons and those concerned with accounting for self-awareness. He sees this distinction as crucial when confronting the questions facing a philosophical theory of consciousness. He describes the difference between these two approaches in the following way:

> One of the merits of the *person-approach* [language of the observational community about persons] . . . is that it has forced on us the realization that that we have two sorts of questions we can ask about the identity of selves, and this enables us to see where the traditional theories fall down. The lesson to be learned is that a theory of self-identity is *not* to be evaluated in terms of whether the self can be the subject of ascriptive sentences. On the contrary a theory of self-identity attempts to offer an account of a self even when such a self is not yet thought of as a language user – a self ascriber. Just as the having of experiences is not dependent on one's ability to report their occurrence, so being a self is not dependent on one's ability to use first-person and third-person sentences. Thus the difference between the *person-approach* and the *self-approach* comes to this: the former asks what we must *take* ourselves to be, given the condition that we are *language-users*; the latter asks what it is to be a subject to which experiences occur, quite independently of this condition. The two approaches operate on entirely different logical levels, and both approaches are, I believe, equally legitimate.[1]

The preconditions of use of the relation 'mine' could be understood in two different ways according to this distinction. On one reading, we could follow the "persons-approach" where the relation is to be investigated as an element of public language about the unique situation

---

[1] C. O. Evans, *The Subject Of Consciousness* (London: George Allen & Unwin, 1970), p. 33.

belonging to persons. We could ask what conditions must be true for this identifying feature of public language to be the case. The framework of our investigation would be the framework of the external observer of the *use* of the relation, but not necessarily of the *user* of the relation. On the second reading, we could follow the "self-approach" asking for an analysis of what it means for the subject *qua* subject to experience consciousness in this way (an investigation of the constitution of self-awareness). Then the question would be how I experience myself in relation to the elements of consciousness which I recognize as objects apart from myself. We may find that analysis of one reading leads quite naturally to analysis of the other. Nevertheless, Evans is right to suggest that these two possibilities operate independently.

In some ways we have already begun the analysis of the relation 'mine' as a function of the persons-approach. The arguments of Coburn and Pike show that descriptions of the abilities and capacities which we use to denote a being as a person have temporal presuppositions. Here the effort to show temporal dependence was drawn from a public language of personal identity. But we allowed the possibility that theologians might object that public language of personal *human* identity was not applicable to personal *divine* identity. Therefore, we must examine the self-approach in an effort to show that the logic of self-awareness demands a temporal foundation.

If I observe the relation between the knowing subject and consciousness, I recognize that there is a dialectic in consciousness consisting of elements as objects and myself as subject. That is to say, I am aware in consciousness of myself and my "doings."[1] In everyday

---

[1] Evans, (*Consciousness*, pp. 22, 25) makes the point that considering the acts of the self as *behaviors* leads one to view that matter from the persons-approach which is concerned with the conditions necessary for

experience, this relation between subject and object is so fundamental that I simply proceed with various thoughts, behaviors and actions which allow me to do what I wish without ever giving the relation any consideration. I may busily engage in thinking, deciding, anticipating and acting at any particular moment without being explicitly aware of the intimate connection between these activities and the fact that they are mine. However, I can, at any moment, reflect on the fact that I am the being creating and sustaining these activities and thereby make explicit this tacit constituent of my being a self. It is a fundamental element of my self-awareness that I have the logical capacity to make this relation explicit. In order for this to be the case, certain preconditions must be fulfilled. And in order for such a relation to occur at all, other interconnected preconditions must also exist.

First, then, let us examine those preconditions necessary for my being able to make explicit the usually tacit relation between my doings and the fact that they belong to me. A minimal account must include:

1. a capacity for awareness of action called 'mine' (identification)
2. an ability to remember the action so specified
3. a capacity to connect the remembered and identified action with my own consciousness (my self-awareness apart from all others)
4. an ability to recognize that the connection is one of generation or sustenance.

---

the identification of *other* entities as persons, and not primarily with the identity of the self as self. Hopefully, "doings" avoids some of this. On the logic of *my* intentions see John King-Farlow, "Could God be Temporal?: A Devil's Advocacy," *Southern Journal of Philosophy*, 1, (Summer, 1963) pp. 23-24.

The first of these conditions merely points out that the relation in question has some content which I must be able to recognize. There is something which the possessive 'mine' brings into focus. So I must have the powers necessary to initially recognize and identify this content whether it be a physical or mental act. Such a precondition recognizes that I have the sensory and intellectual systems suitable for performing this identification. But recognition of the relation is not simultaneous with the content of its content for I first record the doing and then record that the doing was in fact mine. The tacit relation accompanying the doing may be simultaneous with the doing but the explicit recognition of the relation is another, distinct act of consciousness. There is of necessity some temporal duration in the identification precondition.

The second precondition has already been shown to depend on an assumption of temporality. Remembering is recalling the past and that can only be true of an entity which has a past. As I remember that such-and-such a doing is mine, I recognize that some time has elapsed since it occurred, that there is a temporal gap between my recalling the event now and the moment when I was "in the midst" of it. And if I am to assert that such-and-such a doing is mine, then I must be able to recall that doing when I reflect on the connection that it has with my consciousness. So the second precondition is as radically temporal as the first.

Thirdly, I must be able to connect the identified and remembered action with my own consciousness. The identified and remembered action is placed within a temporal scheme. It occurred at some time and is remembered at some time. And for me to make the connection with the time of occurrence and the time of remembering is to place myself as the active agent at each of these times. It is to recognize that it is I who acted and remembered and am even now reflecting upon that action and memory. Again, this condition can only be fulfilled if it is fundamentally temporal.

Finally, my ability to recognize the aforementioned connection is the ability to see that it is a connection between the doing, the memory and *my willing* such a doing. The doing is mine insofar as I am the one who is creator and sustainer of it. And both the creation and sustenance of these elements are temporally locatable since they are synonymous with the temporal doing themselves. In each case, the conditions of my being able to make explicit the quality of 'mine' of personal experience (of self-awareness) presuppose a temporal framework.

Self-Consciousness

But according to the distinction introduced by Evans, this analysis could be interpreted as a persons-approach argument for it uncovers the temporal presuppositions which lie behind those activities and capacities which are used as intersubjective criteria for the identification of others as persons; it does not directly deal with the internal relation between the self and items of consciousness. In this sense, the argument thus far will not negate the theologian's claim that a timeless God could appropriate all of these things timelessly. In other words, we have not as yet shown that *self-awareness* must be temporal. In order to complete the argument, we must account for both approaches to the concept of consciousness. Only then will we be able to assert that any self-conscious being must be temporal.

When we constructed the case for the *via negativa*, we suggested that a timeless God would have to know things (including the fact of His own existence) timelessly. According to the definition of Aquinas and Boethius, this should be taken to mean that God knows instantaneously and perfectly whatever He knows. Thus, we could infer that a timeless God would be instantaneously and perfectly self-aware. We should further notice that self-awareness entails a knowing, conscious subject. Anything which we should wish to claim was self-aware would have to be conscious and be conscious of itself as the subject of that consciousness. Our analysis of the relation 'mine' points precisely to this condition of self-awareness. I cannot genuinely use the possessive pronoun 'my' without being conscious of myself as subject and being conscious of the object of the pronoun. But the argument we wish to pursue is incomplete as it stands for even though we have an analysis of the relation 'mine', we do not have an analysis of the term 'conscious'.

Identification of consciousness presents no difficulty to the knowing subject. But although I have immediate recognition of myself as conscious, I find that (to paraphrase Augustine) if no one asks me what it is to be a conscious self, I know; but if I wish to explain it to someone who asks, I do not know. Let us adopt as a tentative definition of 'conscious' the one offered by Evans:

> To be conscious is, *inter alia*, to perceive, to feel emotions and sensations, to have images and recollections, and to have desires, intentions and thoughts.[1]

While this definition is hardly debatable with regard to human consciousness, it finds only severely truncated compatibility with the divine consciousness of a timeless God. Aquinas would certainly object to implying that God felt emotions and sensations and it is probable that he would wish to alter the concepts of desires and recollections as well. But even the *via negativa* tradition would allow that God was conscious in the sense that He perceives, has intentions, images and thoughts (although all

---

[1] Evans, *Consciousness*, p. 48.

non-temporally qualified).   In other words, if God is conscious even in some *timeless* sense, He must still be conscious of something (even if it is only of Himself as conscious).   And this could be fairly characterized under the conditions of the *via negativa* as the instantaneously whole and perfect consciousness of everything God knows (consciousness of His own mind).   What we have represented in this description is consciousness of a total state consisting of a single, unchangeable and unchanging element; namely, everything that can be known.   The consciousness of a timeless knower "would constitute a perfectly static consciousness in which no existing element perished and no new element appeared".[1]   The task of our analysis is to show that the logic of this state of consciousness requires a precondition of temporality.   We will then have good reason from both external theories of the identification of persons and from internal theories of the structure of self-awareness for believing that consciousness must be temporal.

Attention, Consciousness and God

Evans supplies us with the framework for our analysis of consciousness of a single element in his discussion of attention.   He notes that the range of consciousness extends from the possibility of a single element (called "pure sensuous consciousness") to the state of reverie, i.e. from consciousness of a single, immutable, uniform state to consciousness that is in a state of total accidental association of disconnected thoughts (e.g. James Joyce's *Ulysses*).   Since our concern with the consciousness of a timeless God limits the present discussion to the case of a single element, we shall not have to worry about this full range.   Nevertheless, it should be

---

[1] Ibid., p. 69.

noted that a completely integrated theory of human consciousness must account for this scale even if the extremes exist only as logical possibilities. What is important to us is the fact that the entire range of consciousness is given structure by varying degrees of attention.

Following James Ward, Evans comments on the relation between attention and consciousness. Ward suggests that attention and consciousness are identical since "we cannot be aware of anything without giving it some attention, and this is for the simple reason that to be aware of it is to attend to it".[1] We may wish to be more cautious and suggest that the two are simultaneous concomitants of each other. It is clear that attention is always attention *to something* and it is an absurdity to claim that one is conscious of something but not paying *any* attention to it. While there are certainly degrees of attention such that some objects of consciousness lie at the very periphery of the conscious realm, we obviously cannot claim that consciousness can be aware of anything which it gives no attention to whatsoever. Moreover, attention is necessarily distributed between a foreground and a background for attending to something always involves the item of attention set against the background of other items.[2] In this respect, consciousness shows marked similarities with perception. Focusing on one feature of the visual horizon does not thereby eliminate all other features. It is only insofar as the other visual features provide a background field that any particular item can become a center of focus.

The distribution of attention between foreground and background is an essential feature of every self-conscious being for the object of consciousness is projected onto the foreground while the tacit relation 'mine'

---

[1] As cited in Evans, *Consciousness*, p. 73.
[2] Cf. Evans, *Consciousness*, pp. 80-92.

indicating the self remains in the background. What we need to ask is this: is it logically possible to maintain the idea of consciousness and self-awareness for a *timeless* being where the object of consciousness is a single, immutable state? We may justifiably suppose that a timeless God would have His attention fixed on a single, immutable state (namely, all that can be known). The object of God's consciousness is everything in an all-at-once embracing whole (where the obvious temporal connotations of this phrase will be overlooked). But this picture of God's consciousness has two immediate problems. First, if the object of God's consciousness is everything, then God is attending to everything and because this attending is timeless, it cannot be characterized by varying degrees of attention nor by attention to various parts. God must attend to everything all-at-once in the same degree. But if attention only makes sense in terms of foreground and background (in terms of simultaneous greater and lesser degrees), what remains as the background element in God's consciousness? Evans summarizes the problem this way:

> If our consciousness were such that we were never aware of anything except the objects of attention, we could not know that we were attending: we would have no contrast between attention and nonattention. Let us imagine the possibility of a consciousness the total temporary state of which consisted of but a single element. The question could then be raised whether it would be meaningful to talk of that element of consciousness holding the attention of the person who experienced it. If it could, we should have to be prepared to explain in what respect *attending* to that element of consciousness differed from simply *having* it.[1]

---

[1] Evans, *Consciousness*, p. 105.

Evans argues that a consciousness consisting of a single element would be consciousness which lacked background (lacked any unprojected elements). But without background, there would be no means of distinguishing foreground. Since foreground is the crucial focal object of attention, it follows that a consciousness of a single element could not view that element as an object of attention. This further entails that the notion of self (the subject remaining in the background of any projected object of attention) would be totally absent from such a consciousness.

> Were such a homogeneous consciousness to exist, its existence could not be reported first-hand at the time, for to report the occurrence of the state would of necessity mean that a self must be aware concurrently of the state, and this would entail the existence of unprojected consciousness, which, *ex hypothesi*, does not exist. The only first-hand evidence of the existence of a homogeneous consciousness would come from the subject's memory of normal consciousness returning in the wake of some indescribable state of consciousness.[1]

Although Evans allows the possibility of such an abnormal experience, he says that such an experience could be reported only *after* the experience by a self who "has some dim recollection of a form of experience in which awareness of self was completely absent".[2] The logical possibility of such a consciousness is hardly consolation to the proponent of the *via negativa*.

The second problem for the traditional picture of a timeless God arises in conjunction with this issue of self-awareness. The fact that the *object* of God's consciousness is everything implies that there is also a subject whose

---

[1] Evans, *Consciousness*, p. 170. Notice Evans' choice of "indescribable". This seems to be the fate of the best reading of the *via negativa* on the subject of God's self-consciousness.

[2] Ibid.

consciousness this object stands in relation to. That subject is, of course, God Himself. And the subject of this consciousness cannot also be the simultaneous object of this consciousness. In other words, every object of consciousness implies a subject which is *not an element of the object of consciousness at the same moment.* If the subject turns attention to itself, then it automatically creates a new object of consciousness (the original knowing subject of the subject-object relation) which is not the object of consciousness of a new reflecting subject. There can be no object of consciousness without this implied subject. And that entails that there are always at least two levels of consciousness in self-awareness. The relation of self-awareness is a second order state of consciousness for it logically requires that there be an original object and subject which is then reflected upon by turning attention to the subject of that relation. For this reason, awareness of self in a single element consciousness is impossible. Thus, God could not be wholly and perfectly conscious instantaneously of both the object of His consciousness and Himself as the subject of that consciousness for that would require that He give maximal attention (since all attention is focused on the single state) to both object and subject in the same timeless instant. If the objection is proffered that God could give maximal attention to the object of His consciousness and to Himself as subject in the same timeless instant because no notion of simultaneity or duration need apply to the realm of timeless being, that seems to imply that subject and object become one in God's consciousness.[1] This seems to be the direction of the identification of God's knowledge with His essence, as St. Thomas readily admits. But it makes any attempt to speak

---

[1] We could also suggest that this objection is a *petitio principii*, trading on a use of timeless which becomes increasingly obscure, if not meaningless.

of God as a conscious person hopelessly confused for persons do not and cannot merge subject and object and still retain the reflective, second order operation of *self-awareness*. Therefore, it appears that the claim that God is a conscious, self-aware person entails that God must be able to shift attention from the object of His consciousness to Himself as the subject of that consciousness. This is the minimal logical requirement of the concept of self-awareness. Self-awareness presupposes attending to the subject of a *previous* subject-object relation. In this way, self-awareness creates its own duality of consciousness; it creates its own foreground and background. And this means that there must be some change ascribable to any being which is self-aware.

Finally, Evans' remark that this form of consciousness could at best be reported as a recollection implies patently temporal conditions which are not available in the hypothesis of a timeless God. Self-awareness requires being able to turn my attention from the presence of one conscious level to another. Consciousness requires the constant tacit presence of background (unprojected elements) as the realm of the experiencing self. And it seems merely *ad hoc* to reply that God's consciousness is to be characterized by the expression 'having' rather than 'attending'. That would simply shift the argument to a request to produce the appropriate distinctions with the logic of 'having' which would allow non-simultaneous, unprojected reflection upon a prior projected object of a subject-object relation. Some minimal degree of attention is required for there to be any consciousness at all.[1] And consciousness *of the self as subject* creates its own duality. Therefore, self-awareness necessarily implies mental transition. It follows that any

---

[1] Cf. Evans, *Consciousness*, p. 92.

being which is self-conscious must exhibit change (of at least the mental sort). In other words, self-conscious beings logically must be temporal beings.

We have shown that consciousness presupposes temporality on two levels. First we examined the logic of those activities and capacities which we normally take as necessary conditions denoting conscious, personal beings. We found that use of these descriptions retained implicit necessary assumptions of temporality. Secondly, we looked at the expression "I exist" as a fundamental claim of personal self-awareness. We were able to show that the existence of persons required certain preconditions. In particular, my assertion that I exist implies a capacity to use the relation 'mine'. Since the necessary conditions of identifying anything as a person are activities and capacities each of which is capable of being recognized by the knowing subject as an object of the relation 'mine', the relation 'mine' is a fundamental relation of conscious personal being. We argued that this relation is also grounded in temporal presuppositions. We saw that it connects descriptions arising from the minimal logical conditions denoting a person with the internal experience of being a self. We found that the experience of being a self depended upon two elements in consciousness – attention and second order reflection. These elements also presuppose temporality. The concept of self-awareness creates its own dialectic for the transition from the object of attention to the subject of the experience. The logic of persons leads us to the conclusion that anything which is a person (and the logical capacity for self-consciousness is taken as an essential element of what it means to be a person) must be fundamentally temporal. In order for the necessary conditions of self-awareness to be fulfilled, the being in question must have temporal location and extension. No entity which does not logically have temporal location and extension could be understood as personal.

Reinterpreting the *Via Negativa*

Having shown that God must be temporal and must exhibit change if He is to be understood as personal, we have at last completed the critiques of the *via negativa* tradition. Our arguments demonstrate that the picture of God produced through incorporation of Greek metaphysics and the Greek idea of perfection cannot be reconciled with the idea of a personal divinity. With this in mind, we can now answer the questions raised through the analysis of the two trends in Greek thinking about the divine. That analysis left us with the following query:

> Can Ultimate Reality as described by the Greek tradition be consistently united with an explanation of a first principle of causation?

This question really asks if the terms 'infinite', 'necessary', 'simple' and 'eternal' (timeless) are logically compatible with the expression 'prime mover'.

From one perspective, it seems as though no conceptual difficulty could arise for the combination of these themes. After all, the Greek idea of the prime mover is merely the instantiation of the rational deduction of the attributes of pure Being. The prime mover is infinite, eternal, simple and necessary. And as long as time was defined in terms of actual change, there seemed to be no difficulty in postulating a timeless, immutable beginning of all time and change. This Greek heritage was incorporated into the Christian tradition. By leveling our attack at the resulting theological picture, we have produced the necessary material to challenge the Greek solution as well. We have shown that time without change is a logical possibility. Moreover, we have shown that the Christian

God must be temporal not merely as a being who exists in a changeless but temporal state but as a being who exists in a state which exhibits actual change. This provides both the ontological and epistemological basis for the claim that time cannot have a beginning. Theologically, the reason behind this claim is simple. Since the Christian God is everlasting, His consciousness is everlasting. And since actual change is a concomitant of the presence of consciousness, both change and time must be everlasting conditions of the existence of a divine being who is a person. This gives us theological grounds for rejecting the logical compatibility of the two trends of Greek metaphysics as they are incorporated in the *via negativa*. The original philosophical argument for the possibility of a stationary state undermined the definitional equivalence between time and change. That meant that we could postulate an indefinite temporal past without change as a possibility. But the possibility of such an extension was not enough to overcome the idea of a *first* cause of a *first* change. With the addition of the theological argument, we now have reason to deny the assertion that there is a first change (where change is interpreted in the wider context of both physical and mental events). This denial follows from the analysis of what it means for God to be a person.

It may still be objected that a non-personal principle could offer the hoped for synthesis of the two themes of Greek metaphysics. But this is little help to the *via negativa* theologian. In addition, the breakdown of the distinctions between eternal-changeless and finite-changing categories of reality creates serious problems for the non-personal first principle as well. A "first cause" thesis in the absence of a personal deity will have to be related to the possibility of some temporally extended but changeless period. *Timelessness* may have to be relegated to the realm of logically necessary (analytic) truths. Parmenides' insight reveals the difficulties of consistently maintaining a logical relation between causal first principles and categories of pure Being. At best the Greek tradition would have to show that strong immutability was not incompatible with temporality. At worst, we should find that the idea of a timeless, perfect principle which is the changeless source of all change is rationally incoherent.

Essentially, we have shown that nearly every predicate of the *via negativa* will have to be re-evaluated and reinterpreted in terms of a God who is forever temporal and constantly changing. Initially, this means a restructuring of the notions of God's infinity, simplicity, necessity and eternity. This implies the collapse of the doctrines of immutability and impassibility.[1] And as a result of that collapse we are led to the final part of this study; the reinterpretation of omniscience and freedom.

The object of our study is specifically concerned with the implications that temporality has for the concept of omniscience. Consequently, the reinterpretation of the

---

[1] On page 30, we distinguished between two possible readings of the project of the *via negativa*. There we remarked that a successful analysis and criticism of both of these attempts to use the *via negativa* predicates as a basis of theology would require that two distinct things be shown: (1) that insofar as these attempts tried to say something positive about the nature of God they failed, and (2) that insofar as these attempts tried to maintain a second order logical thesis about the nature of religious language they were mistaken. Much of the foregoing critique has been aimed at the first of these critical projects. In the process, we supplied the material necessary for meeting the second challenge as well. We have shown not only that there are serious conceptual and logical problems for the combination of the *via negativa* terms but also that the very concepts which these terms try to deny of God must be applied to Him if we are to understand God as personal. In other words, we have shown that Aquinas was wrong to suggest that these human categories mark the limits of religious language. Instead, we have seen that these categories logically must be applied to God or we shall be consigned to inconsistency, incoherence and silence.

predicates of the *via negativa* falls outside the scope of our concern except in those areas which directly affect theories of divine knowledge. Nevertheless, the intermediate results of this study are so wide ranging and penetrating that it is worth taking the time to at least set the stage for the reinterpretation of the fundamental attributes of the divine nature. Very briefly, then, we must recognize that God's infinity will have to deal with the fact that temporality can no longer be considered a limitation for personal existence. This recognition alone will force the theological collapse of the Neoplatonic dualism. Since temporality and change are just as much a part of God's existence as they are of Man's, any dualism equating time, change, materiality and imperfection with finitude in opposition to infinite, timeless, immutable and perfect divinity will have to be rejected. Perfection can no longer be seen as logically excluding time and change. And theologians who continue to assert that God is perfect will have to work out what that means within the confines of temporality. In many ways, the basic dualism between Being and Becoming will also collapse. For reasons which we will presently consider, we will not necessarily be forced to suggest that God's essence is changing but we shall certainly have to reconsider whether the Aristotelian categories of eternal essence and changing accident still apply to divine *personal* being. And that will also force a reconsideration of the necessity of God. If God is temporal and changing, in what ways is it possible to continue to suggest that His existence is necessary? Is the non-existence of a temporal God a conceptual possibility? Does temporality demand contingency? Obviously, if God changes, the doctrine of simplicity will have to be reworked. The categories of potentiality and actuality, of composed and uncomposed being, will have to undergo radical alteration. In some fundamental way, we shall have to treat God after the model of human personal being. And that means talking about God's enduring identity through change. The development of a theology of God based on this sort of dialectic makes the doctrine of simplicity as found in the *via negativa* untenable. Since so many of the doctrines of the *via negativa* are conceptually tied together, the collapse of the notions of timelessness and immutability introduce the possibility of a major theological shift (a theological revolution?); something which we could see only dimly as a possibility in our discomfort with the idea of impassibility but which grew upon us in the realization that the general pattern of the *via negativa* became increasingly inadequate. Now it is clear why those early difficulties were so intractable. Attempts to force the Biblical picture of God into the metaphysical straight jacket of the Greeks could only lead to conflicts for at bottom, Greek metaphysics was concerned with a logic of static ideas and the Hebrew-Christian God is fundamentally a God of dynamic relationships.

Weak Immutability

But before we actually turn to an analysis of the doctrine of divine omniscience, there are two challenges which we must face. The first of these is a reconstruction of the doctrine of immutability within the framework of temporality. If we are to understand the notion of omniscience as temporally conditioned, we must first pay some attention to the larger question of God's changes. With that in mind, we can immediately rule out several possible reconstructions of this doctrine. As we argued earlier, a weak thesis of immutability is deficient if interpreted within the confines of a static state. We have shown that not only must God exist in an endlessly temporal state but He must experience change in that state. Therefore, the weak thesis must be modified to allow for this necessity. We may suppose that God is changing without accepting the implication carried over from the *via negativa* that any change requires a change in the essence of God. Strong immutability with its dependence on the categories of potentiality and actuality could not entertain any change involving God because it viewed all change in the divine as a change which affected the perfect essence of the divine. That is to say, change was seen as either positive or negative but not as simply alteration without essential or accidental connotations. This strong view of immutability was based on the Greek idea of perfection – eternal and complete in itself. To suggest that God must experience change if He is to be a person implies that the notion of perfection in this form must be abandoned. However, this does not force us to give up *every* conception of perfection. It is reasonable to suggest, for example, that perfection for personal agency is associated with correctness of choice (moral perfection). This retains the dynamic elements essential to self-conscious being and allows the continuous experience of change. What it requires is this: God can experience change and yet be perfect as long as the choices God makes are always the best possible choices.[1]   This could be interpreted as suggesting that God's perfection consists in His constantly reaffirming His character as God by choosing those actions (initiating changes) which are maximally best in any situation. We must reject the explanation of the *via negativa* that the anthropomorphic passages of the Biblical view are, as a whole, to be discounted and viewed as strictly metaphorical. When Scripture speaks of God changing His mind, reacting with emotion, sympathizing with His creation or altering His plans, we have every right to consider at least some of these to be accurate descriptions of the divine being who is personal. Without

---

[1] Cf. Richard Swinburne, *The Coherence of Theism* (Oxford: Oxford University Press, 1977), Chapter 11 on perfect goodness and moral obligation in relation to the free will and perfection of God.

them, God would be reduced to a static principle. But with them, Christianity asserts that God does in fact share a fundamentally common aspect with Man. And it is not demeaning to the status of God to suggest that He too shows the signs of personhood for God's expression of personality is the cornerstone of the dynamic relationship of faith.

Once we have established the possibility of change without the entailment that change must mean loss of perfection or alteration in essential character, we can reformulate the weak thesis of immutability in the following manner:

> As the revealed corpus and the intuitions of the tradition suggest, God does not change. But this is a statement about His character, His moral worth and His moral status, not a statement about the entire range of His activities and capacities or the logic of His nature. There may be logical connections between God's exercise of free will and His moral perfection[1], but the ultimate ground of those connections is the contingency resident in the free will of God. This means that God chooses not to alter His general purposes, His good will and loving concern and His own moral obligation but it does not mean that He could not change that even if He wanted to. It means that He has changes of feeling, specific choices and actions and *reactions* to this human community. And since the general context in which God operates is in flux (due partly to the contingent nature of human choices), God's individual decisions must constantly reorient His actions and reactions in order to accomplish His goals and purposes. Immutability is a statement of God's continued trustworthiness, not a statement of the logic of His eternal nature.

---

[1] On considerations of other kinds of necessity affecting God, see Swinburne, *Coherence*, Chapter 13.

This weak thesis of immutability reaffirms the Biblical assertion that God is true to His promises and that 'truth' has a pragmatic and moral connotation as well as a logical one.   But it makes this affirmation as a contingent statement.   There is *no logical necessity* for God to continue to maintain His steadfast character.   He could choose to be other than He is.   Ultimately, this means that God has the freedom to choose not to be God.

In spite of the difficulties which this theory of divine personhood overcomes, it is not without its own problems.   We have already alluded to one of these in the assertion that there is some sense in which God might choose not to be God.   This cannot be dealt with in detail until after we have given an analysis of the problems associated with human free will.   There is another difficulty which arises directly from the general theory of self-awareness.   In this study we can at best only recognize its presence.   Our general theory of self-awareness leans heavily on the necessity of change in the recognition of personal existence.   Here one might raise problems about God's incorporeality, arguing that some unusual and possibly damaging qualifications will have to be placed on the general theory if we are to avoid potential conflicts with analogues to human *embodied* persons.   Certainly, some arguments are needed to show that the idea of an incorporeal person is not incoherent.[1]   Evans himself suggests that the general theory of self-awareness provides a basis for this sort of analysis.[2]   But considerations of these questions take us too far afield from our topic of freedom and omniscience.   We must turn our attention to a critique of the traditional presentation of the relations

---

[1] Cf. Swinburne, *Coherence*, pp. 111-125.

[2] Cf. Evans, *Consciousness*, pp. 131-134 for introduction of the idea of "quasi-embodiment" as a potential solution to this problem.

between freedom and knowledge in order to see what effects an analysis of the personhood of God has on the doctrine of omniscience.

SECTION THREE

TIME AND OMNISCIENCE

CHAPTER 9

TIMELESSNESS AND FOREKNOWLEDGE

The previous conclusion presents us with an important theological puzzle. We have seen that the Christian idea of God necessarily entails that God is temporal in a way which requires actual states of change. This conclusion stands in contradiction to the history of the development of the doctrine of immutability, for timelessness is an essential characteristic of the traditional understanding of changelessness. Our analysis of the conditions of consciousness only reflects what must certainly have been obvious to classical philosophers and theologians. Change as the life-blood of the stream of consciousness is nothing new. But the nearly unanimous voice of the *via negativa* tradition considered God to be non-temporal. Confusion of epistemological and ontological distinctions in dealing with the definition of time is not enough by itself to account for this theological consensus. The remaining explanation must come from the connection between timelessness and omniscience. The problem of foreknowledge and free will provides the focus for our inquiry. Considerations of this problem show how crucial the doctrine of timeless eternity is to the claim that God knows every true proposition.

Boethius' Solution

No better representative of the classic view on foreknowledge could be found than Boethius. Not only was his formulation of the problem and solution decisively influential in theological history, he is also cited again and again in recent philosophical discussion of the issue. His introduction of the problem comes from the fifth book of the *Consolation*.

> For if God foresees all and cannot in any way be mistaken, then that must necessarily happen which in his providence he foresees will be. And therefore if he foreknows from all eternity not only the deeds of men but even their plans and desires, there will be no free will; for it will be impossible for there to be any deed at all or any desire whatever except that which divine providence, which cannot be mistaken, perceives beforehand. For if they can be turned aside into a different way from that foreseen, then there will no longer be firm foreknowledge of the future, but rather uncertain opinion, which I judge impious to believe of God.[1]

Boethius' solution is as simple as it is brilliant. Boethius could deny neither God's knowledge of human actions nor His infallibility. But he also believed that some human actions were certainly free. He reasoned that the heart of the problem was the claim that God's knowledge was temporally *prior* to the human act. Boethius resolved this conflict by noting that as long as God was strictly timeless, it would be impossible to contend that His knowledge of human activity was prior to the actual human behavior. A claim about prior knowledge is temporally conditioned, and as such, could not be appropriate of a timeless God. If God is strictly timeless, reasoned Boethius, His knowledge of human events is not prior to their occurrence since His knowledge is not *prior* to anything. It just is (tenselessly). Since it is unqualified by any expression of past, present or future, it is not *fore*-knowledge at all. Boethius calls it "knowledge of a never-passing instant".[2] There is no necessity imparted to the temporal occurrence of some human act because God knows of it for God knows of it not

---

[1] Boethius, *Consolation*, Book V, Part III, p. 395.
[2] Ibid., V, VI, p. 427.

as future but as present and as present any act is (by logical necessity) what it is.   Boethius invokes the following illustration of this point:

> And therefore it [God's knowledge of human actions] is called not prevision (*praevidentia*) but providence (*providentia*), because set far from the lowest of things it looks forward on all things as though from the highest peak of the world.[1]

The Crucial Analogy

Several analogies similar to the one proposed by Boethius have been introduced to explain how it is that God can be cognizant of all those contingencies which are future to us, yet not determine those events.   Regardless of the details of the various suggestions, they all assume that spatial positions have relevant features which are essentially the same as temporal positions.[2]   In order to see the implications of this assumption, let us examine a version of a Thomistic analogy.[3]

Imagine that God views the temporal order from a high tower.   The temporal order is represented by a long line of men.   Each man stands looking back on the line, seeing clearly his near neighbors and more dimly those further from him (his immediate and distant past) but not

---

[1] Boethius, *Consolation*, Book v, Part III, p. 395.

[2] As Capek (*Concepts of Space And Time*), p. xxvi) remarks, "From Zeno to Russell . . . the fallacy of 'spatialization of time' is one of the most persistent features of our intellectual tradition".   See Capek's introduction for discussion of this fallacy and for evidence of connections between concepts of time and change as part of the philosophical views of space.   As an example, see John Leslie, "The Value of Time," *American Philosophical Quarterly*, 13 (April, 1976), pp. 109-121.

[3] Aquinas, *Aristotle On Interpretation: Commentary by St. Thomas and Cajetan*, trans. By Jean Oesterle (Milwaukee: Marquette University Press, 1962), pp. 117-118.

seeing anyone ahead of him (the future). However, from God's perspective, the entire line is clearly visible in such a way that God not only sees every individual man and that man's neighbors but also observes the entire line in a single glance.[1] This implicit assumption in this description is that time and timelessness have certain features similar to space. The attractiveness of the analogy depends on two possible interpretations. Initially we might understand the analogy to claim that God's position is "outside" the temporal sequence.[2] Here God's view of the entire temporal stream depends on the application of the prepositions 'inside' and 'outside' to temporality. Just as a shift in spatial position allows greater vision, so the shift in time/timelessness is supposed to allow greater knowledge. But the use of these prepositions introduces the first problem with this analogy. The first part of the analogy depends on two distinct spatial positions. The argument moves from one restricted position (in the line) to another unrestricted position (in the tower). There is no attempt to argue from spatiality to non-spatiality since that would produce the obvious absurdity that the *position* of the knower in the tower was *not spatially locatable*. But the second part of the analogy violates this common framework, for it suggests that God's position in relation to the temporal order is not a different but nevertheless temporal location but is rather altogether removed from time. I can easily imagine that I might be *spatially* located in some position where I could see the entire line of men.

---

[1] A point needs to be made concerning the importance of the perceptual basis of this analogy. Unless backward causation is possible, no being could *see* the future since that would imply that the future caused him to see, entailing that the cause followed the effect. This is quite different from the claim about knowing the future but traditional arguments use the visual analogies rather indiscriminately.

[2] Cf. Thomas Aquinas, *Summa Contra Gentiles* (London: Burns Oates and Washbourne, 1924), Book I, Chapter 57, pp. 140-141.

But that would not, and could not, mean that I was therefore located "outside" space. In this interpretation, it is the fact that I have spatial location which allows me to assert my special knowledge. I am not removed from space because I do not share the same position as the men in the line. If I were, any assertions which I might make about the spatial relations of the men in the line would become logically questionable since it would not be clear how I could justify my claims. The analogy here confuses spatial and temporal categories. But suggesting that God is "outside" time, the analogy implies that time can be located *somewhere* and that God views time from a stance outside that place. A timeless God cannot have temporal position or extension. But the analogy derives its strength from the notion that timelessness does have positional relation to the temporal, even if that relation is nothing more than "outside of". This mistake cannot be overcome unless it could be shown that time and timelessness have the same coordinate system as space.[1]

The second interpretation of this analogy seems much more plausible precisely because it attempts to show common coordinate system features. It depends on the relational ordering of space and time. The line of men can be seen as a one-dimensional series. The tower is not outside space but simply outside the linear sub-space represented by the line. Since space is a multi-dimensional continuum which can admit ordered sub-sets, this presents no conceptual difficulties. The analogy suggests that the temporal/timeless relation can be understood along the

---

[1] Following the elaboration of the Special Theory of Relativity, some might argue that time and space must have the same coordinate system. But Newton-Smith has shown that this is not necessarily the case, even though it may contingently be the case under some interpretations of the Special Theory. See W. H. Newton-Smith, *Structure of Time*, Chapter 8.

same lines as the space/sub-space relation, i.e. that time admits the same multi-dimensional continuum as space so that we might talk of a one-dimensional temporal order being known from another dimensional order, "the never-ending present".   To be logically satisfactory, this interpretation must be grounded on an argument that time admits multi-dimensional orders.   Some possible orders peculiar to aberrant temporal topologies are obviously excluded by requirements imposed by the notion of timelessness, e.g. orders belonging to branching or cyclical time.   But multiple parallel and discontinuous topologies might produce orders which meet the requirements of the analogy.   The spatial argument suggests that the one-dimensional linear order could be mapped onto a two-dimensional order.   Could the order of our time be mapped onto a timeless order with similar success?   The difficulty seems to be that time admits one a one-dimensional structure.   That is to say, in any given temporal topology, of any two temporal instants A and B, either A is before B or B is before A or A and B are simultaneous.   Newton-Smith argues that an unordered topology is logically coherent but it has very significant consequences for other aspects of that possible world.[1]   In our temporal topology, the ordered relation 'earlier than' seems to be essential.   But in a possible world without an ordered topology, concepts like causality and agency would have to be drastically altered. This means that the relations between such a possible world and our own would be very strange indeed.   Looking at that world, we should not be able to tell which events followed which.   And from that world, it would be impossible to describe our one-dimensional order since there would be no fixed referents or relations in the possible world.   It is difficult to see how this sort of multiple time structure

---

[1] Cf. W. H. Newton-Smith, *Structure of Time*, Chapter 9.

could account for God's timeless knowledge of our temporal realm.

In addition, timelessness presents an even greater problem. Even if it is merely a contingent empirical thesis, the order of our world seems to be one-dimensional. But the order of the timeless world of God's eternity is not two-dimensional, as the analogy suggests. It is non-dimensional. It has no extension or duration. It contains no events which are before or after. It is an eternity which "synchronizes with every time or instant of time . . . Accordingly, whatever exists in any part of time, is coexistent with the eternal as though present thereto . . ."[1] Nevertheless, theologians have wanted to say that God timelessly knows the entire ordered structure of our time as it is ordered. The problem is that timelessness is not simply a different-ordered relation; it is a topology without any direction at all (ordered or not).[2] But it is supposed to have an intrinsic relation to an ordered realm, i.e. it is supposed to be simultaneous[3] with every temporal event. This picture is just incoherent. It requires that the temporal order of this world be mapped onto a single (non-temporal)

---

[1] Aquinas, *Summa Contra Gentiles*, Book I, p. 141.

[2] Simultaneity is, of course, a temporal order-relation and as such, is strictly inadmissible as a description of timelessness. Be that as it may, it is hard to imagine how theologians could describe timelessness without illegitimately borrowing some temporal terms.

[3] In his concluding chapter, Newton-Smith (*The Structure of Time*, Chapter 10) points out that the standard topology (one-dimensional linear order) for time is the richest topology, i.e. deviant topologies can be embedded in a one-to-one order preserving map from the deviant topology to the standard topology. But the reverse is not the case. This is particularly crucial for the present analogy since it implies that the standard order temporality can be mapped onto the timeless order and preserve the order structure of God's knowledge. If Newton-Smith is right, and I see no reason to doubt him, the analogy in question calls for an isomorphic mapping procedure from a richer to a less rich order. Such mapping appears to be impossible.

point which is simultaneous with every ordered event but is itself neither divisible nor before or after any point of the temporal order. The spatial picture which permeates this view collapses when exposed to the logical requirements governing our temporal order. Timelessness cannot accommodate a one-dimensional order as a sub-set of itself. The two views have no isomorphic correspondence. And no theological interpretation of the analogy could allow an isomorphic mapping and continue to maintain that God was not temporally conditioned. With either interpretation, the analogy fails.[1]

---

[1] In later discussion we will treat the problem of temporal indexicals in relation to a theory of temporal omniscience. However, one attempt to handle the difficulties with temporal indexicals follows directly from this sort of analogy and should be mentioned here. Paul Helm ("Timelessness and Foreknowledge," *Mind*, LXXXIV (October, 1975, 516-527) suggests that asking what God knows *now* is equivalent to asking what God timelessly knows by someone who is temporally located in the present instant. Helm takes the indexical expression as a reference to the questioner, not as a reference to God. On this ground, the answer that God timelessly knows now exactly what He timelessly knows at all other times (namely, everything that can be known – past, present and future), is really a response to the *formation* of the question by a *temporal agent*. Helm suggests that the foreknowledge problem can be treated with the help of this understanding of the indexical. He argues that while 'I foreknow that *A*' is necessarily false for a timeless being, the statement 'He foreknows that *A*' uttered by a temporal being and ascribed to a timeless being is not necessarily false for the timeless being. This apparently gives grounds for a genuine case of timeless *fore*knowledge where the timelessness refers to the knowledge of all true propositions believed by a timeless omniscient being and the foreknowledge refers to the temporal location of any temporal questioner. Helm's suggestion might be workable if it could be shown that there is justification for speaking of God as timeless, but that seems incompatible with 'person'. Moreover, his attempt to account for timeless knowledge leans heavily on the dubious spatial similarities examined above. And as we shall shortly see, the *general* conception of a timeless knower is itself logically suspect.

Timelessness and Omniscience

In spite of the conceptual mistakes in this argument, a proponent of the classical solution might feel that there is still considerable merit in Boethius' suggestion even if we cannot make the relation clear. After all, if the notion of timelessness is abandoned, the problem of foreknowledge and free will becomes even more intractable for if God is temporally locatable, it is patently obvious that some of His beliefs about the future occur prior to those future events. And if God is infallible in His beliefs, it seems logically inevitable that the future events referred to in those beliefs must be determined to be what they will be.

In recent years the logical structure of this problem has received considerable attention. But the issues raised by an analysis of the structure of the argument based on locating God temporally are not the same as those raised by arguments based on timelessness. A solution to the foreknowledge problem can be reached only after thorough consideration of both of these possibilities. By itself, the critique of the analogical basis for timeless knowing is not sufficient to put this position to rest. Let us, therefore, turn our attention to the additional difficulties facing accounts of a timeless knower. To complete the argument for God's essential temporality, we will need to show not only that temporality is demanded by consciousness but that the alternative – a timeless knower – is, apart from problems with the putative analogy, logically incoherent in itself. Demonstrating this claim will require a full scale evaluation of the traditional doctrine of omniscience.

We can formulate the classic doctrine of omniscience in the following points:

> (1) God knows all things perfectly in both manner and extent. This follows from the fact that God is infinite (without limitation) and perfect (absolutely complete).

(2) Perfect knowledge is not a quality or a habitual capacity but a direct intellectual intuition. Accordingly, God does not gather or acquire knowledge by inference, comparison, verification or abstraction. He knows everything wholly and simultaneously in the abiding instant.[1]

(3) Because God is without potentiality, His knowledge consists of the identity of intellect and what is known. There is nothing that God can learn as His knowledge eternally embraces all that can be known as it actually is.

(4) God's act of knowing is not something distinct from Himself for this would imply that God's knowledge stands apart from His essence. Since God is altogether simple in every attribute, it follows that God's "act of knowing is his essence and his being".[2]

(5) Since God's being is His act of knowledge, He must know everything perfectly as each thing first exists as an idea in the mind of God.

(6) God knows all things that actually exist as actually existing and all things that potentially exist as potentially existing. This is the direct result of the method of God's knowing, i.e. God knows from the perspective of divine eternity which takes in the whole of time simultaneously.[3]

(7) Since God knows everything perfectly, He must also know all that can happen to each thing.

---

[1] Cf. H. P. Owen, *Concepts of Deity* (London: Herder and Herder, 1971), pp. 30-32.
[2] Aquinas, *Summa Theologiae*, Vol. 4, "Knowledge In God" (Ia. 14-18), trans. By Thomas Gornall (London: Blackfriars, 1964), p. 17.
[3] Ibid., p. 33.

Specifically, this implies that God can know of corruption and evil for the very fact that God knows goodness means that He must also know evil possibilities as the corruption of goodness.

(8) God's knowledge is immutable as is appropriate to His nature.

(9) God's knowledge is infallible as a consequence of His nature.

Drawn as they are from the framework of the *via negativa*, none of these points about God's knowledge is particularly surprising. Let us briefly summarize these under two categories. The *extent* of God's knowledge embraces everything that ever was, is or will be. It includes knowledge of possible but non-existent entities, of evil as a privation of good, of individuals, of propositions and of God Himself. Moreover, each of the things known to God is known perfectly in whatever manner it is. God's knowledge embraces everything from its pre-existence (as an idea in the divine mind) to its final destiny. The *manner* of God's knowledge is wholly unlike human knowing. God's knowledge is on the same level as His being. There is no distinction between who God is and what He knows as though the object of God's knowledge could be set against what it means for God to be a subject-self. Consequently, God has no need to acquire knowledge in any way. He knows by direct intellectual intuition. This intuition perfectly embraces everything that can be known. As a result, God's knowledge is both immutable and infallible.

It is the thesis that God knows by direct intellectual intuition which brings out the relationship between omniscience and timelessness. Not all of the arguments which are used to support this claim entail a doctrine of timelessness but the general intuition behind the belief that God knows all true propositions (past, present and future) is that God "sees" all the temporal events from an eternal "now". It is this intuition which we need to examine.

Three Arguments

The description of God's knowledge as direct intellectual intuition has traditionally been supported by three different arguments. These are the argument from creation, the argument from perfection and the argument from eternity. Elements of each of these are cross-referentially important to the structure of any single argument, but we may for the most part treat them as distinct approaches to the question, "In what manner does God know things?" The argument from creation relies on previously established conclusions concerning the nature of the divine being.[1] As pure act, God must embrace within His thought everything that is to be, for everything that is (as either real or possible) must first exist as an idea in the mind of God. Thus, God knows each and every thing as it will be in the same manner in which He knows His own mind. Since God knows His own mind non-inferentially, by direct intuition, He therefore knows each and every thing in a direct intuition of His own thought. In one sense,

---

[1] Consider Aquinas citation (*Summa Theologiae*, Vol. 4, p. 29) of Augustine (*De Trinitate*, XV, 13, p. 485), "God does not know all creatures, spiritual and corporeal, because they exist; but because he knows them therefore they exist". Aquinas also remarks that "God's knowledge is the cause of things. For God's knowledge stands to all created things as the artist's to his products. But the artist's knowledge is the cause of his products, because he works through his intellect; and so the form in his intellect must be the principle of his activity, as heat is to the activity of heating . . . Now it is clear that God causes things through his intellect, since his existence is his act of knowing. His knowledge, therefore, must be the cause of things when regarded in conjunction with his will. Hence God's knowledge as the cause of things has come to be called the 'knowledge of approbation'" (*Summa Theologiae*, Vol. 4, p. 31).

this argument is no threat to freedom. Even if God knows all possible situations (because He knows all the possible things which could make up any situation), it still remains open whether any of those possible situations will actually come to be. Knowing possibilities entails nothing existentially binding. But this Thomistic account is meant to give grounds for God knowing future actualities as well (although Aquinas did not consider these to be future *from the perspective of a timeless God*). The premise that everything that is, was or will be must first exist as an idea in the mind of God is understood as the premise that God *qua* Creator knows the entire history of each thing before its creation. This seems reasonable as long as events are viewed as sets of various properties and relations of entities and God is the sort of being who can see "all-at-once" the entire sequence of temporal moments constituted by these sets. In other words, this argument depends on the assumption that any event can be known in advance of its occurrence. This assumption is so far without justification.

The second argument for the idea of direct intellectual intuition depends on the idea of divine perfection. God's perfection can be understood in two ways, both of which contribute to the doctrine of omniscience. First, perfect may mean without defect or error.[1] This is the theological basis of the assertion that

---

[1] Aquinas, *Summa Theologiae*, Vol. 4, pp. 23-25, says, "It has been shown above that all that makes for perfection in any creature is to be found first in God, and is contained in him in an eminent degree . . . And thus all things are to be found first in God, not only as regards what they have in common but also as regards what they all have as distinct from one another". Aquinas concludes, "Therefore, since the essence of God contains all that makes for perfection in the essence of every other thing, and more besides, God can know all things in himself with a knowledge of what is proper to each. For the nature proper to each thing consists in its participation in the divine perfection in some degree. But God would not know himself perfectly if he did

God's knowledge is infallible. Secondly, perfect may be understood as absolutely complete. Here the argument follows from God's infinity. Since He is unlimited in *every* way, He cannot experience restraints on His knowledge.[1] Whatever God knows must be identified with His very essence which is necessarily unlimited. God's knowledge necessarily must be complete and exhaustive. He must know everything that can be known. Traditional theology has interpreted this to mean that God's knowledge includes knowing the truth concerning every conceivable proposition. Specifically, it means that His knowledge is not limited by time or space; that it has neither temporal nor spatial perspectives although it includes any knowledge statements which do have temporal and spatial perspectives. Knowledge which is unlimited in terms of time and space cannot be knowledge which is gathered through the processes typical of human beings. For God to learn anything would imply that at some time His knowledge was incomplete. Under these circumstances, God's knowledge would not be perfect if anything could be

---

not know all the ways in which his perfection can be participated by other things; nor would he know perfectly the nature of existence if he did not know all the degrees of existence. Hence it is clear that God knows all things in what is proper to each and makes them different from one another."

[1] "God has knowledge, and that in the most perfect way. This will become evident if we note that the difference between knowing and non-knowing subjects is that the latter have nothing but their own form, whereas a knowing subject is one whose nature it is to have in addition the form of something else; for the likeness of the thing known is in the knower. Thus, clearly, the nature of a non-knowing subject is more confined and limited by comparison with knowing subjects; . . . It is clear, then, that a thing's freedom from matter is the reason why it is able to know; and the capacity to know is in proportion to the degree of freedom from matter. . . . since God is immaterial in the highest degree, . . . it follows that he has knowledge in the highest degree" (Aquinas, *Summa Theologiae*, Vol. 4, p. 7).

added to it. Therefore, there can be no learning or accumulating processes for God's knowledge. If God's knowledge is to have any analogy with human thought at all, it must be like the immediate awareness we have of our own bodies or mental operations. Of course, while human embodiment may be thought of separately from the self (at least as a logical possibility), this sort of separation is not logically possible between God and His knowledge.[1]

The central issue in this argument is the assumption that time presents no limits (epistemological or otherwise) to God. The traditional doctrine of perfection treated time as a property of finitude. We have shown that treatment to be inadequate. The consequent implication that time is a constituent in God's existence means that this present argument offers no *justification* for the claim that God knows everything, past, present and future. We shall show that if time is a factor in God's existence, it is a limiting factor.[2] However, the full argument for this contention

---

[1] We shall treat this stipulation later in comments of the idea of "essential omniscience" as outlined by Pike. See below.

[2] W. H. Newton-Smith (*The Structure of Time*) has argued that the topology of time is not *necessarily* linear. He examines the possibilities of closed time (cyclical), branching time and multiple times, concluding that these possibilities present no internal logical incoherencies. This would indicate that the structure of time as we know it is an empirical matter, not to be settled by *a priori* arguments. However, even if Newton-Smith is right about the logical possibility of aberrant temporal topologies, these possibilities do not give justification to a temporal/timeless dichotomy, as we have seen. Nevertheless, they do raise a further question about the claim that time is a limiting factor. Is it possible to construct a theory of knowledge based on one of these other topologies which would allow God unlimited *temporal* omniscience? For example, could God exist in a parallel but distinct time from our own which would allow Him to know every future event of our temporal order? We cannot speculate on the possibilities here, but we should notice that alternative logical possibilities for temporal topologies affect an understanding of the doctrine of omniscience only if time is, in fact, non-linear in the

must wait until we have elaborated the third traditional support for the idea of God's direct intellectual intuition.

The last argument of the proposal of timeless omniscience is based on the doctrine of eternity. Aquinas summarizes the direct relationship between eternity and omniscience:

> God knows all things that are in any way whatever. But nothing bars things which absolutely speaking are not from being in some way. Things *are* in the unqualified sense if they are actually existent. But things that are not actually existent exist potentially as producible either by God himself or by a creature: whether in active power or in passive potentiality; whether in potentiality as matters of opinion or of imagination or as expressed in any other way. Therefore whatever can be produced or thought or said by a creature, and also whatever God himself can produce, all is known by God, even if it is not

---

required sense for only then will we be concerned with the *actual* relationship between a different topology and states of knowledge. In this regard, even Newton-Smith agrees that the empirical evidence points toward a *linear* topology for any present experience of time. Since the doctrine of omniscience must be worked out in regard to the actual structure of time, we will operate with a linear topology. Different topologies present interesting logics but it seems clear that in those possible worlds temporal existence would still be a limiting factor for any conception of agency, action and deliberation [Cf. Richard Gale, *The Language of Time* (London: Routledge & Kegan Paul, 1968), p. 131, *pace* David Lewis, "The Paradoxes Of Time travel," *American Philosophical Quarterly*, 13 (April, 1976), 145-152. Newton-Smith suggests that a faculty of pre-cognition logically similar to our present faculty of memory is not *incoherent* in spite of the major revisions such a faculty would require in our linguistic usage and ordinary conceptions of the world (Cf. Newton-Smith, Chapter 9 and Gale, Chapters 7 and 8). But while he disagrees with Gale over the logical conceivability of such a claim, he agrees that such a world could not be similar to ours. Relative to our world, such a faculty is not possible. Therefore, no account of temporal omniscience for this time could rely on an expansion of the pre-cognition faculties in aberrant topologies.

actually existing. In this case it can be said that he has knowledge even of non-existent things.

Yet we have to take account of a difference among things not actually existent. Some of them, although they are not now actually existent, either once were so or will be: all these God is said to know by *knowledge of vision*. The reason is that God's act of knowledge, which is his existence, is measured by eternity which, itself without succession, takes in the whole of time; and therefore God's present gaze is directed to the whole of time, and to all that exists in any time, as to what is present before him. Other things there are which *can* be produced by God or by creatures, yet are not, were not, and never will be. With respect to these God is said to have not knowledge of vision, but *knowledge of simple understanding*.[1]

Knowledge of vision results from God's non-temporal view of the temporal order. In the picture that Aquinas describes, God views all of the passage of time at once (although not strictly "at once" since this is a temporal expression). He "sees" everything that has been, is and will be in the one 'moment' of the instantaneous whole of eternity.[2] H. P. Owen draws the following picture of the relationship between timelessness and omniscience:

Theists who follow Aquinas adopt the second of these alternatives [that God knows the world as a "single, timeless present"]. In the eyes of God, they say, events that happened in 200 B.C. are as much present as my existence. The argument in favor of this view is this. If God is eternal, and if all his acts express his essence; his consciousness must be in all respects eternal; but if he knew the world in its temporal form his consciousness (and so his being) would be temporally conditioned.[3]

---

[1] Aquinas, *Summa Theologiae*, Vol. 4, p. 33.
[2] Aquinas gives a fuller elaboration of this direct, intuitive knowing based on eternal *perception* of the temporal order in *Summa Contra Gentiles*, Book I, Chapters 56-57, pp. 139-146.
[3] Owen, *Concepts of Deity*, p. 33.

Owen certainly sees the correct implications of this view, and of its operating possibility. We have already shown that the description of God as a timeless being is not reconcilable with the logic of the concept of person. On this ground alone we would be justified in rejecting the picture of knowledge of vision drawn by Aquinas. But for the purposes of drawing out other significant features of the purported connection between timelessness and omniscience, we will turn our attention to the internal logic of this position and ignore other difficulties. Some substantial contemporary objections have been made which are directly applicable to the idea of a timeless knower. We shall find that these objections not only support the conclusions we have drawn from our previous discussion of divine personhood but also undermine the intelligibility of the idea of a timeless omniscient being.

Pike on the Timeless Knower

Owen himself raises some queries about the logic of a timeless knower. Concerned with the apparent difficulties of maintaining that a timeless God has knowledge of a temporal realm, Owen asks:

> First, if time is real how can it be known timelessly? It is easy to understand that God, in knowing himself, knows timelessly all that possibilities that the world actualises; but he does not thus know them *as actual*; and if their actuality is objectively temporal I find it very hard to see how we can meaningfully speak of them as being timelessly known.[1]

Nelson Pike deals with the same issue in much greater detail. He considers whether or not it makes sense to suggest that a timeless knower could know such obvious temporal facts like "Today is Tuesday". Pike says that

---

[1] Ibid., p.31.

there is no immediate logical difficulty in saying that a timeless knower might know facts like "2+2=4". As long as the description of the fact known "requires no mention of temporal relations or temporal extension"[1] it may reasonably be claimed that a subject without temporal location or extension could know such a fact. According to our earlier distinction, we might say that a timeless knower logically could have knowledge of strictly timeless facts. But even if we find this sensible, that does not account for the entire range of facts that may be called timeless.[2] As Lucas suggests, failure to distinguish between omnitemporality, strict timelessness and permanence (those things which might change but just do not) has resulted in confusion in both logic and theology.[3] Pike's concession that a timeless knower might know facts that have neither temporal relations nor position allows us at best to believe that timeless knowledge is knowledge of logically necessary (analytic) truths. One might well wonder if this is at all helpful as regards the doctrine of omniscience for it certainly does not seem to be compatible with the account of God's knowledge of the temporal order.[4]

Pike is concerned, however, with the compatibility of timeless knowing and temporal facts. He points out that the traditional doctrine of omniscience holds that God cognitively grasps the entire matrix of temporality in a single act. This includes the facts of the temporal *ordering*

---

[1] Pike, *Timelessness*, p. 88.

[2] Cf. Arthur Prior, "The Formalities of Omniscience," in his *Papers on Time and Tense* (Oxford: Oxford University Press, 1968), pp. 26-44.

[3] Lucas, *Treatise on Time and Space*, p. 75.

[4] It would seem to account for God's knowledge of temporal contingencies if, of course, temporal facts were not contingent from God's perspective (i.e. when God *sees* them they are present and thus necessary). Although such a possibility will be discussed later, it should be clear that *strict timelessness* would require modification to accommodate this suggestion.

so that it is reasonable to say, for example, that God knows with being temporally qualified that Caesar was assassinated before the reign of Napoleon. It would be something like knowing that the statement, "Caesar was assassinated before the reign of Napoleon", is timelessly true because it expresses a fixed, necessary relation of this temporal order. But if this reasoning satisfies questions about knowing the relations of the temporal order, it does not seem to help with questions about knowledge of specific temporal events (e.g. that Lincoln is being assassinated *now*). Here Pike cites Arthur Prior's suggestion that a timeless being could not know statements of facts temporally locatable only in the present (e.g. "Today is Tuesday"). The argument contends that any being who knows what today is would have to have temporal position in order to know this. In other words, to know that today is Tuesday is to know the meanings of these temporal indicators and a necessary condition of knowing the meanings of these temporal indicators is having temporal position. For me to know that today is Tuesday implies that I exist at the temporal moment which is Tuesday. So a timeless being could not know expressions of facts that require temporal indexical reference.[1]

Pike agrees that all of this seems true. But he does not see it as damaging to the claim that a timeless being could not *know* such things. He offers the following reply:

---

[1] For a succinct example of this argument see Norman Kretzmann, "Omniscience and Immutability," pp. 413-414.

A timeless individual could not have an item of knowledge
that *he* could formulate or report in a statement such as, 'The
first scene is now on the screen' or 'Today is the twelfth of
May'. This is because statements of this sort serve (in part) to
identify the temporal position of the speaker relative to some
event or circumstance such as, e.g., the occurrence of the first
scene on the screen, the first of the year, the birth of Christ,
etc. . . . I cannot see, however, that this observation gives
warrant for the claim that there is something that a timeless
individual could not know. As uttered by a timeless being,
statements such as, 'The first scene is now on the screen' and
"Today is the twelfth of May' do not report facts at all. There
is nothing here that *could be known* – either by the timeless
being *or by anyone else*. Of course, as uttered by a *temporal*
being, statements of this sort report facts. But we have not
been given reason for thinking that the facts in question could
not be reported by a timeless being in statements free of
temporal indexical expressions. Two things have not been
shown: (1) that true statements in which temporal indexical
expressions are used (e.g., 'Today is the twelfth of May', as
uttered by Coburn on the twelfth of May) cannot be
formulated in statements having equivalent meanings but
which are free of temporal indexical expressions; and (2) that
if there are no such meaning-equivalent formulations of
statements utilizing temporal indexical expressions, the facts
reported in these statements cannot be reported in statements
free of indexical expressions. Thus, so far as has been
effectively argued to the contrary, what is known by a timeless
being might well exhaust the class of knowable facts . . . Prior,
Coburn and Kretzmann[1] claim to have identified a range of

---

[1] Cf. Prior, "Formalities of Omniscience", Coburn, "Professor Malcolm
on God" and Kretzmann, "Omniscience and Immutability".
Kretzmann's argument is the clearest. He grants that an omniscient
being could be said to know "simultaneously" every contingent event
in the form "event *e* occurs at time *t*" but he claims that this version of
omniscience is drastically incomplete. While such a being could know
that my writing these words occurs at time *t* and my reading them
occurs at *t+n*, such a being could not know that I am writing these
words *now*. Since Kretzmann's argument concentrates its attention on
the temporal indexicals alone, it does not explore the implication of
granting God non-temporal knowledge of the fixed order. In this

facts that a timeless individual could not know. But this claim
has not been established. So far as I can determine, all that
has been established is that there are certain *forms of words*
that a timeless individual could not use when formulating or
reporting his knowledge.[1]

The argument behind Pike's rebuttal is slightly
suppressed in this passage. He makes a strong distinction
between a statement and a sentence. He agrees that a
timeless being could not express the indexical sentence of a
temporally located being for the sentence, "Today is the
twelfth of May", is not something that could be uttered
sensibly by a timeless being. For a timeless being, such an
utterance would be incontrovertibly false. Since no
timeless being can have the implied temporal position
necessary to make such a knowledge claim, Pike argues
that such a temporal indexical sentence could never be a
possible item of knowledge for a timeless being in the first
place. That is to say, since it would be necessarily false
from a timeless perspective, no temporal indexical sentence
could ever have been a fact that some timeless being could
have known and therefore, no temporal indexical sentence
could ever have been a possible item of knowledge for a
timeless being. But Pike concludes that there is nothing
here that could have been known – either by a timeless
being *or by anyone else.* This carries the argument one step
further. It seems to be true that if such a sentence could
never be a fact for a timeless being, then it can be no
disgrace to the status of a timeless knower that it is not
known timelessly. But the doctrine of omniscience
requires more of God than that He knows timelessly only
patently timeless facts. It requires that God know *all* facts
(but He may, of course, know them all timelessly). If that
is the case, and temporal indexical expressions constitute

---

regard, we shall see that both Kretzmann and Pike concede too much to
the traditional formulation.

[1] Pike, *Timelessness*, pp. 94-95.

facts (even if only for temporal beings), then they become something that God apparently cannot know. Pike admits that temporal indexical expressions *report* facts for temporal beings. But he suggests that the fact is something entirely independent of the indexical expression. And the reason that he can claim that there is *no fact here at all* (even for temporal beings) is that he assumes that temporal indexical expressions add no essential information about the event which they report and thus have no empirical or sensible content. It seems obvious that these expressions supply some sort of information that contributes to temporal knowing. But it is, according to Pike, not the sort of information that constitutes a fact. That is to say, he claims that it has not been shown that the same *facts reported* by temporal indexical sentences could not be *reported* without temporal relations. On this ground, he holds that the class of putative facts so expressed does not prove to be a counterexample to the claim that there is an omniscient timeless being. He suggests that this way of talking is simply a manifestation of temporal operations and that there is not reason to believe that such facts could not be reported in non-temporal ways as well.

But Pike has introduced this conclusion about the nature of facts without offering any substantial support. His objection to the argument offered by Kretzmann, Prior and Coburn is that they have not isolated a class of *facts* at all. Pike agrees that temporal indexical expressions are unique, but he disagrees that they are unique referring devices. He suggests that temporal indexical expressions are *subjective* in that they refer only to the speaker and not to the event. He admits that temporal indexical sentences sometimes *report* facts. But he maintains a hard and fast distinction between the reporting of a fact and the fact itself. The fact is the event in question. It is the same event no matter how or when it is reported. It just happens that temporal beings do report such events with sentences

216

involving temporal indexical reference. But that does not entail that timeless beings could not report the same fact in some timeless way.[1] If the argument is correct, Pike has shown that no counterexamples have been isolated.

Gale on Time and Tense

The point which Pike makes regarding the difference between the temporal indexical report of some fact and the fact itself and his assumption that temporal indexicals are subjective, i.e. carry no factual information on their own, is so crucial to the entire structure of the analysis of omniscience in both its temporal and its timeless contexts that it is worth considering in detail. Pike's claim has been attacked by Richard Gale.[2] Gale shows that "temporal notions are implicitly involved in all of the basic concepts by means of which we think and talk

---

[1] In effect Pike is arguing that all temporal references in statements of fact are in principle capable of being eliminated. Our critique in the following section will deal directly with this thesis. But there is a deeper and more subtle philosophical move here. It concerns the previously mentioned spatialization of time. A possibility resident in the logician's view of tenseless truths (which we will discuss shortly) is the picture of time seen as a river. Use of that metaphor has disastrous consequences (e.g. those events in the future are *now* already part of the river of time and are flowing inexorably toward us as the future becomes the present). Timeless statements concerning the temporal order seem to imply that events always are (in some sense) even though they are not yet present to us. Because this view has important consequences for our later arguments concerning temporal omniscience and restricted foreknowledge, we will forestall elaboration here. Pike's claim for a *timeless* knower can be dealt with more directly. But the spatialization of time will be treated when we defend our forthcoming proposal of temporal omniscience.

[2] Gale, *The Language of Time* and Richard Gale, "Indexical Signs, Egocentric Particulars, And Token-Reflexive Words," *Encyclopedia of Philosophy*, IV, 151-155. Also see David F. Pears, "Time, Truth and Inference," *Proceedings of the Aristotelian Society*, LI (1950-1951), 1-24.

about the world".[1]   By following Gale's arguments
concerning McTaggart's paradox of time, we will see that
Pike's analysis is based on a faulty premise – a premise that
not only supports his view of timeless omniscience but also
stands behind certain reconstructions of omniscience in
temporal contexts.

McTaggart's paradox is based on two ways of
ordering temporal occurrences.[2]   The first way builds its
order on the notions of past, present and future. This is the
class of ordinary language expressions that recognizes time
as dynamic and speaks in tensed terms.   Any particular
event in this series can change its tensed description – it
can move[3], so to speak, from the distant future to the near
future to the present and into the near past to the distant
past. This series McTaggart calls the *A-series*.   In contrast,
the *B-series* is an order based on the relation between
temporal events.   In particular, the generating relation
'earlier than' produces a permanent ordering in which
moments of each event do not change tense but take on the
character of a logically (timelessly) true description.
McTaggart raised the question: How can these two ways of
talking about time be reconciled with each other?   While
our concern is not specifically aimed at the reconciliation
of the dynamic and static concepts of time, we can
recognize the significant parallels between McTaggart's
theses and questions about the epistemological and
ontological aspects of temporal events.   For example,
Pike's claim that no one has shown that true statements in
which temporal indexical expressions are used "cannot be

---

[1] Gale, *Time*, p. 5.
[2] Cf. The descriptions of these two orders in Leslie, "Value of Time",
pp. 109-111; and in Richard Gale, ed., *The Philosophy of Time: A
Collection Of Essays* (London: Macmillan, 1968), pp. 66-69.
[3] The existential and spatial connotations of this description will have
to be treated with great care, as we shall see.

formulated in statements having equivalent meanings but which are free of temporal indexical expressions" is tantamount to saying that no one has shown that *A-series* expressions cannot be reduced to *B-series* expressions without loss of meaning. And Pike's second objection (that even if there are no meaning-equivalent statements, no one has shown that the same fact cannot be reported in statements free of temporal indexical expressions) is equivalent to the claim that no one has shown that the events described in the *A-series* are more fundamental than, or independent of, the *B-series*. If we can express an *A*-statement about a contingent event in terms of a *B*-statement without loss of meaning, then we will have shown that *A*-statements are not essential to event reports (and do not constitute facts).

The purpose of Gale's analysis is to meet precisely these objections.

> . . . it will be the aim of this book to show that the logic of ordinary temporal discourse is such that tenseless expressions are logically dependent upon tensed ones, and also that the fundamental concepts which we employ in talking about the world involve tensed concepts, they could not be expressed except in a tensed language.[1]

To fulfill this goal, Gale mounts an argument that *A*-determinations are ineliminable.[2]   Gale defends the following theses:

(1) The *B*-Series is reducible to the *A*-Series since *B*-relations can be analyzed in terms of *A*-determinations;

(2) temporal becoming is intrinsic to all events;

---

[1] Gale, *Time*, pp. 7-8.
[2] Gale's treatment is not the first on this topic. Extensive bibliographic materials can be found in Gale, *Time*, pp. 17-33 and in Gale, ed., *Philosophy of Time*, section two.

(3) there are important ontological differences between the
    past and the future; and
(4) change requires the *A*-Series.[1]

Our immediate concern is with the first thesis for it
is in direct opposition to the claims of Pike. Gale suggests
that much of the intractability of the debate between
proponents of the conflicting theories is the result of the
fact that no adequate criteria have been established for the
determination of *A*- and *B*- sentences. The general intuition
behind *A*-sentences is the idea of temporal passage and the
truth-value of statements containing indexical expressions.
Thus, any criterion of an *A*-sentence will have to capture
the temporal restrictions of indexical reference and at the
same time reflect the fact that such sentences cannot be
freely repeated without a change in truth-value. To cover
those cases which could be counter-examples to a criterion
which only specified these two features, Gale also provides
restrictions against sentences which make necessarily true
or false statements through the use of tensed expressions
(e.g., "This bachelor is now married") and sentences which
are not freely repeatable solely in virtue of some non-
temporal indexical expression (e.g., "I am John Jones" or
"This is the place where *S* is always doing φ "). Once these
restrictions are incorporated into the criterion for an *A*-
statement, the intuitions behind the temporal references of
A-statements can be expressed like this:

> Any statement which is not necessarily true (false) is an *A*-
> statement if, and only if, it is made through the use of a
> sentence for which it is logically possible that two non-
> simultaneous uses of this sentence make statements differing
> in truth-value, even if both statements refer to the same things
> and the same places.[2]

---

[1] Gale, *Time*, p. 24.
[2] Ibid.

B-sentences, on the other hand, express an intuition about the timeless truth of mathematical logic. In this case, any event report must be ultimately either true or false. It <u>is</u> (tenselessly)[1] the case that "either *p* or not *p* at time *t*." And so the *B*-sentence must be freely repeatable, i.e. it must make a temporal determination (describe a temporal relation) under conditions that preserve the truth-value of the statement whenever it is uttered. A *B*-statement expresses an event-report that is independent of the indexical reference of the speaker. Gale formulates the criterion for identification of a *B*-statement as follows:

> Any statement is a *B*-statement if, and only if, it describes a temporal relation between events and is made through the use of a sentence for which it is the case that if it can now be used to make a true (false) statement then any past or future use of this sentence also makes a true (false) statement.[2]

It is apparent that the *B*-statement criterion does not fit precisely the attempt of Pike to reformulate temporal indexical expressions as timeless truths. Sentences like 'Today is the twelfth of May' or 'The first scene is now on the screen' certainly fit the description of *A*-statements. But there is a complicating difficulty when we try to match Pike's claim about the timeless transposition of these indexical sentences with the criterion for a *B*-relation statement. The *B*-statement criterion calls for a temporal relation between events that can be freely repeated *at any time* without change in truth-value. That is to say, the *B*-relation is really *omnitemporal*, not strictly timeless. Pike make no distinction between these two senses of timeless. As a result, when he offers an example of a timeless

---

[1] Where necessary, we will distinguish the tenseless 'is' (see Rescher's "atemporal *is*", p. 154) by underlining <u>is</u>.

[2] Gale, *Time*, p. 51.

statement which captures the fact reported in the temporal indexical sentence, 'The first scene is now on the screen', he actually gives a statement which meets the requirements of the *B*-relation criterion; namely, 'The first scene is (tenselessly) on the screen at 3:47 p. m. on the sixth of September'. This statement is freely repeatable without change in truth-value no matter *when* it is uttered. But it does not follow from the fact that it is true *at any time* (omnitemporally true) that it qualifies as a strictly timeless truth. As we have seen, strict timelessness requires that the expression have no temporal connections whatsoever (that it is nonsensical to raise questions about its possible temporal connections). But it is not nonsensical to ask, "How long was the first scene on the screen?" or "Was the first scene on the screen before Queen Victoria dies?"

Confusions between omnitemporality and strict timelessness will be important throughout the analysis of Pike's argument. But for the present, we shall consider only the claim that *A*-statements can be rendered in terms of *B*-relations. After all, if the *A*-statement is not translatable into an omnitemporal *B*-relation without loss of meaning or information, it should be obvious that it could not be translated into some variation of a *B*-relation that would meet the more rigid demands of strict timelessness. If such a rendering does not communicate the same information to a statement that could be freely repeated at any time, how could it communicate the same information to a statement that has no temporal relations at all? Since Pike's example shows that he really considers *B*-relations to be the appropriate meaning-equivalent statements, we can deal first with the omnitemporal claim before we try to identify the further difficulties associated with strict timelessness.

What happens when we try to convert the *A*-sentence, 'The first scene is now on the screen', into a *B*-statement? In order to meet the criterion of a *B*-statement, we have to express the fact reported by this *A*-sentence in such a way that the sentence reporting the *B*-relation expresses a tenseless truth about the event and is freely repeatable without a change in truth-value. Gale argues that in general both standard methods of accomplishing the reduction of '*S* is now φ ' fail. If we attempt to move from '*S* is now φ ' to '*S*'s being φ is (tenselessly) simultaneous with this token', we fail to produce the required reduction because the use of 'this token' produces an expression that qualifies as an *A*-sentence. If we revise this expression by replacing the indexical word with a metalinguistic symbol, the sentence '*S*'s being φ is (tenselessly) simultaneous with *theta*' qualifies as a *B*-statement but then the question is whether the *B*-statement *analysans* gives an adequate analysis of the *A*-statement *analysandum*.[1]

Gale suggests that the *analysans* can give an adequate analysis of the *analysandum* only if the *analysans* at least entails the *analysandum* (i.e. only if the event-report of the *A*-statement is deducible from the event-report relation of the *B*-statement). But in the cases we are concerned with these conditions are not fulfilled. If, for example, we take the *B*-statement offered by Pike, we see that the sentence, 'The first scene is (tenselessly) on the screen at 3.47 p. m. on the sixth of September' does not entail that 'The first scene is now on the screen' without the additional information that 'Now it is 3.47 p. m. on the sixth of September'. And, of course, this additional piece of information is an undisputed *A*-statement. Gale argues for the general case:

---

[1] Cf. Gale, *Time*, p. 54.

that S's being ϕ <u>is</u> simultaneous with *theta* (the occurrence of a token of 'S is now ϕ') does not entail that S is now ϕ. These B-statements describe a B-relation between S's being ϕ and a certain token event without entailing that either one of these events is now present (past, future). That they do not convey or entail information about the A-determination of an event can be seen by the fact that whenever someone uses the sentence, 'S's being ϕ <u>is</u> simultaneous with *theta* (the occurrence of a token of "S is now ϕ"), he has not forestalled the question whether S's being ϕ (or the occurrence of *theta*) is not present (past, future). The same considerations hold for the B-Theory's attempt to analyse an A-statement into a B-statement through the tenseless ascription of dates, e.g. 'S is ϕ at t_7'.[1]

Gale concludes that "because an A-statement cannot be rendered by a B-statement without loss of factual or informative content A-determinations cannot be reduced to B-relations".[2] This argument shows that there are significant pieces of information that can't be expressed without indexical reference. This overturns Pike's claim that it has not been shown that true A-statements cannot be reformulated as B-relations, for Pike's notion of "having equivalent meanings" implies that the concept that explains entails the concepts to be explained. But Pike also claims that even if A-statements cannot be formulated as B-relations, that does not entail that the facts reported by A-determinations cannot be reported by B-relations. This claim seems very strange indeed. For if Pike admits that there are no meaning-equivalent expressions, then he must admit that the meaning of the A-statement is not captured in the B-relation. And if some part of the necessary information needed to express meaning-equivalence is missing from the B-relation, how can he still insist that the B-relation statement reports the *same* fact as the A-

---

[1] Gale, *Time*, p. 55 and the extended argument of pp. 54-69.
[2] Ibid., p. 69.

statement? This could only be the case if the indexical expression is not considered relevant to the reported fact. Since this is the piece of information missing from the *B*-relation, Pike can only claim that the same fact is reported in spite of this absence if he believes that the missing piece has no bearing on the actual fact reported.

There seems to be some support for this view. Imagine the event of the first trans-Atlantic balloon crossing. That event is what it is regardless of the temporal perspective of any sentence reporting it. If the first trans-Atlantic balloon crossing occurs on August 17, 1978, then it seems reasonable to say that the event of the first trans-Atlantic balloon crossing is the same regardless of whether it is reported now (24 April 1979), at some time earlier than August 17, 1978 as a possible future event or at the time of the event. Nothing empirical seems to be added to the event by imaging that it is happening *now*.[1] The first trans-Atlantic balloon crossing happens on some particular date prior to other events and after still other events and no temporal position of the subject uttering a statement of this event can alter that relation. But reasoning in this way depends on the premise that *A*-determinations, because they are not empirical or sensible, add nothing to the factual content of an event. This is an assumption which must not go unchallenged.

If the premise that indexical expressions add nothing to the event report is true, then it implies that *B*-relations are at least independent of *A*-determinations. Since we have already seen that *A*-determinations are not reducible to *B*-relations, we have shown that *B*-relations are not more fundamental than *A*-determinations. But we have not shown that *A*-determinations are more fundamental than *B*-relations, i.e. we have not shows that *B*-relations can

---

[1] Cf. Gale, *Time*, pp. 70-71.

be reduced to *A*-statements. If we could demonstrate the logical priority of *A*-statements, then it would follow that *B*-relations depend on *A*-statements and that would mean that no full event-report could be given independently of the information contained in the *A*-determinations about the event. This would overthrow Pike's second claim and destroy the assumption that factual content is independent of *A*-statement information.

Gale notes that if it is possible to define the generating relation of the *B*-series (earlier than) in terms of 'past, present and future', then it will follow that the *B*-series is reducible to the *A*-series and that no *B*-relation could exist without an *A*-statement. But the history of this attempted reduction shows that efforts failed when proponents tried to construct a *B*-series in terms of a *pure A*-series. A *pure A*-series is determined by an unqualified past, present and future – "a past, present and future that do not admit of degrees"[1], while an *impure A*-series is determined "not only by an unqualified past, present and future but also by more past and more future".[2] The generating relation, 'earlier than', is definable in terms of an impure *A*-series of disjuncts. Thus:

> *P* is earlier than *Q*. ≡ . *P* is past and *Q* is present or *P* is past and *Q* is future or *P* is present and *Q* is future or *P* is more past than *Q* or *Q* is more future than *P*.[3]

---

[1] Gale, *Time*, p. 91.

[2] Ibid., p. 93.

[3] This analysis may be open to some objections concerning its precise relation to McTaggart's definition but those objections can be overcome without disturbing Gale's position. Cf. George Schlesinger, "The Reduction of *B*-Statements," *Philosophical Quarterly*, 28 (April, 1978), 162-165; L. Nathan Oaklander, "The 'Timelessness' of Time," *Philosophy and Phenomenological Research*, 38 (December, 1977), 228-233 and Gale's reply, pp. 234-238.

The definition of the *B*-series relation in terms of an impure *A*-series shows that every *B*-relation is some impure *A*-statement.   Moreover, it also shows that the generating relation of the *B*-series and the generating relation of the *A*-series is the same and that the *A*-series is both necessary and sufficient for the report of temporal facts.   Gale concludes that the fundamental nature of the *A*-series, in its impure form,

> shows that our concept of time involves in addition to the three unanalysable concepts of past, present and future the notion of a structural order, and it was because of the latter that we had to introduce the concepts of *more past* or *before*.[1]

Gale's argument reveals that *A*-statements are both necessary and ineliminable for the expression of temporal facts.   Though the information that *A*-statements contain may be neither sensible nor empirical, it is nevertheless significant.   To suggest, as Pike and other *B*-theorists do, that such information is irrelevant because it is not empirical is to define *facts* arbitrarily as only empirical or sensible.   Unless *B*-theorists can give coherent arguments that would compel us to accept this premise, their assumption must be rejected for we have good reasons for believing that the information supplied by the *A*-statement is essential for understanding the full description of the temporal event.   If the *B*-series can be reduced to the *A*-series but not conversely, then it follows that there are certain truths that can only be expressed in terms of the *A*-series.   Gale has shown that *B*-relations are definable in terms of impure *A*-statements (that *B*-relations always contain some *A*-statement) and this supports the view that facts are more than the class of statements referring to empirical data.   Moreover, the reduction of *B*-relations to

---

[1] Gale, *Time*, p. 99.

A-statements shows that *A*-statements are more fundamental than *B*-relations and that there could not be knowledge of a *B*-series without knowledge of an *A*-series.

We can justify this claim by considering two possible worlds. The first arises from a closed view of time. It is temporally repeated, i.e. at some point in time everything exactly repeats itself.[1] In these circumstances, it would be impossible to distinguish between repetitions of any individual without specifying temporal location (i.e. which of the repeating cycles is now the case). And the *B*-series would preserve the essential *order* of events in such a world but could never distinguish which of the repeated event-orders was now the case. The second possible world is a world in which there is spatial reduplication. Similar difficulties arise in this case because the *B*-series could not distinguish between exact multiple replicas in the same time but in different spaces. Full descriptions of events must be able to eliminate these possibilities. And this is possible only if some spatial/temporal frame of reference is included in the knowledge of the event ordering (e.g. names or space-time place holders). *A*-statements fix the frame of reference in relation to the speaker and thereby eliminate repeating and reduplicating ambiguities. Thus, a full description of an event requires knowledge of an *A*-statement frame of reference, whether explicit or implicit.[2]

---

[1] This possible world should not be confused with the usual, and logically unacceptable, idea of cyclical repetition; namely, that the *same things* occur again. All that this world specifies is that new instantiation exactly like the past ones occur again.

[2] Cf. Gale, ed., *Philosophy of Time*, pp. 80-81 where he points out that some have argued that ordinary language is irreducibly tense-structured precisely because it must of necessity refer to unique objects and events.

Generally, then, *A*-statements are the only ultimate guarantee of temporal and spatial uniqueness.[1]

Pike's underlying assumption that facts are only empirical is an unwarranted straight jacket.[2] Consequently, his claim that no class of facts has been isolated by Kretzmann, Prior and Coburn is false. In this sense, it is also false for Pike to claim that there is a hard and fast distinction between reports of events and the events themselves. Insofar as reports of events contain temporal indexicals, they contain pieces of information about events which cannot be ignored.

A Critique of Timeless Omniscience

Gale's argument shows that temporal indexicals cannot be reduced to omnitemporal tenseless relations without loss of information. If this is the case, Pike's attempt to show that temporal indexicals can be transformed into statements that a strictly timeless being could know seems even more difficult to believe. In spite of these mistakes, we can follow the rest of Pike's analysis with two goals in mind: first, to disentangle the confusions and ambiguities which result from the failure to distinguish

---

[1] This argument applies to both space and time. Anthony Quinton ("Spaces and Times," *Philosophy*, 38 (1962), 130-147) raises the possibility of a "mathematician's space" – a space where the speaker has no location. But this discontinuous space does not seem to have a temporal analogue (*pace* W. H. Newton-Smith, *Structure of Time*, Chapter 2). A time in which I have no place (or to which I have no relation) does not appear to be a real time at all, for without the ordered relation 'earlier than' it is difficult to see how the discontinuous time scheme could be established as actually the case, and with the relation the alternative time scheme appears to be no longer discontinuous.

[2] Cf. David F. Pears, "Time, Truth and Inference", p. 18 where he remarks, "Moore said that there are temporal facts. Anyone who is thorough about the reinstatement of temporal verbs is really saying that there are no non-temporal facts".

strict timelessness from omnitemporality, and secondly, to see if any support can be given to the idea of a strictly timeless knower from any other quarter.

In order to examine Pike's argument in an effort to accomplish these two tasks, we must return to the point we left before considering the work of Gale. Pike offers the following description of a way in which a timeless being might report an event referred to in an *A*-statement.

> A timeless individual might know that at a certain point in time, the first scene was on the screen. He might identify this temporal point in a variety of ways. He might say, for example, that it was 3.47 p.m. on the sixth of September. In order to pin it down in a different way he might add that it was the moment at which Pike said: 'The first scene is now on the screen.'[1]

He claims that even though the meaning of the sentence, 'The first scene is now on the screen', uttered by a temporal being might not be the same as the meaning of the sentence, 'The first scene was on the screen at 3.47 p.m. on the sixth of September', uttered by a timeless being, the fact reported would be the same. According to Pike, this claim is based on the similarity of justification.

> If called upon later to justify my original comment, I would point to the fact that at 3.47 p.m. on the sixth of September – the moment at which I said: 'The first scene is now on the screen' – the first scene was on the screen. This is precisely what the timeless being would point to if challenged to justify his report.[2]

This supporting argument reveals the impact confusions about omnitemporality and timelessness have on Pike's thinking. In order to explain the "timeless"

---

[1] Pike, *Timelessness*, p. 92.
[2] Pike, Timelessness, pp. 92-93.

reporting of a temporal fact, Pike operates as though the strictly timeless knower of the *via negativa* has omnitemporal relations to the temporal order. If God is strictly timeless, then no temporal relation or implication of a relation can be ascribed to Him. Moreover, the traditional doctrine of eternity treats timelessness as an instantaneously whole and perfect "moment", a concept that is later expressed as God's eternal present. In these circumstances, Pike admits that uttering the sentence, 'The first scene is now on the screen', is necessarily false. But the same conditions make any reference to the past also impossible. God can neither have a past nor a future, nor even a present in the normal sense of the word. How then could God be challenged *later* to justify a report that the first scene *was* now on the screen. From God's eternal present, there are no temporal order relations relevant to Him. Eternity is a single instant which "overlaps" all temporality.[1] Under these conditions, God's knowledge of any temporal event must be tenselessly simultaneous with all other events. Strict timelessness limits us to the use of the tenseless is and only the is. Anthony Kenny is right about the consequences of this position when he says:

> . . . the things which happen at different times are all present together to God. An event is known *as future* only when there is a relation of future to past between the knowledge of the knower and the happening of the event. But there is no such relation between God's knowledge and any contingent event: the relation between God's knowledge and any event in time is always one of simultaneity. Consequently, a contingent event, as it comes to God's knowledge, is not future but present; and as present it is necessary; for what is the case, is the case, and it is beyond anyone's power to alter.[2]

---

[1] Cf. Aquinas, *Summa Contra Gentiles*, Book I, pp. 140-141.
[2] Anthony Kenny, "Divine Foreknowledge And Human Freedom," in Anthony Kenny, ed., *Aquinas: A Collection of Critical Essays* (New York: Doubleday, 1969), p. 261.

Kenny directs his remarks to knowledge of future contingent events, but we can see the argument will apply to any temporal indexical event-report. That is to say, for every event, if there is no beginning to time, then that event is future to some previous time and is therefore known as future by any knowing subject temporally located prior to the occurrence of the event. But if we take seriously the timeless description of God's knowing, we will be forced to speak of God's knowledge only in terms of the tenseless is (the 'is' of the eternal present, as it is sometimes called, retains certain temporal links which, strictly speaking, should not be allowed). Therefore, it would be an error to say that God knows that a man _will land_ on Mars. We should in fact say that God knows that a man _is landing_ on Mars. The difficulty is obvious. The second of these two statements seems false (for no one is now landing on Mars) and as false could not be known, even by God.[1] The same tenseless grammar must be rigidly applied to Pike's argument. God cannot report that the first scene _was_ on the screen if all events are simultaneously present to Him. Of necessity, He will have to report that the first scene is on the screen and that it is on the screen at the same tenseless moment as the man is landing on Mars and Caesar is being assassinated. Pike has already admitted that such a description taken in the present tense would be necessarily false for a timeless being. But he fails to apply the

---

[1] An objection could be raised here. If we suppose that God knows (tenselessly) all true propositions in their (tenselessly) true states, (e.g. as they are either true or false in a logical sense where these are treated as the logician's categories), then we might be able to imagine that God knows in the tenseless state these temporal (but only from our perspective) facts. But there are crucial ontological and epistemological assumptions involved in this position. The difficulties associated with this argument will be treated in the next chapter since they affect both timeless and temporal omniscience.

requirement of strict timelessness to the remainder of his argument.   He treats eternity as though it were omnitemporality and thus he is able to introduce past tense statements into the reports of God's knowledge.   Strict timelessness would require that the reports would not admit to temporal questions.   And omnitemporality seems to require that the reports be reducible to tenseless *B*-relations.

Pike has unwittingly satisfied the very requirements which are the basis of his objection to Kretzmann, Prior and Coburn.   We can see that (1) if statements of the knowledge of a timeless being must be strictly limited to the tenseless is and must not admit of temporal questions, then it follows that such statements are necessarily without any possible temporal connections.   This fulfills the requirement that true statements of temporal indexical expressions cannot be formulated in statements of equivalent meaning without the temporal indexical referent. We may also notice that (2) if every knowledge report of a timeless being is simultaneously present with every other knowledge report because the facts known by a strictly timeless being are all simultaneously present, then every knowledge report must be a present knowledge report of a present fact (or, more accurately, a tenseless report of a tenseless fact).   It makes no sense to suggest that God can distinguish the parts of a tenseless moment which is a simultaneous and undivided instant.   And we have already seen that the *via negativa* holds God's knowledge to be synonymous with His essence which is without parts (simple).   It would seems that the *parts* of the temporal order do not show any readily understandable way of being reconciled with a timeless instant.   There is good reason to believe that facts reported by temporal indexical expressions could not be reported without these expressions nor could they be distinguished as *parts* of an order in a tenseless eternity.   Therefore, a *timeless* being could not report such facts even if reformulated timeless *B*-relations were possible. The first claim shows that a timeless God could not use temporal indexical expressions and that these expressions cannot be reduced to some meaning-equivalent timeless statements. The second claim shows that the facts referred to by the temporal indexical expressions cannot be reported without some temporal indexical reference and so could not be reported or known by a timeless being.

Problems caused by the failure to distinguish between strict timelessness and omnitemporality are increased by accepting the idea that the fixed order of temporal relations (*B*-series) can be known in a strictly timeless manner. Initially, Pike suggests that there is no apparent difficulty in saying that a timeless (sense unqualified) knower might know a fact such as '2+2=4'. This example fits the traditional picture of God as strictly timeless since the mathematical truth is also strictly timeless. But Pike moves directly from this example to the fact 'Abraham Lincoln was assassinated sometime after the battle of Gettysburg'. In this case, Pike wishes to show that a strictly timeless being can know the truth of this relation since it expresses a tenseless relation between two temporal events (the *B*-statement equivalent being, 'The Battle of Gettysburg is (tenselessly) earlier than the assassination of Lincoln'). Pike offers an argument from Boethius to account for God's strictly timeless knowledge of this temporal relation.

> Boethius said that God 'beholds' the whole matrix of temporally ordered events and circumstances. God does not behold them one after another; He grasps them in a single act of cognition. God knows every detail of the temporally ordered matrix—including all of the temporal relations between the events and circumstances involved. But, of course, God's cognition is not, itself, temporally qualified.

> Though God is aware *of* temporal events, His awareness is
> not, itself, a temporal event . . . For the present purposes, we
> can assume that this line of thinking is acceptable.[1]

But we have seen that it is precisely this line of
thinking which is not acceptable. Pike's example must be
revised in order to meet the requirements of strict
timelessness. Following Kenny, we recognize that a
strictly timeless God could never know that Abraham
Lincoln *was* assassinated sometime after the Battle of
Gettysburg. Pike obviously has a *B*-statement in mind here
but, unfortunately, has been careless in its formulation. If
we revise the statement (as above), the temporal relation is
set in a tenseless context, but we can immediately see that it
fails to support Pike's claim about the nature of timeless
omniscience. In its tenseless form, this statement is a *B*-
relation. Its truth-value remains constant in an
omnitemporal context, i.e. in relation to the given order of
our history. But that does not imply that it is a strictly
timeless truth for such truths appear to be analytic.
Moreover, it is only omnitemporally timeless insofar as it is
reducible to some disjunction of *A*-statements. And such a
reduction shows an intrinsic relation to temporality which
God's eternity cannot allow. If Pike wishes to uphold
Boethius' description of God's omniscience, he must show
that this tenseless omnitemporally true relation can be
formulated in a strictly timeless fashion. And that would
amount to showing that it could be reformulated in such a
way that it would be meaningless to raise any questions
with temporal reference about its truth. It would have to be
formulated in such a way that it could not be contradicted
by any temporal assertion. To be strictly timeless, such a
statement would have to be removed from every
conceivable connection with temporality. Pike has not

---

[1] Pike, *Timelessness*, p. 88.

given us such a reformulation and it is difficult to see how he could.   What he has provided is an attempt at a *B*-relation (and a lackadaisical one at that).   But even this attempt, transposed into a pure *B*-relation, will not support Pike's thesis for Boethius' doctrine.

Gale's argument shows that any *B*-relation contains some *A*-statement, that the *A*-statement is more fundamental that the *B*-relation and that the *B*-relation cannot be known without the implied *A*-statement. Therefore, Boethius' doctrine that God knows all temporal relations without His knowledge itself being temporally qualified is false. If God knows the tenseless relation, 'The Battle of Gettysburg is earlier than the assassination of Abraham Lincoln', then that implies that God also knows the *A*-statement disjuncts which define that relation.   To suppose that God could know the *B*-relation but not know the *A*-statement would be to suppose that there is in fact a class of statements (facts) which an omniscient God does not know. This would certainly be incompatible with any traditional understanding of the doctrine of omniscience. If the tenseless relation is definable in terms of past, present and future and the impure form, then an omniscient God must know that such an entailment does hold and that amounts to knowing *A*-statements (the knowledge of which requires temporal location). Moreover, since knowing the truth of the *B*-relation is knowing the truth of an omnitemporal relation, God's knowledge of the *B*-relation implies temporal extension. Boethius' argument that God can know the entire matrix of temporal relations without temporal qualification is not only false, it is logically incoherent. And Pike's acceptance of this line of thinking produces nothing but confusion for his discussion of timeless omniscience. We must reject the claim that God is aware of temporal events or temporally conditioned relations without His awareness being temporal. We must also reject any attempt to speak of timeless knowing with temporally conditioned terms like 'earlier than', 'later', 'before' or 'simultaneous'. It would appear that strictly timeless omniscience is limited to knowledge of strictly timeless truths. And since these are most likely limited to the class of logically necessary analytic statements, it is difficult to see how a timeless knower could know what is happening at this moment.

The problem with a timeless knower is not limited to a problem about translating temporal indexicals into timeless relations. Pike's mistake concerning *B*-relation reductions and his acceptance of Boethius' claim that God knows the temporal ordering stems from a strong sentence-statement distinction coupled with a logician's view that every statement of the form, 'event *E* occurs at time *t*', has a definite truth-value for every *E* and every *t*. If we imagine that here is some event *E* which is a possible event at some time in the future *t*, and omniscience is understood to mean knowledge of all true, then it seems to follow that God would know (tenselessly) whether the expression, 'event *E* occurs at time *t*', is true or false. And since God knows the truth about these expressions as tenseless truths, He knows such truths at any point in time which we might choose to ask Him. In Pike's view, the assertion that there is a timeless knower presupposes this framework. This form of the argument has received a great deal of attention from logicians, in particular Arthur Prior. He identifies certain equivocations and ambiguities regarding the words 'true' and 'is' which greatly influence the outcome of this argument. But his remarks are equally applicable to timeless and temporal omniscience. Therefore, we will postpone this discussion until we can treat all of its ramifications.

By careful analysis of the problems associated with claiming that a timeless being could have knowledge of temporal facts, we have shown that strict timelessness cannot account for the usual knowledge attributed to God under the doctrine of omniscience. Strict timelessness seems to rule out all except strictly timeless truths. While more needs to be said about the difference between temporal and logical truths, we should not be surprised by this intermediate result. For we have already demonstrated that consciousness presupposes temporality and that implies that any knowing subject (any conscious subject) is able to have knowledge of the temporal order precisely because temporality is a fundamental constituent of its existence. In other words, if consciousness implies temporality then the knowledge claims of any self-conscious being imply temporal indexical reference. The other side of the coin has also been shown; that no timeless being (no being without temporal location) can claim to have knowledge of temporally conditioned facts. If consciousness is a temporally conditioned phenomena, then no timeless being could be conscious. This seems to agree with the remarks of Kenny on the futility of attempting to give tense-logical accounts of the knowledge claims of a timeless being. It is little wonder that theologians have had difficulty expressing the concept of the timeless knowledge of temporal events with logical consistency. The claim that we can easily understand God timelessly knowing all the possibilities of the world because God knows His own mind timelessly is hopelessly confused. We have seen that God's knowledge of Himself presupposes temporality. In these circumstances, attempts to defend a doctrine of timeless omniscience must fail.

We have successfully argued that Boethius' solution to the foreknowledge problem is inadequate in at least three major respects. First, it fails to reckon with the argument that consciousness entails temporality. Secondly, the underlying analogy offered in support of the proposal contains fundamental category mistakes. Thirdly, even if we ignore these criticisms, we find that the notion of a timeless knower cannot account for knowledge of the temporal order.   We must conclude that if God is conscious, then He is temporal; His cognition is temporally locatable and His existence is not discontinuous with our own.   If God does have a unique perspective on the temporal order, that perspective is not the result of His position "outside" time. God's unique perspective, and the basis of omniscience, will have to be worked out within the confines of temporality. God may have unique knowledge, but He is not timeless.

CHAPTER 10

TEMPORALITY AND FOREKNOWLEDGE

The Problem Remains

The failure of the doctrine of timeless omniscience makes the problem of foreknowledge even more pressing. Now it is impossible to circumvent the issue by claiming that nothing is temporally prior to God. If God is temporal, then some of His cognitions certainly seem to be prior to some events. Any solution to the question of free will must confront a God whose knowledge is temporally locatable. But under this condition, the problem appears to be irresolvable. Pike expresses the general framework of the problem in terms of six working assumptions:[1]

> {1} 'God is omniscient' is a necessary statement.
> {2} If an individual is omniscient, that individual believes all true propositions.
> {3} If a given individual is omniscient, than that individual believes nothing that is false.
> {4} Omniscience is an essential property of any individual possessing it.
> {5} If a given individual is God, that individual has always existed and will always exist.
> {6} If an individual exists at a given moment in time, then in order to count as omniscient, that individual must hold any belief he holds at that moment in time.

---

[1] Pike, *Timelessness*, pp. 54-56.

From these six assumptions (which we will entertain for the moment without further explanation or critique), Pike outlines the general problem structure. The schematic representation of the argument is as follows:[1]

(1) 'Yahweh is omniscient and Yahweh exists at T1' entails 'If Jones does A and T2, then Yahweh believes at T1 that Jones does A at T2' (Assumptions II and VI).

(2) If Yahweh is (essentially) omniscient, then 'Yahweh believes P' entails 'P'. (The doctrine of divine infallibility from Assumption III and IV.)

(3) It is not within one's power at a given time so to act that both 'P' and 'not-P' are true.

(4) It is not within one's power at a given time so to act that something believed by an individual at a time prior to the given time was not believed by that individual at the prior time.

(5) It is not within one's power at a given time so to act that an individual existing at a time prior to the given time did not exist at the prior time.

(6) If Yahweh believes at T1 that Jones does A at T2, then if it is within Jones's power at T2 to refrain from doing A then either: (1) It was within Jones's power at T2 so to act that Yahweh believed P at T1 and 'P' is false; or (2) it was within Jones's power at T2 so to act that Yahweh did not believe as He did believe at T2; or (3) it was within Jones's power at T2 so to act that Yahweh did not exist at T1.

(7) If Yahweh is (essentially) omniscient, then the first alternative in the consequent of line 6 is false (from lines 2 and 3).

(8) The second alternative in the consequent of line 6 is false (from line 4).

(9) The third alternative in the consequent of line 6 is false (from line 5).

---

[1] Pike, *Timelessness*, pp. 59-60.   Pike's reference to various assumptions (e.g. Assumption III) are to those listed above, see footnote 1.

(10)   Therefore: If Yahweh is (essentially) omniscient and believes at T1 that Jones does A at T1, then it was not within Jones's power at T2 to refrain from doing A (from lines 6 and 7-9).

(11)   Therefore: If Yahweh is (essentially) omniscient and exists at T1, then if Jones does A at T2, it was not within Jones's power at T2 to refrain from doing A (from lines 10 and 1).

The conclusion of this argument seems to be the logically inescapable denial of free will. Apparently, the only avenues open to a theistic proponent of free will are modifications of one or both of the key doctrines -- omniscience and infallibility. There are several possibilities. We could claim that God is not omniscient (there are things which He should know but He just does not). But this is too radical a departure from any ordinary conception of the Christian God. In fact, on Pike's account of the working assumptions, this claim is logically inconsistent with the very idea of God. In cases where the tension between omniscience and free will proved intolerable, the usual historical treatment upheld omniscience and considered free will an illusory but necessary element of the human condition. On the other extreme, we could claim that God is not infallible (some things He thinks He knows are false). In its strongest form, this possibility implies that God is genuinely mistaken in His beliefs about the future. But, again, this is too radical a treatment. Some sense of infallibility follows from the doctrine of omniscience. These radical positions are not only inconsistant with the history of Christian doctrine, they are, in fact, unnecessarily excessive. In order to maintain continuity with the Christian tradition, we must seek a modification that requires the least possible alterations in the historical understanding and still accommodates the remaining logical problems.

Possible Solutions

There are several moderate positions. We could suggest that God is restricted in His infallibility, i.e. that He is fallible with regard to some of His beliefs but infallible with regard to others (in particular, He has fallible knowledge of future free acts).[1] This view would allow us to continue to talk about God knowing with certainty those future events that are now present in their causes (determined by present conditions, etc.) without committing us to the thesis that all future events are now present in their causes. But this raises the question, "Why is it that God does not know some propositions (and, in particular, these propositions) concerning future events?" In other words, the position requires another level of explanation, namely, an explanation that tells us what it is about future free acts that entails God now has only fallible knowledge of their outcome. The logic behind this question leads us to two possible modifications of the doctrine of omniscience. Both of these are compatible with the above position of restricted infallibility; in fact, restricted infallibility follows as a logical consequence from either one.

The first holds that God has fallible knowledge of future free acts because He chooses to limit His knowledge in order not to inhibit freedom. There are two possible readings of this suggestion, one of which seems to involve a circular argument.[2] We will examine the more plausible

---

[1] Pike attempts another solution based on a distinction between necessary and contingent infallibility. We shall discuss this suggestion in the next chapter and show that it is unsatisfactory.

[2] On one reading, both Lucas (*Freedom Of The Will*, p. 75) and Swinburne (*Coherence*, p. 176) suggest that God chooses to "compromise" His knowledge for the sake of freedom; that He chooses not to know certain things about the future. But Kretzmann is right when he says that omniscience is not logically similar to omnipotence.

of these under the forthcoming treatment of the Ordinary Language objection.   There we will argue that this restriction of omniscience is, at best, unnecessary and, at worst, internally inconsistent.   The second possible modification of omniscience also gives an explanation of the above position of restricted infallibility but it does so on entirely different grounds.   It does not invoke an argument about God's choice nor a discussion of the necessary conditions of freedom.   If it is true, it is true on grounds that are independent of the postulation of human free will. It suggests that God does not know with certainty *some* future-tense propositions because, of logical necessity, no one, not even God, could know these things.   This is a much stronger thesis than the restriction by choice. Consequently, it requires considerably more elaboration and defense.   If it is true, it makes the first version of restricted omniscience unnecessary and, in some cases, it makes the framework supporting that restriction false.   If it can be supported, it gives a strictly logical justification to our modification without involving a *petitio principii* or *ad hoc* considerations.

A Tense-Logical Proposal

The theist can deny neither omniscience nor free will.[1]   This seems to entail that he also cannot deny

---

It is the condition of knowing, not a power or capacity to know. Either God knows all that can be known or He does not. If God chooses not to know something, this implies that the choice is based on alternative present cognitions and that implies that He knows what it is that He chooses not to know.

[1] We may not wish to prejudge the case with talk about *human* free will.   Our solution does not depend on there actually being such freedom.   But the theist has almost always claimed that God's choices were free.   This seems to follow from God's temporal existence for a God who knew that outcome of His own choices in advance could not be said to deliberate, consider, decide, intend, etc. (Cf. Gale, *Time*, p.

infallibility.   In addition, we have argued that God is temporal, thereby eliminating the classical solution to the foreknowledge problem. But the foreknowledge problem depends on the premise that God knows now all true propositions about future contingent events. The solution that we will defend does not claim that *all* future propositions are unknowable.   It only claims that one particular class of future propositions are, in principle, unknowable.   Moreover, it claims that these are unknowable because they are neither true nor false prior to the actual occurrence of the event to which they refer. Neither temporal omniscience nor infallibility requires us to accept the claim that God knows at t_1 the truth or falsity of every statement of the form 'Event E occurs at t_n' where t_n is after t_1. These two doctrines require only the following assertions. If 'E occurs at t_2' is true at t_1, then God must know that it is true, and if 'E occurs at t_2' is false at t_1, then God must also know that. But if 'E occurs at t_2' is *neither true nor false* prior to t_2, then there is no logical requirement compelling us to claim that God should know anything about the occurrence of event E. And without this premise, the foreknowledge problem dissolves.[1]

This solution depends on two major hypotheses; one that deals with the kind of events in question and the

---

131.) There is a theological tradition that "solves" the foreknowledge problem by accepting determinism, claiming that human freedom is an illusion. This position is not consistent with that of the church fathers who considered the problem a real one. We will see that it is also an unnecessary concession.

[1] According to Richard Taylor, this solution was originally put forward by Levi ben Gershon (1288-1344). Taylor's article, "The Problem of Future Contingencies," *Philosophical Review*, LXVI (January, 1957), 1-28, claims the solution stems from Aristotle's notion of real contingency. Ben Gershon had access to Aristotle through Averroes and there seems to be no reason to suppose that he might not have been influenced by such an argument.

other that deals with the assignment of truth-values to propositions about those events. These give rise to several objections against such a proposal. We may identify these objections as follows:

> {1} the Ordinary Language objection
> {2} the Definite Truth-Value objection
> {3} the Dating objection
> {4} the Logical Fatalism objection

In order to defend our proposal against these, we will adopt the following general strategy. We will show that the *Ordinary Language* objection is a real one but that it is addressed to a much stronger thesis than ours. However, examination of this will give rise to several crucial distinctions that will be usefully applied to variation of this objection which do have consequence for our proposal. Once these distinctions are articulated, the basis of restricted omniscience by choice can be examined. We will see that problems with this position lead us directly to the second objection that concerns the assignment of truth-values and temporal indexical expressions. We will argue that the *Definite Truth-Value* objection can be reduced to the problem of *Logical Fatalism*. As a by-product of this discovery, we will be able to meet the objection concerning the *Dating* of temporal indexicals. Finally, we will show that *Logical Fatalism* is itself untenable. It should be noted, however, that two additional, and perhaps more far-reaching, objections arise outside the context of this logical treatment. We will consider then in the next chapter. Only then will our defense of the tense-logical proposal be complete.

The Ordinary Language Objection

Briefly, the objection can be put as follows:

Ordinary language contains many examples of cases where we wish to say that we know what is going to happen in the future. While the amount of evidence for these claims varies, it seems reasonable to suggest that such examples are correct normal usage. But our proposal apparently entails that these ordinary language claims are either mistaken or misguided. The claim that future contingent statements are neither true nor false prior to the occurrence of the events seems to restrict normal uses of 'know' and 'true' too much to be justified.

The basic objection posed by considerations of ordinary language is fairly straightforward. We quite naturally conclude that we can have a good deal of knowledge about the future. I might claim with good evidence that there is going to be an eclipse in 1998 or that the tide will be at minus five feet at 7 A.M. tomorrow. With somewhat less evidence, I might say that I know that the Iranian civil war will begin before the next week or that Jones will cut his lawn next Saturday. All of these examples seem to be appropriate use of the verb 'to know'. If I can have such knowledge of the future, it seems reasonable to suppose that God can have good reasons for believing some things about the future (and, one would imagine, undoubtedly much better knowledge than my limited understanding allows).

Several distinctions need to be made concerning these sorts of cases. The first pertains to the classes of events under investigation. When we consider the problem of foreknowledge and free will, we are not particularly interested in events like eclipses and tides. Predictive knowledge of these sorts of events can be explained in terms of causal conditions. Of course, if the actions of human beings that we usually call free choices are also causally determined in a manner similar to the eclipse of the sun, then it follows that God (or anyone else apprised of the correct antecedent conditions) could know in advance those sorts of behaviors. How we know causally determined events has a bearing on future contingencies but without establishing a full thesis of causal determination, the context is only tangential. Moreover, our claim does not suggest that God could not have knowledge of this sort of future event. This objection is true but not germane.

The disturbing point of the Ordinary Language objection is that there is also an appropriate use of 'know' with reference to future activities of free agents. But this use of 'know' must be distinguished from the use that belongs to traditional positions on omniscience. According to the traditional doctrine of omniscience, God's knowing is infallible. That is, if God knows that p then it follows that p. This is a logically necessary connection. Omniscience means knowing all true propositions and if God knows that p (p is true) then it logically cannot be otherwise. God's knowledge is certain knowledge. But ordinary language claims about future contingent events do not seem to carry this sort of entailment. This is to say, these sorts of claims about the future carry implicit possibilities of error. "I know that Jones will cut his lawn tomorrow" could lead to "I thought I knew but I was wrong" or "I told you I knew". Part of the reason behind the weaker claim involved in this sense of 'know' stems from the fact that future contingencies of this sort have usually been understood as events the occurrence of which depends on how some agent will choose. So when I say, "I know that Jones will cut his lawn tomorrow", I am usually making a probability claim based on present evidence. And while I may be right, it does not follow from my making the claim that I must be right. Gale points out that the truth or falsity of these sorts of knowledge claims lies in their pragmatic implication and that this implication is a very strange one, relying on conventions.

The queer thing about the pragmatic implication is that it is
not what someone says -- the statement he makes -- that
pragmatically implies some other statement but his saying --
his using a sentence in a certain context. More precisely:
(P) The use of sentence s in context c pragmatically implies
that q if, and only if, the use of s in c enables the hearer to
infer that it is most likely the case that q and s is usually used
in c when it is the case that q and there is a convention that a
speaker should not use s in c unless it is the case that q and if
this convention were to be publicly disavowed by the speaker
it would frustrate the achievement of the perlocutionary acts
for which s is usually used in c.[1]

In fact, predictions based on causal evidence could be seen
as knowledge claims of the same type where the claim has
a much higher degree of probability because the evidence is
much better. The sorts of events that are our principle
concern in the issue of foreknowledge are events which
normally could be interfered with by agents. Thus, if Jones
tells me what he is going to do, if I regularly observe him to
be a man of his word, if he is in the habit of cutting his
lawn on Saturday, etc. , all of this supports my claim to
know what will happen tomorrow. But any number of
things can occur which would falsify the claim, including
the fact that Jones can *deliberately* frustrate my prediction.
I am not claiming to know with certainty when I claim to
know that Jones will cut his lawn tomorrow. As we shall
see, if Jones' action is really contingent, it cannot be
described under the strong sense of 'know' which belongs
to traditional notions of omniscience.

In contrast, the traditional doctrine of omniscience
asserts a logical connection between God's knowledge and
His infallibility such that whatever God believes to be true
could not, under any circumstances, be false. God's
knowledge of p entails p. Even Aquinas recognized that

---

[1] Gale, *Time*, p. 142.

future contingent acts could not be *known* in this strong sense by God if they were really contingent and future. Thus, he relied on eternity as timelessness to remove the contingency through removal of the future element of these events. According to Aquinas, for God these events are not future, but *present* and therefore can be known with certainty.[1] This use of 'know' is much stronger than the typical use in ordinary language for it rests on epistemic necessity and timelessness.[2]

Some have argued that God's omniscience should be understood in the weaker sense of 'know'; that His knowledge of the future is fallible.[3] They have claimed that there is no difficulty in supporting that God knows the

---

[1] Cf. Aquinas, *Summa Theologiae*, Vol. 4, pp. 47, 49, 51.

[2] Richard Taylor, "Future Contingencies", pp. 9-11, gives the following meanings of four crucial terms involved in our proposal. (1) logical necessity corresponds to analyticity and logical contingency means the statement in question is neither analytic nor self-contradictory, (2) epistemic necessity corresponds to what is known to be and epistemic contingency corresponds to some statement about an event which is not known to be or not to be, (3) causal necessity corresponds to an event determined to be by antecedent conditions and laws while causal contingency corresponds to an event of which neither the occurrence or non-occurrence has a cause, (4) temporal necessity (unalterability) applies to any event that has happened (already occurred) and temporal contingency applies to any supposed event which has not yet occurred. According to the traditional doctrine of omniscience, God's knowing that *p* necessarily entails that *p* (but see Kenny, "Divine Foreknowledge", pp. 258-260 for the distinction between *de dicto* and *de re*). That God may know that *p* because *p* is logically necessary or causally necessary are both compatible with the present proposal. The question is the range of events covered by temporal contingency and their connections with causal contingency and epistemic necessity.

[3] Lucas and Swinburne could both be read in this way although certain additional claims that Swinburne makes about the assignment of truth-values to future contingencies cause problems for his account. If Lucas' suggestion concerning God's choice is seen as a proposal of *fallible* knowledge, I find nothing disagreeable with it.

future in the same way that we do, i.e. based on the evidence at hand as probable but not certain. As such, His knowledge claims would be open to possible refutation. There is a good deal of argument to recommend this position and we have conceded it as an implicit part of restricted infallibility. But it is a radical departure from the traditional connection between *knowing* and *necessity*. Since the intention of this study is to examine the logic of the traditional view, we will leave this present path unexplored for the moment. However, it will become apparent that certain features of the ordinary language use of 'know' have significant influence on key argument and positions in the objections concerning temporal indexicals and truth-values. Moreover, the claim of fallible knowledge does not answer the second-order inquiry, "Why is it that God does not know these things with certainty?" That question can be answered only by exploring the traditional connection.

We can further this examination by considering a related difficulty posed by Swinburne. He suggests that the usual understanding of 'true' also stands in opposition to the claim that future contingent statements are neither true nor false prior to the event occurrence. This objection leads directly to a discussion of truth-values and temporal indexicals. Swinburne notes that we may not *know* any particular future contingent statement to be true or false until the occurrence of the event referred to , but he claims that such statements *are* either true or false regardless of my knowledge of them. In order to examine this contention, we must make some remarks about the uses of the word 'true'. Lucas and others have pointed out that in ordinary language the word 'true' has a pragmatic context or an "operational import".[1] When I say that something is

---

[1] Lucas, *Freedom Of The Will*, p. 67. Also see Lucas, "True," *Philosophy*, XLIV (July, 1969), 175-186 and Gilbert Ryle, "It Was To

true, I make a claim to its trustworthiness, I promise its certainly and I vouch for it. Thus, in ordinary language I am able to say, "This is true" at one time but not at another. Tensed expressions (e.g. 'will be true', 'was true') connected with 'true' rely on this operational quality. But logicians have required a different conception of 'true' when they speak of the truth or falsity of some statement. Logical truth is independent of time. In mathematical logic, every proposition must either be true or false regardless of the temporal position of the speaker or the temporal reference of the statement. Accordingly, the logical notion of truth does not allow the expressions 'was true', 'will be true', 'became true', etc.[1] Without stipulating the different contexts for these two uses of 'true', it is easy to pass from one to the other with the greatest of consequences.

One of these consequences deals with the spatialization of time. If we examine the pattern of events from the perspective of the logician, it is easy to imagine that each of the tenseness truths about the history of the time scheme picks out some ontologically real entity or event. After all, each timeless truth refers to some event. The truth of the statement, "The Battle of Gettysburg <u>is</u> (tenselessly) earlier than the assassination of Lincoln", depends on the occurrence of the events specified and their relation to each other in the temporal order. So it would seem that making a purportedly true statement about some future event actually picks out some event which now stands in the wings ready to come on the stage of the present. This is to view time as a real line already filled with event-content which moves through a point called the "present" from which we observe its passage. This view

---

Be," in *Dilemmas* (Cambridge: Cambridge University Press, 1969), p. 20.

[1] Gale, *Time*, Chapter VIII.

suggests that I can pick out various temporal points in the same way that I pick out spatial points so that my point of reference is arbitrary and has no truth-value bearing on the temporal point of the event under consideration. But 'now' does not pick out a temporal point in the same way that 'this' or 'here' picks out a spatial point since 'this' picks out one of many possible equally available spatial perspectives which 'now' is restricted by the one-dimensional temporal order. "There is no temporal field of vision corresponding to a spatial field of vision, since events which are earlier and later than each other by definition do not coexist".[1] It is misleading to suggest we can freely orient our perspective to any point in time. That would be to conceive of time in the same terms as space.[2] And if we were to conceive of time in this spatialized manner, we would prejudice any possible understanding of future *contingency* before we began the inquiry. For if this picture is true, then the future has only epistemic contingency (we just do not happen to know *now* what it will be) and logically contingent (neither analytic nor self-contradictory). There is no possibility that the future exhibits real causal or temporal contingency because everything is really already there (and has always been there according to the implication of the tenseness <u>is</u>) waiting to be revealed. In this crass form, this view embraces fatalism. But the appeal of the straightforwardness of mathematical logic draws many to view time in this way in spite of the fact that they disown fatalism. However, unless this is exposed, it leads directly to major difficulties concerning the real contingency of the future. Taylor puts the argument like this:

---

[1] Gale, *Time*, p. 201. Also see Richard Gale, "'Here' And 'Now'", in Eugene Freeman and Wilfrid Sellars, eds., *Basic Issues In The Philosophy Of Time*, (LaSalle, Ill.: Open Court, 1971), pp. 72-85.
[2] Cf. Gale, *Time*, pp. 200-203.

... (a) if an event of a given description is really contingent in the sense given, i.e. not yet nomically [causally] determined, and (b) if the outcome of things, i.e. the occurrence or nonoccurrence of the event in question, has not already been decided merely by the lapse of time, such that it irrevocably has happened or has failed to happen—in short, if the thing in question is a future contingency—then (c) any statement asserting or denying that it will happen is not (yet) true but also not (yet) false.[1]

We can see that this is not a general claim about all future events. It says only that if there are events such that they are both temporally and causally contingent (which is, of course, exactly what "free" acts are supped to be), then no statement concerning such a purported event can be assigned a truth-value, either temporally or timelessly, prior to the actual occurrence of the event. To make such an assignment is to assume something which implies the denial of real contingency. Any argument which makes such an assumption will ultimately be circular or question-begging.

     Consequently, if I assert that Jones will mow his lawn tomorrow and by that I mean that it is epistemologically certain (the proposition is true), then I cannot assert that the statement is causally contingent, and/or temporally contingent and/or logically contingent. For real contingency entails epistemic contingency. No proposition about an event that is yet to occur the occurrence of which depends on the undetermined future choice of an agent could be known now to be the case or not to be the case (although, obviously, it could be known now {to be or not to be} the case since this is tautologically true; and it could be *known* in the weak sense of 'know'). The remainder of this chapter and the next chapter will attempt to defend this view of contingency.

---

[1] Richard Taylor, "Future Contingencies", p. 14.

Unfortunately, these are not the only difficulties which plague attempts to understand the ordinary language usage. In addition, there are two possible understandings of the future tense. Lucas[1], following Reichenbach[2], provides a diagrammatic analysis of the distinction between *oratio recta* and *oratio obliqua*. If we adopt the following symbols:

E is the date of the occurrence of an event
S is the date of the utterance spoken about the event
R is the point of reference adopted by the utterance

we can distinguish between the future cases:

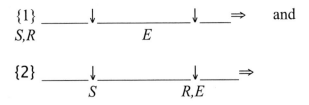

and

The first is an example of a case where the future is already fixed in its causes at least in terms of the language employed. It is the future tense of prediction which implies, no matter how good the evidence, that I have some reason to believe that such-and-such will be the case. Unless I specify otherwise, you are entitled to assume merely from the fact that I have made the prediction that I have good reason for believing something about the future.[3] These are reasons which I have *at the time of the utterance*, regardless of the actual outcome of the event. But the

---

[1] Lucas, *Treatise on Time and Space*, pp. 292-299.
[2] Hans Reichenbach, *Elements of Symbolic Logic* (New York: Macmillan, 1951), pp. 287-298.
[3] See Gale's formulation of the convention, above page 229.

second case does not carry such an implication. Here the case is more like a bet on the races. As Lucas comments:

> If I bet you that Eclipse will win the Derby, I am not warranting that he is going to: I am staking only my money, not my reputation, on the event. If he wins, my guess turns out to be correct, but its correctness depends entirely on whether he wins, not at all on the soundness of my reasons for backing him.[1]

These important distinctions lie behind the analysis of the objection put forward by Swinburne:

> In normal use, propositions about a named future time (including claims about any future free actions) are true or false—timelessly. We may not *know* them to be true or false, until the occurrence of that of which they speak. But what I claim may be true, even if I do not know it to be true, and even if what I claim has yet to occur.[2]

If Swinburne is correct about the implications of ordinary language, then the thesis that some future contingent statements are neither true nor false until their event-referent occurs must be false. Of course, we could insist on a special use of 'true' which would make this thesis valid, but Swinburne points out that special pleading would violate the normal usage and that would seriously impair the strength of the solution.

However, if we pay close attention to the previous distinctions which we have made, we find that Swinburne's argument is not as convincing as it first appears. Swinburne suggests that a claim made about the future may be true without my knowing it to be so. We must first ask what he means by 'claim'. Is this claim to be understood as a prediction or as a bet? It could easily be either. But in

---

[1] Lucas, *Treatise on Time and Space*, p. 293.
[2] Swinburne, *Coherence*, p. 175.

his context, there is no point in suggesting that the claim is like a bet. Future contingencies of this class carry no implication of timeless truth. A bet on Eclipse does not mean that *at any given moment* (omnitemporally) either Eclipse will win the race or Eclipse will not win the race, for if either of these were true (timelessly) then it would appear that either one or the other was always going to be the case so that nothing could ever have been done to change the outcome. A bet on Eclipse means only that of two possible alternatives, *at some particular moment* either Eclipse will or will not win the race. If the winning or not-winning of the race is really contingent, then one cannot assume that any timeless truth-value can be assigned to the statement concerning the outcome of the race in spite of the fact that a timeless truth-value can be assigned to the disjunction of the two possible outcomes. The event is certainly not logically necessary nor epistemologically necessary. It is not temporally necessary and if it is really contingent it is not causally necessary. The statement contained in a bet only specifies the condition of the Law of the Excluded Middle, and is tenselessly true on that basis alone. But this is a bare tautological sense. It does not follow that the Law can divide its modality regardless of the temporal reference of the statement.[1]

If we imagine that Swinburne makes his claim in the sense of a prediction, then we must assume that at the moment of the claim he has good reason for believing that his claim is true rather than false. But he goes on to say that this claim may be true *without my knowing it* to be so. He cannot mean this in the weak sense of 'know' for the

---

[1] Symbolically, if $(pt_n)t_m$ is '(the occurrence of p at t_n) viewed from the perspective t_m', then at t_1 I can say both $(pt_2 \lor \sim pt_2)t_1$ and $(pt_2 \lor \sim pt_2)t_2$. And $(pt_2 \lor \sim pt_2)t_2 \supset (pt_2)t_2 \lor (\sim pt_2)t_2$ but $(pt_2 \lor \sim pt_2)t_1$ does not entail $(pt_2)t_1 \lor (\sim pt_2)t_1$. See Lucas, *Treatise on Time and space*, pp. 282-295.

predictive claim is based on precisely that interpretation. In order to make the prediction, he must know it to be true in the weak sense. But this entails that the claim is fallible. And if the claim is about some real contingency, this is exactly what we would expect. So Swinburne (on this reading) must mean that I may not know it to be true with certainty. This interpretation fits the previous remark that ordinary language propositions are timelessly true or false, i.e. they are true in the logician's sense that their truth-values cannot be altered due to the temporal position of the speaker or the utterance. Such propositions cannot be strictly timelessly true for they are obviously not analytic. They must be omnitemporally timelessly true, i.e. they must be true *at any time*. And Swinburne is right that some future tense statements are omnitemporally true but epistemologically contingent. For example, I do not happen to know if there will in fact be an eclipse of the sun in 1998 but that there will be an eclipse of the sun in that year is certainly now either true or false since it is a causal result of the present orbits of the moon and the earth. If it is true, it is true by virtue of causal necessity. But the premise operating behind the idea of future free acts is that they are not causally determined, logically determined or temporally determined. Nevertheless, Swinburne's claim is that they may be epistemologically contingent yet omnitemporally true. If we suppose that statements concerning such acts are either true or false because 'true' ('false') always means 'timelessly true' ('timelessly false'), this assumption merely begs the question. Moreover, we have shown that here is a legitimate sense of ordinary language which operates in the temporal modes of 'true'.

I suspect that Swinburne's remark is predicated upon the following sort of argument. There appears to be something counter-intuitive in saying that my assertion, "Jones will cut his lawn tomorrow", is neither true nor false now. For tomorrow, if Jones cuts his lawn than I would wish to say that yesterday the claim I made *was true* even though I may not have known it to be so and even though I may not have had any evidence whatsoever for my claim (in this sense, whether the claim is a prediction or a bet makes no difference).[1] Therefore, the claim has a truth-value when I make it even if I do not know which it is.

But this argument confuses meaningfulness and truth. Regardless of the question of evidence, my assertion that Jones will cut his lawn tomorrow is meaningful. For example, I could specify its truth-conditions. But it does not follow from its meaningfulness that it has a truth-value now. If tomorrow Jones does cut his lawn, then *retroactively* it can be assigned a truth-value. But the assignment of truth-value must be *retroactive and tensed* [2] if the event in question is a real contingency. If its truth or falsity really rests on the contingent activity of an agent, then the truth-referent of the assertion is the occurrence of the event today. Yesterday the event did not yet exist. To assign the statement a truth-value (even hypothetically as a present but unknown possibility) is to assume that the possibility of retroactive assignment gives grounds for tenseless, omnitemporal assignment.[3] But this ignores the *tensed* language of 'true' and the presupposition of real contingency. If future free acts are really contingent, they cannot be supposed to have truth-values prior to the occurrence of the events since there is nothing in virtue of which the assignment could be made except the possibility of later, retroactive assignment. The fact that I do not

---

[1] Swinburne's remark that the occurrence of the event *makes* the statement true could be seen as support for this interpretation.

[2] Cf. Gale, *Time*, p. 150, ". . . if we can meaningfully speak of events becoming present or taking place then by the same token we must also be able to speak meaningfully about statements predicting the occurrence of such events as becoming true."

[3] See Gale's distinction between metalinguistic endorsing statements and metametalinguistic statements; Gale, *Time*, pp. 137-150.

know if they are true or false beforehand is not a result of my ignorance but a result of the logic of this kind of event. They are epistemologically contingent because they could not, in principle, be otherwise.

By distinguishing carefully between the uses of 'know' and 'true', we see that if Swinburne's claim is taken as a bet, it produces nothing which would give grounds supporting the thesis that all future contingent statements are now (and always were) either true or false. On the other hand, if we take his claim as a prediction, the resulting epistemological contingency does not entail omnitemporal truth. His argument apparently attempts to combine the weaker sense of 'know' with the stronger (logician's) sense of 'true'. This combination could be successful only if it rested on a thesis of logical fatalism[1], a thesis which rests in turn on an illicit modal transformation. While we may appreciate the point that a good deal of ordinary language does speak as though truth is timeless, we must conclude that this situation cannot be applied *carte blanche* to every future tense statement.

Because Swinburne analyses 'true' in ordinary language as 'timelessly true', he solves the problem of foreknowledge by placing restrictions on omniscience as a result of God's own choice. Since his position entails that all future contingent statements do have definite truth-values, he is constrained, under the condition of omniscience, to assert that God *could have, in principle,* knowledge of every future free act. But this seems to imply the denial of freedom. Swinburne's qualification which allows free will is based on God's volitional act (i.e. God's choice to allow freedom is a choice which necessarily limits what god *does* know, not what He *could* know). But it is choice which determines the limits of knowledge, not

---

[1] The central premise of logical fatalism is that whatever is the case was always going to be the case and, therefore, is necessarily the case.

the limits of knowledge which determines the range of choices.[1] Since Swinburne believes that God's knowledge is not restricted because of logical conditions placed on the assignment of truth-values to future contingencies, he has a stake in the argument from temporal indexicals recently put forward by Kretzmann.[2] Swinburne must show that the temporal indexical does not represent a unique referring device that has epistemological restrictions. The general form of this objection we have called the *Definite Truth-Value* objection.

The Definite Truth-Value Objection

This objection can be summarized as follows:
Every proposition has a definite truth-value (even if we do not as yet know which value is the correct one). Future contingent propositions have definite truth-values. These do not change with respect to the temporal indexicals contained in the statements which indicate temporal position or the speaker or the utterance. Since God knows every true proposition, He knows now the definite truth-value of every future contingent proposition.

This objection is closely related to the first objection. But it also extends the argument from ordinary language. We have see that it must be qualified in order to become a counter-*solution* but as it stands, it is in direct opposition to the central premise of our proposal. Swinburne defends this objection against the argument proposed by Kretzmann.

---

[1] Swinburne's solution is based on a purported symmetry with the doctrine of omnipotence. We shall return to this solution after we have discussed temporal indexicals. At that point we will have a good case for rejecting the proposal.

[2] Kretzmann, "Omniscience and Immutability", pp. 409-421.

Kretzmann argues that there are some propositions which can be known only at certain times or by certain persons. Kretzmann claims that the proposition that 'it is now t_1' (e.g. 2 October) can only be known at t_1 (*viz.* On 2 October). This proposition, Kretzmann claims, is not the same proposition as the proposition that at t_1 it is t_1 (e.g. that on 2 October it is 2 October), which can of course be known at any time. But if there is an instant of time t_1, there must (logically) be some instant of time before t_1 – for before t_1 either there was something or there was nothing, and so there was a time at which there was something or nothing. Hence there must be a time at which no person could have had the knowledge, expressed at t_1 by the proposition that 'it is now t_1'. So, generally, since for any instant of time there is at least one other, at each instant any agent will be necessarily ignorant of a truth expressible at another instant by stating that it is 'now' that instant. So at any instant an agent must necessarily be ignorant of something.[1]

Swinburne attempts to counter this with the same pattern of arguments used by Pike in defense of the timeless knower. He argues that Kretzmann's use of indexical expressions presents only part of the possible range of expressions of this type. He cites Castaneda's formulation of quasi-indexical expressions and urges that the use of quasi-indexicals makes plausible the claim that two temporally and/or spatially distinct subjects can have knowledge of the same fact. He concedes that the same fact cannot be reported by two temporally distinct subjects *in the same words* but he holds that it can nevertheless be reported. Swinburne believes the problem can be resolved by carefully distinguishing the logic or *oratio recta* from that of *oratio obliqua*. He says:

---

[1] Swinburne, *Coherence*, p. 163. We will ignore the possible complications which arise over Swinburne's comment that the topology of time is necessarily that of a real line. While there are arguments to the contrary, they do not affect the question of temporal indexicals.

Now Castaneda urges against Kretzmann's examples the following principle:

(P) If a sentence of the form 'X knows that a person Y knows that . . .' formulates a true statement, the person X knows the statement formulated by the clause filling the blank ' . . .'

(P) seems plausible enough. If John knows that Mary knows that 2+2=4 or that George is ill, then John knows that 2+2=4 or that George is ill. If the clause " . . .' of (P) contains quasi-indicators, then when the clause is shifted from the first sentence to the second, the quasi-indicators may have to be replaced by other indexical devices in view of the fact that the subject of the sentence is now different, in order for the clause to 'formulate', i.e. express the same statement. If 'John knows that Mary knows that her house has four bedrooms', it does not follow that 'John knows that her house has four bedrooms', which is an unclear claim of dubious grammar, but rather that 'John knows that Mary's house has four bedrooms.'[1]

Since it is apparent that under these conditions the statement, 'It is now 2 October', uttered by *A* could also be known by *B* at a date later than 2 October (but reported as '*B* knows that *A* knew that it was then 2 October'), Kretzmann's claim that there are some temporal indexical facts which cannot be known by anyone other than the present subject uttering the temporal indexical expressions (or a subject uttering a similar expression at the same time) seems to be false. As Swinburne says, "What *A* knows on 2 October and *B* knows on 3 October is that a certain day which can be picked out in many and various ways, according to our location in time as 'today' or 'yesterday' or 'the day on which *A* thought that it was 2 October' (or even as '2 October') is 2 October".[2] The same fact is

---

[1] Swinburne, *Coherence*, p. 165.

[2] Swinburne, *Coherence*, pp. 165-166. The exact sense on 'is' in the phrase 'is 2 October' is left unspecified in this argument. There are good reasons to believe that Castaneda's principle requires a tenseless use of 'is' here and this creates significant problems, as we shall see.

known by two temporally distinct subjects. But this does not revive Pike's claim that it makes sense to suggest that a timeless knower could have knowledge of such facts but report then differently. What Swinburne has demonstrated is that there is no logical objection to supposing that a knowing subject *at time t* could not be apprised of knowledge of facts referred to by temporal indexical expressions at times *earlier than t*.

However, Swinburne draws a more powerful conclusion from this failure of Kretzmann's objection.

> I conclude that the objection fails. In default of it I suggest that it is coherent to suppose that there is an omniscient person. There would be no reason why it is incoherent to suppose that a spirit, omnipresent and creator of the universe, is omniscient. Such a spirit, if asked, could give you the answer to any question, if he chose to do so. The state of the universe in the past and future would be so clearly know to him—maybe its whole history would be seen by him at glance and be held in his mind—that he would not need to conduct an investigation to find out how things had been years ago or would be in years to come. Just as a man does not need to conduct an investigation to know what he is now looking at, no more does God, in the theist's view, need to conduct an investigation in order to know any thing about the world's history.[1]

Objections to Swinburne

Swinburne's reply to Kretzmann seems to account for cases where we might wish to say that *B knows* now what *A knew* at some time in the past. But this covers only part of Kretzmann's problem. Kretzmann (on Swinburne's own account) argues that a truth expressed at the time t_1 with the indexical expression 'now' could not have been known at a time *prior to* t_1 since it was not true until that

---

[1] Swinburne, *Coherence*, p. 166.

time.[1] And so, generally, if for each instant of time there is at least one prior instant, at each prior instant an agent will necessarily be ignorant of a truth expressible at a later time by stating that it is 'now' that instant. This generalization is not the same as the one Swinburne produces in his discussion of Kretzmann.[2] What we wish to know is this: is it logically coherent to suppose that an omniscient being could know at time t_1 what Jones purportedly expresses in an indexical reference at a later time t_2.

Suppose that on 2 October A knows that 'it is now 2 October'. Is it possible for B to know on 1 October what A knows (will know) on 2 October? It is certainly true that if B does know on 1 October what A knows on 2 October, he will not be able to report that knowledge in the same words used by A on 2 October. Is it nevertheless possible to formulate the supposed knowledge claim of B on 1 October in the quasi-indexical mode in such a way that B's knowledge specifies the same fact known by A?

---

[1] Swinburne is able to draw this conclusion in spite of the fact that he treats in detail only a case of knowledge of a past event because, like Pike, he makes a strong distinction between the temporal indexical *sentence* and the *statement* expressed by that sentence. It is the statement which expresses the fact. The sentence is only a truth-bearer. Swinburne seems to imply that even though sentences might differ in form (i.e. some by containing temporal indexicals and other not), the statement picked out by referring devices in the sentences is the same. Thus, whether I pick out 2 October by 'now' or 'five days ago' or 'next Saturday' makes no difference to the truth claim expressed by the particular sentence. As long as the referring device picks out the same truth (fact), it will express the same content. Therefore, anyone who knows what the referring device picks out will know the fact contained in the statement. This, of course, is true as long as the issue is only one about referring devices. But Swinburne's treatment must suppose that there is nothing unique about temporal indexicals and that every statement can be assigned a timeless truth-value.

[2] Castaneda does argue directly about the case of *future* contingent statements. Since Swinburne cites Castaneda with approval, he may feel that the entire issue is resolved in the principle of quasi-indexicals.

Formulation of knowledge claims according to the quasi-indexical principle seems reasonable enough as long as we pay close attention to the requirement that the principle formulates a true statement. The initial formulation in our example would be:

If a sentence of the form '*B* knows that a person *A* knows that it is now 2 October' formulates a true statement, the person *B* knows the statement 'it is now 2 October'.

But this formulation will not do, for on 1 October *B* does not know that 'it is now 2 October', but rather that 'it will then be 2 October'. We must alter the tense structure of the quasi-indexical if we intend to meet the requirement that it expresses a true statement. Swinburne himself suggests such an alteration when he gives an example of Castaneda's principle for a case of past knowledge (*B* knows on 3 October what *A* knew on 2 October).

> How can *B* report his knowledge? By words such as 'I know that *A* knew yesterday that it was then 2 October'.[1]

He argues that this formulation expresses the same knowledge claim as *A's* previous claim 'it is now 2 October' because, although a different device is used to pick out the day in question, the same thing is being predicated of that day, namely, that the day in question is 2 October.

But we must make note of the fact that the quasi-indexical expression of *B's* knowledge of *A's* previous claim is true because 'it is now 2 October' *was* true for *A* and is therefore necessarily true at the time of *B's* expression. What has been the case cannot now not have been the case. This observation is crucial for the quasi-indexical cannot formulate a knowledge claim unless it

---

[1] Swinburne, *Coherence*, p. 165.

expresses a true proposition. It obviously would not do to suggest that *B* knows that *A knows* that it is now 2 October if in fact it is now 3 October. *B* can only know what *A knew* if the truth of *A's* claim is already established. This information resides in the expression that *A knows* that ' . . .'. Even on Swinburne's account, to suggest that *A* knows that *p* entails that *p* (or that *p* is true).[1] Apparently, the only difficulty in the case where *A's* knowledge claim lies temporally prior to *B's* formulation is showing that *B* can pick out the same fact that *A* has already picked out.[2] But if *B* says, "I know what *A* will know tomorrow", another complication is introduced and the claim will have to be handled in a slightly different way.

The point of Castaneda's principle is to show that temporal indexicals do not present epistemological restrictions which cannot be overcome. The principle claims to be able to formulate a true statement which captures a claim of *A* at one particular time in a claim of *B* at another time. But the principle does not specify the sense of 'true' in its formulation. Swinburne's remarks on the ordinary use of 'true' as 'timelessly true' and his use of 'know' suggest that he interprets the principle to speak of 'true' in the logician's sense. There are good reasons for believing that Castaneda also intends this reading and that the principle would not work without it. But if this is the correct rendering, then use of the principle does not seem tenable in cases of future contingencies for, as we shall see, it claims too much of *B's* knowing.

---

[1] Swinburne, *Coherence*, p. 169.
[2] Gale's argument for the ineliminability of *A*-statements makes this simple version less plausible than it first appears. As we shall see, the shift from 'now' to 'then' coupled with certain requirements of the principle itself raises questions about the extent of the knowledge claims of *A* and *B*.

However, Swinburne's alteration of the tense structure of the principle in the case of *B's* knowledge of *A's* prior claim may suggest a thoroughly temporal use of the principle. Let us suppose that 'true' is to be understood as 'temporally true' (tensed context) and see what results. If *B* employs the principle in a temporal context to express his knowledge of *A's* future claim, it will have to be altered to show this tense change. Following Swinburne, we might suggest:

If a sentence of the form '*B* knows that a person *A* will know that it will then be 2 October' formulates a true statement, the person *B* knows the statement 'it will then be 2 October'.

But if the sentence formulated is only temporally true, then it is true because it is based on evidence which *B* has at the time of his formulation for there is no qualification on a temporally true statement that it should never turn out later to be false. Without the presuppositions that *A's* temporal sentence actually makes a tenselessly true statement, *B's* claim to know that *A* will know that *p* is a fallible claim and, as such, is open to refutation. *A* can fail to come to know *p* and if that were the case, *B's* claim would then be false. While it is perfectly legitimate to say that *B* now believes with good reason that *A* will come to know *p*, this is a claim in the weak sense of 'know' and does not entail the truth of *A's* claim. On a temporal rendering of 'true', the quasi-indexical principle does not meet the objection raised by Kretzmann since he is concerned with what can be *known (true)* in the strong sense of both of these terms. If the quasi-indexical principle is used as a formulation of knowledge claims by a God who exhibits restricted (fallible) foreknowledge, then I have no objection to its intent. But such an interpretation does not show

Kretzmann to be mistaken in his worry over future contingent temporal expressions.[1]

Since Swinburne believes that the quasi-indexical principle overcomes Kretzmann's objection, he must believe that it gives grounds for asserting that future temporal indexical expressions can be formulated in statements which are tenselessly true. Kretzmann argues that a being which always knows what time it is must be in a state of knowledge which "changes incessantly with respect to propositions of the form 'it is now t_n'".[2] For such a being must first know that it is now t_1 and not t_2 and then know that it is now t_2 and not t_1. Kretzmann implies that the being could not know at t_1 the truth of a temporal expression at t_2. If the quasi-indexical principle is to overcome this implication, it must be able to render the temporal claim made at t_2 in an expression which would be true at t_1. We have seen that that expression itself could not be a temporal truth. It must be formulated in such a way that if it is known at t_1, it logically entails the truth of the claim at t_2. Only then would is be possible to say that *B's* knowing entails an expression which <u>is</u> (tenselessly) true in spite of the fact that it is (temporally) not yet true for

---

[1] We may question whether there is a transfer of complete information in the shift from 'now' to 'then'. 'It is now t_1' seems to do more than pick out a date t_1. It also implies that the referential device is simultaneous with the referent. To transfer this information to *B's* expression ('it will *then* be t_1'), we should have to read *B's* claim as the claim that *A* will know that 'the day picked out is t_1 and that *A's* knowing *that* is simultaneous with t_1 and *A* knows that it is simultaneous'. But I am not convinced that this could be given as an analysis of 'then' without violating some other requirements of the quasi-indexical principle. Be that as it may, the issue here is secondary and could be treated apart from discussion of Swinburne's use of Castaneda's principle.

[2] Kretzmann, "Omniscience and Immutability", p. 410, fn. 4.

A. Let us examine an argument for this understanding of the principle.

Suppose that *B* does claim to know what *A* will know. This amounts to saying that *B* knows on 1 October that *A* (necessarily) will know on 2 October that 'it is now 2 October'. For *B* knows that *p* entails that *p* and this means that if the quasi-indexical is to assert a true statement, it must be read in the strong sense of 'know', i.e. knows with certainty. But there is something disconcerting about this claim. Quite simply, it suggests a knowledge claim which *A* is *going to make*—a statement which is not yet true for *A*. On October 1, *A* could not know that 'it is now 2 October'. And unless *B* can guarantee that *A* will make such a claim tomorrow, there seems to be no reason to believe that *A* should ever come to know that 'it is now 2 October'. Unless *B* knows now the definite truth-value of this future contingency, there seems to be no logical necessity in *B's* claim which would prohibit *B* from being mistaken about the forthcoming event. "What has been the case cannot now not have been the case" does not seem to have an equivalent version for propositions of the future tense. The closest parallel, "What will be the case will be the case", lacks the crucial temporal indexical. Certain kinds of claims about the future seem dissimilar to claims about the past because the future could yet be interfered with but the past cannot.[1] For example, I may be wrong about some detail of the death of Queen Anne but I am not wrong about it because the event can still be change or altered. However, my being wrong about a claim concerning a manned Martian expedition could be wrong precisely

---

[1] There is one sense in which interfering with the future is just as impossible as changing the past. While our claim is not as logically sophisticated as it might be, its intuitive character can be given the necessary detail, as in Prior, "Formalities of Omniscience", pp. 40-44 and Gale, *Time*, Chapter VIII and IX.

because, whatever my prediction about the future event, you could exercise steps to frustrate it.

Castaneda on Temporal Indexicals

Castaneda tries to overcome this apparent asymmetry between past and future in his article, "Omniscience and Indexical Reference".[1] He sees the general problem posed by Kretzmann as follows:

> How can a person, whether omniscient or not, believe, know, consider, or in general, apprehend and formulate for himself and by himself a proposition or statement . . . that contains an indexical reference by another person?[2]

On the question of future contingencies, he asks: is it possible for a being X that knows that it is now t_1 and not t_2 and then knows that it is now t_2 and not t_1 to know at t_1 the same set of propositions which he later knows at t_2 ?

There is good reason to suspect that a claim that there are no cases in which a person might formulate a true proposition containing the indexical reference of another person must be mistaken. Swinburne has developed this argument in relation to claims about the past. Castaneda points out that Kretzmann's own account of the beliefs of the being X at t_1 and t_2 are instances of *oratio obliqua* which purport to express the temporal indexical knowledge claims of some other being from the perspective of Kretzmann's indexical position. And since it is certainly not Kretzmann's aim to make some point about his own indexical position but rather to argue about the necessity of any given person's temporal indexical reference to himself, then it must be possible to specify the beliefs in question in

---

[1] Hector-Neri Castaneda, "Omniscience and Indexical Reference," *Journal of Philosophy*, LXIV (April 13, 1967), 203-210.
[2] Ibid. p. 204.

some way which avoids indexical reference to the speaker or else Kretzmann himself would be barred from producing the argument. Castaneda concludes that this leaves open the question whether or not the beliefs formulated by another person at t_1 and not t_2 can be reported without reference to the temporal indexical expressions of *oratio recta*. He suggests that Kretzmann's argument requires an assumption which invalidates the objection it produces. This assumption is tentatively formulated as:

> At t_1 X knows [tenselessly] that it is [tenselessly] then t_1, but not t_2, and at t_2, later than t_1, X knows [tenselessly] that it is [tenselessly] then t_2, but not t_1.[1]

By employing 'then' instead of 'now', Castaneda contends that the temporal indexical reference to the speaker is eliminated while the temporal indexical reference to the subject is retained. This means that the statement above could be made about X at any time by anyone. 'Then', according to this argument, is not an indicator but a quasi-indicator. By applying this quasi-indicator to X himself, Castaneda contends that a statement may be formulated which expresses $X's$ knowledge of the truth of all four propositions in question at time t_1. On this basis, he formulates the general principle of quasi-indicators. Applying this principle to Kretzmann's example, we get the statement:

> If a sentence of the form 'X knows that a person Y knows that at t_2 it is then t_2 and not t_1' formulates a true statement, then the person X knows the statement formulated by the clause 'at t_2 it is then t_2 and not t_1'.[2]

---

[1] Castaneda, "Omniscience", p. 206.
[2] Cf. Castaneda, "Omniscience", p. 207.

Since this statement is supposedly free of temporal indexical reference, X can know the claim made by the statement at any time. In particular, he can know the claim at time t_1, at which time he also knows that it is then t_1 and not t_2. So X can know at time t_1 both sets of propositions: that at t_1 it is then t_1 and not t_2 and at t_2 someone will know that it is then t_2 and not t_1.

That X's knowledge of the truth that 'at t_1 it is then t_1' is unrestricted temporally must mean that the truth expressed in this knowledge claim can be formulated at any time, whether earlier or later than t_1. Castaneda believes that the omnitemporal or tenseless context of this relation makes it possible to express the same fact reported by the temporal indexical expression that 'it is now t_1' without the use of that temporal indexical. Castaneda's suggestion that a use of the term 'then' instead of 'now' removes indexical reference to the speaker but not to the subject may be sound, but it does not solve the whole problem of temporal indexicals. He claims that application of his principle allows us to assert that at time t_1 X knows both sets of propositions. But this raises the question: is it true at t_1 that someone *will know* that it *is* then t_2? Since there is no logical guarantee that there will be any cognitive agents in existence at t_2 to know that it is then t_2, such a claim about the future must remain undetermined—unless Castaneda takes this claim to be about the necessary truth that at t_2 it is t_2 (a claim which obviously does not depend upon any existing cognitive agent). The quasi-indexical principle requires that the claim formulated be a true statement, but as we have noted, it does not specify the context of the word 'true'. We must assume that Castaneda requires the same logical strength of his principle that he did of his reformulation of the missing basis for Kretzmann's objection. If this is so, we have good reason to suppose that Castaneda wants to speak of logical (timeless or tenseless) truth. That seems to mean that the claim that X

knows that someone will know that 'at t_2 it is then t_2' is really a claim to know the necessarily true statement that 'at t_2 it is t_2'. But this is not the problem which motivated Kretzmann's objection. There is little philosophical merit in stating that the knowledge claims of another person can be formulated without temporal indexical reference because they express necessary truths. He must mean that the claim of Y at t_2 is true (in some sense) *at t_1*. With a little reflection on our previous discussion of the senses of 'true', we can see what he has in mind. It is necessarily true at t_2 it is t_2. But at t_2, Y's claim that 'it is now t_2' is also temporally true. The claim of Y at t_2 expresses in tensed language (which is not freely repeatable) what seems to be a tenseless truth (which is freely repeatable). And on that basis, it seems that we could express the tenseless truth at any time and say the same thing that Y can say temporally only at t_2 . But this conclusion incorporates a tensed sleight-of-hand for it transforms the future subject at t_2 into the certainty of the tenseless <u>is</u>. To see this, we need to specify each sense of 'know' and 'true' in the two possible readings of Castaneda's principle. If the principle is read in a temporal context, it seems to say:

> If a statement of the form 'X knows (temporally) that a person Y knows (temporally) that at t_2 it is (temporally) then t_2 and not t_1' formulates a true (temporally) statement, then the person X knows (temporally) the statement formulated by the clause 'at t_2 it is (temporally) then t_2 and not t_1'

But this formulation is not quite correct for the temporal sense of 'know' is a weak sense and so does not entail the truth of Y's claim. To be correct the principle should read:

> . . . that a person Y will know that it will be t_2 at t_2 , then Y will know that 'it is (temporally) now t_2'.

This reading is undetermined as to whether anyone will know something at t_2. As such, it does not give grounds for the proposal that *the fact known at t_2* can be expressed tenselessly at t_1. It is ontologically uncommitted as to whether or not there is a fact. However, if the claim is strengthened so that the required tenseless sense of true does follow, i.e. :

> . . . *X* knows (tenselessly) that someone knows (tenselessly) that it is (tenselessly) then t_2

then the use of 'know' entails the fact that someone must know at t_2 that 'it is now t_2'. And this could only be the case if the future contingent proposition about such an event actually does have a definite truth-value prior to the actual occurrence of the event. Castaneda's principle cannot be used to establish the claim that I can know now what Jones will know tomorrow because the principle assumes the truth of this claim in order to provide us with the required degree of certainty.

We can see how important these confusions between the senses of 'true' are in applying this principle by examining one other case. Castaneda takes the example where Kretzmann argues that if the Chrysler Building is now 1,046 feet high but later a forty foot tower is added, then my knowledge of its height ceases to be 'knowing that it is 1,046 fee high' and becomes 'knowing that it is 1,086 feet high'. So, at time t_1 I know that the building is '1,046' but at t_2 I no longer know '1,046' but rather '1,086'. Castaneda argues that this does not amount to a change in knowledge for it is possible to formulate the knowledge claim expressed at t_2 in terms of a knowledge claim at t_1. He suggests:

> Kretzmann knows at t_1 that: the Chrysler Building is 1,046 feet high at t_1 , and t_3 it *will* have a 40-foot antenna extended

from its tip, and that the man who makes the extension *knows* at t_2 that the Chrysler Building *is* 1,086 feet high then.[1]

Castaneda claims that if Kretzmann knows this, then he clearly knows the fact reported in the claim at t_2 that '1,086', and therefore no knowledge change results from t_1 to t_2. Of course, the reporting *words* (the temporal indexical expressions) will be different in the two cases (incorporating a shift from 'now' to 'then'), but the truth of the fact reported remains the same.

However, we need to ask: does Kretzmann really *know* that at t_3 forty feet *is* added and that someone at t_2 knows that it is added? Castaneda has moved from the hypothetical to the certain by suggesting that if it *will* be the case that the tower *will be* 1,086 feet high, then it *is* the case that it *is* forty feet higher. *If* it is true that forty feet will be added, then it *will be* true that the building *will be* 1,086 feet high. But that is not the same as suggesting that it *is* 1,086 feet high. Castaneda can only know (in the strong sense) the claim derived by application of his principle if he views that claim as entirely a matter of logical truth. Thus, he supposes that it is true that forty feet is added. By *retroactive* assignment, it seems to follow that if this *is* true, then it was always going to be true. And if it was always going to be true, then the expression of its truth at some time prior to the actual addition of the forty feet is also true for it is the case that forty feet will be added and what is the case cannot not be the case. So it seems that Kretzmann can know the truth of the statement prior to its actual occurrence and, therefore, indexical reference ceases to be problematic. But reasoning like this totally confuses the distinction between the temporal context of 'true' and the logical context of 'true'. And once this distinction is clarified in relation to the knowledge of future

---

[1] Castaneda. "Omniscience", p. 209. (Italics mine)

contingencies, Castaneda's claim that Kretzmann knows *now* the truth of an event at t_2 (some time in the future) simply begs the question. In this case, the problem with temporal indexicals is reduced to the problem of *Logical Fatalism.*

Logical Fatalism

This problem has a very ancient logical as well as theological heritage. Aristotle struggled with the issue when he asked about the truth of a statement concerning a sea battle which is going to be fought tomorrow.[1] The general objection can be stated as follows:

God's temporal omniscience must include knowledge of the definite truth-values of all logically necessary propositions regardless of the temporal positions of the events referred to by those propositions. Since whatever is the case was always going to be the case, God always must have known whatever was going to come to be. Therefore, God knows now, at this temporal designation, all *future* contingent statements.

The statement 'it is now 2 October' made by *A* on 2 October is true for it is necessarily true that it is 2 October on 2 October. And the necessary truth of the statement 'it is now 2 October' made on 2 October does not change if *that statement* is referred to at some time before or after its actual utterance. It would, of course, be false to suggest that 'it is now 2 October' could be uttered truly on any other day except 2 October. But someone might argue that if it is the case that *A knows* that it is 2 October on 2

---

[1] Aristotle, *On Interpretation*, trans. by Harold Cooke, in *The Organon: Categories, On Interpretation, Prior Analytics* (Cambridge, Mass: Harvard University Press, 1949), IX, pp. 135-141.

October, then it is also the case that *A* was going to know that it would be 2 October on 2 October. For if it were not true that *A* was going to know that it would be 2 October on 2 October, then it could not be the case that *A* knows on 2 October that 'it is now 2 October'. And if it is the case that *A* is going to know that it will be 2 October, then it is true to say that 'it is now 2 October' is a statement which *A* will certainly know. And if 'is it now 2 October' is something which *A* will certainly know, then there is no difficulty with the claim that *B* knows on 1 October that 'it is now 2 October' is something which *A* will know on 2 October. The temporal position of the secondary subject's point of reference to *A's* claim can have no bearing on the truth or falsity of *A's* knowledge. That is, *A's* claim is true (*A* knows that *p*) because it is uttered on 2 October. And since the fact that it is the case that *A* knows that it is now 2 October on 2 October shows that it is necessarily the case that *A* was going to know that it would then be 2 October on 2 October, the reference to *A's* claim made by *B* is entirely independent of any particular temporal position of *B*.

We may examine Arthur Prior's formulation of this problem as a guide for our critique:

What is the logical status of the claim that whatever is the case has always been going to be the case?

Prior amplifies this question with the following argument:

(1) Suppose that it is now possible that a certain thing, say *p*, should come to pass *n* time-units hence.
(2) Then it *will* be true when that time comes (whatever actually happens then) that this thing *was* possible now.
   (2a) Or Negatively, it *will* be false then that the things *was* at this present time booked to fail to come to pass.

(3) It will also be false then that it *is* failing to come to pass (since if it were then failing to come to pass, it would now have been going to fail).

(4) But if it will then be *false* that it *isn't* coming to pass, it will be *true* that it *is* coming to pass.

(5) So, from the mere possibility of a future event we can by these steps infer that it will actually occur.[1]

Examination of this argument shows just how important the earlier ordinary language distinctions are. Statement (1) asserts something which falls into the context of ordinary tensed discourse.   In other words, the possibility of something coming to pass in the future is resident within the temporal concept of 'true' for here it is appropriate to say, "*P will* be true" (*P* has a possibility of *becoming* true). If we designate this temporal context by the symbol T_t for 'True in a temporal (tensed) context' in contrast to T_L for 'true in a logical (tenseless or timeless) context', then we can say that statement (1) is T_t. But when we try to determine the context of truth for the second statement in this argument, the issue is not clear. The second statement needs to be separated into its constituent elements. "Then it will be true when that time comes (whatever actually happens then) . . ." asserts that whatever is the case at that time is the case—a tautological truth.   'What *will* be the case *will* be the case' is framed within the context of T_L regardless of its use of the future tense for what it claims is timelessly true (and freely repeatable since it specifies no content). But the second part of the statement is set in T_t since it refers to the original possibility described in statement (1).   Use of the temporal 'will be' helps the argument slide from T_L to T_t. Statement (2a) incorporates the same equivocation since it is merely a negative restatement of (2). And (3) moves from the ground of (2a)

---

[1] Cf. Prior, "Formalities of Omniscience", pp. 40-41.

in the context of T_L to a statement about the present temporal condition of such an event (in the context of T_t) by asserting that what is timelessly false (the negation of a tautology) has some temporal connection with what will be the case as a result of a present possibility. So, (4) concludes the argument by invoking the Law of the Excluded Middle, arguing that if proposition p is false, then its opposite, not-p, must be true. Since p is in this case a statement that the possible event is not going to come to pass, it appears that we must conclude that not-p is true, i.e. that the event in question is going to come to pass. By requiring that all of the propositions under discussion be either true or false in a timeless sense, statement (4) moves the remaining elements of the T_t context into the realm of T_L.

Confusions concerning the two senses of the future tense also play a role in this argument.   David F. Pears argues that propositions which introduce possible future events derive their logical strength from the connection made with the present tense of a secondary clause. For example, "The sun will rise tomorrow if and only if tomorrow's sunrise is an event which will happen" seems so appropriate a statement that one hardly notices the shift from the future tense to the present tense. But the assertion that the sunrise *is* an event supplies the apparent strength to the supposed future possibility. The use of the present tense suggests that the sunrise of the future is somehow contemporary and that makes the future possibility appear to be just as certain as any other *present* event.   The proposition may be restated using parallel future tense constructions as "The sun will rise tomorrow if and only if tomorrow's sunrise *will be* an event which will happen". This form carries none of the force of the first form because it does not fall prey to the confusion of tenses.   Pears remarks:

For 'being an event' is a sort of ontological diploma awarded
to a possibility which has been successful in the competition
for actuality; and the award must await the result. The main
verb, by detaching itself from the time of the event, has not
left itself free to be attached to the time of the utterance.
When it shuffled off its proper time it shuffled off all time.[1]

As a result of this transformation of future tense
possibility into present tense actuality (a shift from $S
\longrightarrow R,E$ to $S,R \longrightarrow E$), apparent logical certainty is given
to propositions about the truth of future contingencies.
Pears argues that the timeless is is illicitly coupled with the
temporal *will be*.[2] This seems to give warrant to the claim
that the truth of the proposition in question is *now* already
as certain as any logical truth could be. Pears shows that
the same confusion can be uncovered in the more
interesting case: that the truth of hypothetical sentences
determines the future events to which they apply.

In Prior's expanded argument, we are given a
curious mixture of tenses in the constructed hypothetical.
The transition from the proposition, "If it is now possible
that event *p* will come to be in the future, then it will be
true at that time that event *p* was coming to pass now, to the
proposition, "If it is false then that it is not coming to pass,
then it is true now that it is coming to pass', depends for its
logical strength on the assertions which it makes about the
present and the past (and so necessarily true) events. But in
each case the present-ness or the past-ness of the event is
coupled with the future postulation (hypothetical
construction) of the event. Because the future supposition
of the event is treated in the context of the timeless is, it
seems that one can move from this timeless sense of truth
to the claim that the future contingency must now in fact be

---

[1] Pears, "Time, Truth And Inference", p. 5.
[2] This is exactly what we noticed about Castaneda's principle.

presently true as a coming reality. After all, what is logically true cannot not be true. Pears comments:

> Now we should not say that the antecedent event determined the consequent event unless we believed that the hypothetical was true. But from this it does not follow that it is the truth of the hypothetical of the truth of any other sentence which determines the consequent event. Nor could it follow. For the timeless cannot determine. Nor does "determine" here mean "makes the opposite logically impossible", but "makes the opposite causally impossible." For the inference now leads to a novel conclusion and therefore forfeits logical certainty and affects to follow the track of causal necessity.
>
> . . . .
>
> But we should say that it was logically impossible for the consequent event not to happen only if we had been given not only the truth of the antecedent, but also the truth of the hypothetical. But unfortunately we never are given the truth of the hypothetical until we have been given the truth of the consequent . . . So, though we have a lever in the present, we have no fulcrum until the future event has happened. And then the lever and the fulcrum are no longer needed.[1]

Dating Truth-Values

All of this logical analysis justifies our preceding remarks about Kretzmann's objection that at any given time, an agent must necessarily be ignorant of something. At this point we can clear up the *Dating* objection. Pike raises this objection when he says that dating the truth-value of a statement which already contains a temporal indexical expression is "obscuristic".[2] We may state the objection as follows:

---

[1] Pears, "Time, Truth And inference", p. 11.
[2] Pike, *Timelessness*, p. 74.

To say that 'Event statement E is true at t_2' fixes its truth-value. It is simply confusing to continue to debate whether or not 'E is true at t_2' is true at t_1. And if the truth-value of the statement is fixed, then God knows its truth-value.

Pike claims that foreknowledge requires the 'Jones does A at t_2' is true at t_1 so that God knows at t_1 what will occur at t_2. But he claims that this premise is confused for God could know 'Jones does A at t_2' at t_1 without it being true at t_1 that 'Jones does A at t_2'. He dismisses the foreknowledge solution we have been proposing as a confusion about temporal indexicals. However, Pike does believe that God is essentially omniscient (i.e. God knows all true and only true propositions and God would not be God if this were not the case) and he holds a strong connection between knowledge and truth (i.e. knowing that p entails that p).

Therefore, he cannot avoid reference to temporal indexicals by distinguishing between belief in p and the truth of p when he is talking about an omniscient being, unless he makes the same mistakes which we discovered in the Ordinary Language objection. Pike argues as follows: 'Jones does A at t_2' is true. Because it is true, God knows it. But God knows it as a timeless truth. So, while it is true *for us* to say that God knows this proposition at t_1, it is not true that the proposition must be true at t_1. This is because the reference to t_1 is a reference to the temporal location of the questioner (one of us), but not to God or to God's knowledge. God's knowledge of tenseless truths cannot be dated.

By now the general pattern of criticism of such an argument should be clear. First, the argument depends on *retroactive* assignment of truth-values to future contingencies. Secondly, it trades on the same weak and strong distinctions of 'know' which we identified in the analysis of Swinburne's position. Thirdly, its assumption that timeless truths can be formulated which show no dependence on temporal expressions has been shown to be fallacious. Such an assumption clearly invokes a two-logic system in which one level deals with the knowledge of timeless truths and the other deals with temporal reality with the provision that temporal indexicals are not unique referential devices and can be eliminated without loss of information. And finally, Pears comments on the "ontological diploma" of events show that Pike's assumption that 'Jones does A at t_2' is *true* removes the future hypothetical character from this statement. We need not elaborate these criticisms here since their application to Pike's position follows without difficulty from the previous analysis. However, it is important to point out that Pike's mistakes at this point have considerable influence on his later defense of the distinction between necessary and contingent infallibility.[1]

We have shown that the logician will not be able to sustain a reply to Kretzmann based on the requirement of mathematical logic that every proposition must be either timelessly true or timelessly false. It is perfectly appropriate for us to speak of proposition p concerning a future contingency being indefinite in its truth-value now. It is precisely this sort of indefiniteness which gives rise to Kretzmann's observation. It may be necessary for the construction of mathematical logic to *stipulate* that all propositions within the calculus must have explicit truth-values. But it does not follow that the logician can therefore assign truth-values to *all* propositions nor does it follow that *all* propositions have definite truth-values at any given time. On this ground, Lucas is right when he says, "We do not know, and cannot in principle know, what the truth was, until the event in question has actually come true".[2]

---

[1] See below, Chapter 11
[2] Lucas, *Freedom Of The Will*, p. 68.

We may now turn our attention to the theological implications of these findings. We notice immediately that Swinburne has demonstrated only that Kretzmann's argument is invalid when interpreted for statements about knowledge claims based in the past (and therefore know either to be true or false). We have given logical support to Kretzmann's argument when it addresses knowledge claims about future events. And on this basis, the conclusion drawn by Swinburne must be wrong for he clearly implies that God has knowledge of all future states of the world on equal footing with His knowledge of all past states. How else could Swinburne describe omniscience as the ability to answer any question concerning the entire durational history of the world?[1]

Temporal Omniscience

Swinburne's intention in his reply to Kretzmann was to show that it is logically coherent to say of a person *P* that he is omniscient at time *t* if "at *t P* knows of every true proposition that it is true".[2] But this claim is subject to crucial ambiguities which emerge from our previous analysis. If we take account of these, two workable alternatives for a general definition of omniscience are available:

{1} at *t P* knows of every true proposition (every timelessly true proposition and every possible present or past

---

[1] There is, of course, the possibility that God knows all future states of the world because they are causally determined. We have shown only that they are not logically or epistemologically necessary. However, since Swinburne rejects such all-embracing causal determinism, this position cannot serve as justification for *his* claim about God's knowledge of the future.

[2] Swinburne, *Coherence*, p. 162.

temporally necessarily true proposition) that it is (logically) true.

{2} at *t* P knows of every true proposition (every timelessly true proposition and every possible temporally true proposition whether past, present or future) that it is (logically) true.

The first reading suggests that some propositions of the temporal matrix are now necessary truths but others are as yet undetermined. God knows all of those truths of the temporal matrix which are determined (which is all that anyone could know) but God *does not, and could not*, know those which are now indefinite. The second reading considers every true proposition outside of its temporal matrix and suggests that because every proposition which was, is or will be temporally true has some fixed truth-value at some time, all such propositions may be considered as tenselessly true. Thus, God *could* know all true propositions (past, present and future) regardless of whether or not He actually does. Both readings ascribe to God knowledge of what is strictly timelessly true and both readings also allow God knowledge of any future events which are now fixed in their causes.[1] In terms of a general theory, we have the following possibilities:

{1} God knows of all truths which are strictly timelessly true that they are logically true

{2} God knows of all temporal truths which are causally determined that they are temporally necessarily true.

---

[1] For the sake of simplicity, the condition of knowledge of causally determined events will not be treated here. This condition falls outside the scope of the *logic* of the problem and will be treated in the next chapter.

{3} God knows of all other present and past temporally true propositions that they are true, and that, as a result of the order of the temporal matrix, both of these classes of propositions are now temporally necessarily true.

AND EITHER

> {4a} God knows of all possible temporally true propositions (past, present or future) the definite truth-value of each proposition and therefore He knows that they are temporally necessarily true,[1]

OR

> {4b} God does not know (and could not know) the definite truth-value of those possible temporal propositions concerning as yet unrealized and undetermined future events.

Swinburne's remarks support the proposal of {4a}. This blurs the distinction between the contexts of the word 'true'. On this reading it is possible to suggest that what God knows <u>is</u> the case has the same range as what can be assigned the logical status 'true' and this guarantees knowledge of all future (although obviously not future to God) contingent (although again not contingent to God) events.

But our considerations of the logical structure of the fatalist argument reveal that of the two possibilities, only {4b} is applicable to temporal knowers. This point becomes even clearer if we suppose that {4a} is a coherent possibility. For if we suppose that a temporal God does in fact know the definite truth-value of every possible temporal proposition, then that implies that He transcends the noetic limits which other temporal creatures experience.

---

[1] Of course, this condition would have to be qualified to avoid the foreknowledge problem but this qualification comes after the fact that God could know all temporal truths. In that respect, we have suggested that the qualification is unnecessary.

We should then expect that some argument could be produced which would demonstrate how this is possible for a temporally conditioned consciousness. Swinburne makes some suggestions in this direction when he says that God might see the whole history of the world at a glance; that He might hold it in His mind in the same manner that I know what I am now looking at. This description is very close to the suggestions made by Boethius and Aquinas that God "takes in the whole of time; and therefore God's present gaze is directed to the whole of time, and to all that exists in any time, as to what is present before him".[1] It seems to give support to the view that God has a direct intuition of the truth of every temporal proposition because He sees every event in its present occurrence and therefore knows the definite truth-value of every proposition concerning these events. But this is uncomfortably close to the formulation derived from a doctrine of timeless omniscience - a doctrine Swinburne finds inadequate.[2]

Prior makes some remarks which are pertinent to this point. He gives a refined formulation of the traditional Christian doctrine of omniscience. He rightly claims that this traditional formulation has always held the belief that God knows everything that is true. Thus:

(1) For every p, if p then God knows that p.[3]

Prior then raises the question:

In this statement that for every p, if p then God knows that p, are we to understand this verb 'knows' as a verb in the present tense, or are we not?[4]

---

[1] Aquinas, *Summa Theologiae*, Vol. 4, p. 33.
[2] Cf. Swinburne, *Coherence*, pp. 215-222.
[3] Prior, "Formalities of Omniscience", p. 27.
[4] Ibid., p. 29.

Prior raises this question in order to criticize the view of Aquinas on timeless omniscience. But his remarks are helpful in grasping what it means for God to be omniscient in a temporal context as well. He notes that if we choose to interpret the verb 'knows' as an ordinary present-tense verb, we shall also have to treat the verb 'is' in 'God is omniscient' in the same manner. And if, at the same time, we wish to maintain that God's omniscience is permanent and unalterable (in the manner in which Swinburne suggests that God could answer any question we might wish to put to Him), then we will need to expand the formula:

(1) For every p, if p then God knows that p.

to the formula:

(2) It is, always has been, and always will be the case that for all p, if p, if p then God knows that p.[1]

In this way, instantiations of p would range through all past, present and future cases showing that God knows *now* what was, is and will be the case. Prior suggests that anyone who is committed to statement (2) is also committed to statement (3) that:

(3) If, at any time, it was the case at that time that it would be the case that p, then God knew at that time that it would be the case that p.

This raises the question whether or not the believer in God's omniscience as defined in statements (2) and (3) is also committed to statement (4):

---

[1] Formulae (2), (3), (3a) and (4) cited from Prior, "Formalities of Omniscience", pp. 29-30.

(4) For all *p*, if (it is the case that) *p*, God has always known that it would be the case that *p*.

And this, notes Prior, does not follow directly from (3) unless we add the intermediate step (3a) that:

(3a) For all *p*, if (it is the case that) *p*, then it has always been the case that it would be the case that *p*.

So, if (3a) is true, then (4) is true and if (3a) is false, then (4) is false for any doctrine of omniscience which is based on the formula expressed in (2). How, then, might we go about determining the truth or falsity of (3a)? For the truth or falsity of (3a) is clearly the crucial point in determining the logic of the doctrine of omniscience with respect to the future. As Prior says:

> For if (3a) is false, that means that in some cases in which it *is* the case that *p*, it nevertheless *hasn't* always been the case that *p* would be the case, and if this hasn't always *been* true, then clearly neither God nor anyone can have *known* it to be true. So that at this point everything really depends on whether for every *p* that *is* the case, it has always been the case that it would come to pass that *p*, or as I sometimes loosely put it, whether whatever *is* the case *has always been going to be* the case.[1]

Prior's formulation of the argument is in line with Kretzmann's objection. Prior is interested in those cases where the theologian is inclined to say that God knew the truth of some statement in advance of the event referred to by the statement. What Prior questions in the terms of (3a) is the general case of the objection raised by Kretzmann

---

[1] Prior, *Formalities of Omniscience"*, pp. 30-31.

when he says that "at any instant an agent must be ignorant of something".[1]

    With Prior's question we have now come full circle. We began with the Ordinary Language objection, analyzed its impact on temporal indexical arguments, remarked on Swinburne's and Castaneda's critique, noted with the problems could be reduced to the issue of Logical Fatalism, applied that critique to the theological picture of God's omniscience and returned to Kretzmann *via* Prior. With this circle we have been able to show that statement (3a) is, indeed, false. It is not the case that for all *p*, if *p* then it has always been the case that it would be the case that *p*. In at least one significant sense, namely in the context T_t with reference to future contingencies, what will be the case is undecided until it is the case. So it is not true that whatever is the case has always been going to be the case. Prior makes some important observations about the implications that all of this has for discussion of the logical status of statements about future contingencies. He notes that in one sense the future *is just as unalterable as the past* for

> . . . nothing can be said to be truly 'going-to-happen' (futurism) until it is so 'present in its causes' as to be beyond stopping; until that happens, neither 'It will be the case that *p*' nor 'It will be the case that not *p*' is strictly speaking true.[2]

> . . . in an important sense of 'truths' there are no contingent truths; once a thing reaches the status of a 'truth' there can be no going back on it; though there are 'contingencies', i.e. matters of which it is not yet either that they will be the case or that they will fail to be the case.[3]

---

[1] As cited in Swinburne, *Coherence*, p. 163.
[2] Prior, "Formalities of Omniscience", p. 38.
[3] *Ibid.*, p. 42.

It is essential that Prior places the discussion of the unalterability of the future and the impossibility of contingent *truths* in the context of a *tensed* language. For unalterability is a function of 'when it happens' or 'until it happens', not a function of some timeless necessity. And the sense in which there are no contingent truths is also a matter of the truth in question actually coming to pass so that there is 'no going back on it'; no other possibility. In the context of tensed language, none of this compromises the assertion that the future remains open and unknowable. In the same article, Prior says:

> But the presentness, pastness or futurity of states of affairs does of course vary with *time*, i.e. it is itself a tensed matter-- .
> . . So I don't understand what is meant by saying that contingent future occurrences are neither contingent nor future *as* God sees them, though I do understand what would be meant if it were said that they are neither contingent nor future *when* God sees them. How, in fact, could God *know* a state of affairs to be present and beyond alteration, until it *is* present and beyond alteration . . .[1]

A Formal Definition

What do we say then about the supposition that it is possible to give some sense to the notion of a temporal God who nevertheless transcends the noetic limitations of time? We must say that the stronger the claim that God knows the truth of temporally conditioned propositions about future contingencies, the closer such a claim must embrace a commitment to the doctrine of timelessness. And since we have argued that timelessness is not only inconsistent with the idea of personhood but is internally incoherent in relation to acts of cognition, it should be obvious that the only logically acceptable view of omniscience for a

---

[1] Ibid., pp. 43-44.

Christian God is one in which God logically cannot know the definite truth-values of propositions about some future events. As a result of the logic of temporality, knowledge of the future is restricted for any temporal agent. But that does not mean that a temporally omniscient being is restricted in all of the ways in which temporal human agents are. We must, therefore, fill out the doctrine of temporal omniscience in order to counteract any misunderstandings which might result from the rather startling claim that God cannot know certain significant things about the future. In this regard, we may make the following points:

(1) When we say that God is ignorant of the as yet unrealized and undetermined future contingencies, we do not mean that He suffers from some defect of intellect. It is not the case that knowledge of future contingencies could be had but, because of some imperfection, God does not have it. We have shown that knowledge of future contingencies is a logical impossibility given the temporal framework of our world. It is no defect in God's omniscience that He does not know these things. We are only asserting that if there are events which are not causally determined, logically certain and temporally necessary, then knowledge of these events is, in principle, impossible.

(2) It must also be pointed out that the logical limit encountered in the case of future contingencies does not affect the other areas covered by omniscience. It is still possible that God exhaustively and completely knows all strictly timeless truths and all past and present temporal truths. Moreover, it is reasonable to suggest that God knows every conceivable future possibility for God is able to draw His inferences (if this is an appropriate characterization) from an absolutely

exhaustive knowledge of the past and present. Obviously, if an event is a direct casual result of the past and/or present conditions, God would know that such an event is causally determined. In some sense, temporal omniscience does include knowledge of certain future events. And it would be reasonable to suggest that God could know (in the weak sense of 'know') about future contingencies as well, but this must be understood as *fallible* predictive knowledge based on the evidence at hand.

(3) God's omniscience does not stand alone. In relation to omnipotence, it implies that God knows every future act that He intends to do at time t for God's omnipotence can guarantee that such future acts will occur. Nothing except God Himself can prevent God from doing what He decides to do. But this does not mean that God's intentions are permanently fixed and of the same class as timeless truths. For intentions are temporal actions. And as expressions of temporal truths they can change their truth-values as the agent changes his mind. But a change in intention does not entail that God knew something which was false at an earlier time simply because it is not true at a later time. For such a suggestion would merely reinstate the ambiguity we have uncovered concerning the temporal and logical contexts of 'true'. God's knowledge of His own intentions is indexically related to the present moment. It is not a statement of unalterability.

(4) Since the doctrine of infallibility goes hand-in-hand with the doctrine of omniscience, we would expect it to undergo temporal qualification as well. God is infallible in the sense that at any given time t it is impossible that God could be mistaken about what He knows with certainty to be true at time t. Such a

doctrine of infallibility allows for alteration in the tensed matrix of the temporal context of 'true' without suggesting that God was wrong about some belief which He held as true at time t_{-1} but which He does not hold as true at time t.

We can formalize these features in a definition of temporal omniscience in the following way:

Df.   A person P is omniscient at time t if and only if he knows at time t of every proposition which is true at time t that it is true, and he knows of every proposition about a time later than t which is such that what it reports is physically necessitated by some cause at t or earlier, that it is true and he knows the logical limitations entailed by his knowing with certainty only these things.

CHAPTER 11

TWO FURTHER DIFFICULTIES

In order to complete our defense we must now turn to two remaining issues: the thesis of causal determinism and Augustine's counter-solution to the problem of foreknowledge and free will. We have already anticipated some of the results of the forthcoming discussion on determinism by including in the formal definition of temporal omniscience a statement concerning knowledge of events that are physically necessitated. But if the general thesis of determinism is true, it makes any appeal to *divine* foreknowledge unnecessary, as we shall see. Augustine's solution, that God simply knows what we will *freely* choose to do, has already been anticipated in the treatment of some of the issues of the Ordinary Language objection. However, it needs to be handled as a genuine counter-solution because it raises two significant problems for this study: first, it apparently provides a workable solution without requiring changes in the definition of omniscience or reconsideration of truth-value assignments, and secondly, it calls in question the very necessity of this study of time and knowledge.

Determinism

Knowledge of cause and effect can give knowledge of the future in an entirely unproblematic way. There is a case in which limited omniscience allows a certain kind of foreknowledge regardless of considerations about a general thesis of causal determinism. That is to say, if event E at some time in the future (t_2) is the strict causal result of factors a through n and those factors occur at times prior to

t_2 but not after God's present temporal location (t_1), then God knows that event E is completely determined by factors a through n (all of which He knows at time t_1). In this respect and only in this respect, God knows with certainty the true propositions referring to event E in advance of its occurrence. On these grounds, even if determinism as a general thesis is false it is still reasonable to suggest that some events may be determined and that God knows the truth concerning each determined event.

But this possibility of genuine foreknowledge could not be a threat to human freedom unless it could be shown that all of the acts of human beings are determined by prior conditions and strict causal laws. The possibility of genuine foreknowledge within the limits of temporal omniscience requires no commitment to the truth or falsity of such a claim. It only shows that if such a claim is true, there are no logical restrictions preventing God from knowing all future events. In fact, if causal determinism could be shown to be true, we could dispense with *divine* foreknowledge altogether. Laplace could easily fulfill the conditions of omniscience. Given correct antecedent conditions and causal laws, any human agent could infallibly predict every event in the future and know with certainty every event in the past since fully specifiable state descriptions would be available in either "direction" of the temporal order.

In one sense, then, arguments concerning causal determinism do not raise problems for temporal omniscience. However, the general thesis of determinism does stand in contradiction to the notion of human freedom. Because of this, it is appropriate to make some remarks on the issue. These can be, at best, of a most abbreviated nature.

It should be noted that no compelling arguments have yet been given to establish the general thesis of causal determinism. In fact, recent work in the philosophy of science has raised questions about the very possibility of fulfilling the conditions required by such a thesis. There are, for example, serious difficulties involved in the requirement that one have perfect information about any single state of the universe. There are also problems with the notion of the causal regress, the formulation of the system and the implied reconstruction of ordinary language. Theologically, of course, there are substantial reasons for rejecting the general thesis. And on a strictly logical level, Lucas has given an argument based on the implications of Godel's theorem which shows that the thesis is, in principle, impossible.[1] Nevertheless, the philosophical debate continues. It is unnecessary for us to enter into it here. But we can usefully pursue some arguments concerning possible reinterpretations of our previous analysis of truth-values which are directly related to problems of causal determinism. In this regard, the best (and possibly only) example is found in Leibniz.

Leibniz on Hypothetical Necessity

Leibniz' attempt to resolve the conflict between foreknowledge and free will introduces the concept of *hypothetical necessity*.

> They say what is foreseen cannot fail to exist, and they say so truly; but it follows not that what is foreseen is necessary, for *necessary truth* is that whereof the contrary is impossible or implies contradiction. Now this truth which states that I shall write tomorrow is not of that nature. Yet supposing that God foresees it, it is necessary that it come to pass; that is, the consequence is necessary, namely, that it exist, since it has been foreseen; for God is infallible. This is what is termed

---

[1] It would be impossible to cite even a small part of the relevant literature here. I choose, therefore, to refer the reader to a general defense against determinism which I believe to be thorough and adequate. From it, further exploration of the issue follows with ease. See J. R. Lucas, *The Freedom Of The Will*, Chapters 16-28.

hypothetical necessity. But our concern is not this necessity: it is an *absolute necessity* that is required, to be able to sway that an action is necessary, that it is not contingent, that it is not the effect of a free choice.[1]

George Parkinson distinguishes Leibniz' notion of hypothetical necessity from absolute necessity in the following manner:

> 1. Absolute necessity "is simply logical necessity, and for Leibniz a truth is logically necessary when its opposite is or implies a self contradiction".
> 2. Hypothetical necessity is "something which is itself contingent, but which is necessary *given that, assuming that* such and such is the case". [2]

For example, this present state of affairs may be hypothetically necessary if a different state is logically possible but, given the preceding circumstances, only a state such as the one which now exists could actually arise. That is to say, given such-and-such a set of preceding circumstances (which could conceivably have been different), the present state of affairs logically follows.

In relation to our problem, Leibniz uses this notion to undermine the apparent determinism of God's infallible foreknowledge by showing that the actual state of the world is the result of hypothetical necessity, not logical necessity. This means that the present state description of the world could have been otherwise, provided that there were other antecedent conditions. He argues that the possibility of alternative antecedents supports the claim that human freedom exists. God's infallible foreknowledge does not

---

[1] Gottfried Wilhelm von Leibniz, *Theodicy*, trans. by E. M. Hubbard (Indianapolis, Ind.: Bobbs-Merrill, 1966), p. 47.
[2] George H. R. Parkinson, *Leibniz on Human Freedom*, Studia Leibnitiana Sondergheft 2 (Wiesbaden, W. Germany: Franz Steiner Verlag, 1970), p. 8.

imply absolute necessity (which would make any other state description self-contradictory) but only implies that given the preceding conditions (the opposite of which is not self-contradictory), God infallibly knows that such-and-such a state will arise.

Stuart Hampshire raises an objection to this statement by proposing a case where a man is bound by robbers who then proceed to steal his possessions.[1] The proposition, "Jones does not prevent the robbery' (where Jones is the victim), is certainly not a logically necessary one, yet it is hypothetically necessary since, given the preceding conditions, Jones cannot prevent the robbery. Hampshire points out that the statement, 'Jones is *free* to prevent the robbery', still is not true even if the conclusion of the preceding conditions is only hypothetically necessary. Thus Hampshire says that Leibniz' argument fails because 'we need for freedom more than the mere logical possibility of the alternatives, which is all that Leibniz gives us".[2]

Pike adds that Leibniz' application of the logical distinction between necessary and contingent to the problem of foreknowledge and free will is irrelevant to the question of moral freedom. Pike admits that Leibniz is correct in claiming that God's foreknowledge does not make any human action necessary; it only means that "all that will follow from [God's infallible foreknowledge] is that 'Jones does A at T2' is true, not that it is *necessarily true*".[3] But Leibniz' observation here is beside the point, since the contrast with which the problem is concerned is not whether the proposition is necessary or contingent in a

---

[1] Stuart Hampshire, *The Age Of Reason: The Seventeenth Century Philosophers* (New York: New American Library, 1956), p. 167.
[2] Stuart Hampshire, *The Age Of Reason: The Seventeenth Century Philosophers* (New York: New American Library, 1956), p. 167.
[3] Pike, *Timelessness*, pp. 61-62.

logical sense but whether the action is necessary or *voluntary*. That is to say, even if the proposition describing an action is hypothetically necessary in the Leibnizian sense, the question, "Is such a state of affairs described in the proposition necessary or voluntary?", has not been answered. These two dichotomies represent independent considerations. It is just this realization which is reflected in Hampshire's criticism. What is at issue is not logical contingency but the pragmatic ability to act otherwise.[1] As Kenny suggests, "in order for me to be able to do an action freely, it is necessary that it should be within my power not to do that action".[2] In this framework, if an action is necessary, then it is not voluntary. But making this distinction clear has no essential bearing on the logical status of the proposition expressing the action. What we wish to know concerning the foreknowledge problem are the logical consequences for human action which follow from God's foreknowledge, not the logical status of the propositions involved (although the logical status of the propositions can have a bearing on the notion of omniscience, as we have seen). Leibniz' introduction of the notion of hypothetical necessity does not solve the issue of moral freedom. As Pike comments:

> Let it be *contingently* true that Jones does A at T2. Let it be contingently true that Yahweh exists at T1 and (again contingently) that Yahweh is God. It follows that Yahweh is

---

[1] Cf. Leibniz, *Selections*, ed. By Philip Wiener (New York: Charles Scribner's Sons, 1951), p. 332, "For absolutely speaking, our will as contrasted with necessity, is in a state of indifference, being able to act otherwise, or wholly to suspend its action, either alternative being and remaining possible". Leibniz' inconsistency in application of this definition of moral freedom creates the need for a concept like hypothetical necessity.

[2] Kenny, "Divine Foreknowledge And Human Freedom", p. 257.

essentially omniscient. It follows too that Yahweh believes at
T1 that Jones does A at T2.   This latter is a *contingent*
statement. We can now conclude that it is *contingently* true at
T2 that it is not within Jones's power to refrain from doing A.[1]

This objection is not the only difficulty facing the
Leibnizian account. If we take seriously Leibniz' thesis
that this present world is the logical result of the original
preconditions set up at creation, then the only actual
voluntary choice was God's initial decision to begin this set
of preconditions rather than some other. After that creative
act, everything else follows from absolute necessity—a
necessity predicated upon the physical laws established at
the creation.   The only sense in which hypothetical
necessity applies to this world is the sense in which God
could have chosen to begin with a different set of
preconditions. According to Leibniz, every state of affairs
within the temporal order can be pushed back to these
initial preconditions.   Insofar as these preconditions
constitute a system, they entail a general thesis of causal
determinism—a thesis which makes *divine* action
unnecessary.   Without constituting a formal system,
Leibniz' solution fails to produce the required explanatory
sequence.

Ultimately, Leibniz seems to rule out even this
application of hypothetical necessity for he argues that the
principle of sufficient reason allows God only the single act
of creating the best of all possible worlds. Leibniz' notion
of all true propositions being analytic is certainly crucial
here. Such a notion would make propositions describing
events like creation analytic. And this proposition is the
hypothesis upon which all else is conditioned. If Leibniz is
to be consistent at this point, it seems odd indeed that he
should wish to speak of *hypothetical* necessity based on

---

[1] Pike, *Timelessness*, p. 62.

analytic truths.   In fact, given this notion of truth, the postulation of the free choice of God in creating seems somewhat absurd.

Leibniz makes one other move to try to reconcile foreknowledge and free will. In *Discourse on Metaphysics*, he argues that God foresees all the possible future free acts (all of the logically possible alternatives) and then creates only those beings whose future free acts are what He desires.   From the moment of creation, these logically contingent acts become epistemologically certain, but only from God's point of view.

> God in concurring in our actions ordinarily does no more than follow the laws which he has established, that is to say he conserves and produces our being continually, so that thoughts happen to us spontaneously or freely in the order which the notion of our individual substance carries with it in which they could be seen from all eternity.   Further, by virtue of the decree which he has made that the will should always tend to the apparent good, expressing or imitating the will of God in certain particular respects with regard to which this apparent good always has some truth in it, he determines our will to the choice of that which seems the better, nevertheless without necessitating it.[1]

It seems that there is only one way in which this solution can avoid the criticisms which we have already raised.   If Leibniz understands statements about human actions to have different logics for the actor and the observer, then it may be possible to make some sense of the thesis that God determines our choices without necessitating them.[2] Unfortunately, Leibniz' claims that all

---

[1] Gottfried Wilhelm von Leibniz, *Discourse on Metaphysics*, trans. by Peter Lucas and Leslie Grint (Manchester: University of Manchester Press, 1953), p. 49.

[2] Such a suggestion is treated in D. M. MacKay, "On The Logical Indeterminacy Of A Free Choice," *Mind*, LXIX (January, 1960), 31-40.

true statements are analytic, that the principle of sufficient reason restricts God's initial choice and that God stands outside of the temporal order seem to undermine any satisfactory elaboration of this two-logics suggestion. At any rate, Leibniz does not specify how such a suggestion is to be understood.

It should be clear that Leibniz' question concerning foreknowledge and free will has been reduced to the question of whether or not God created the world in such a manner that every action is predetermined. Leibniz' thesis of logical determinacy answers this question in the affirmative. Our analysis shows that these logical considerations can be reduced to causal considerations. But we are under no obligation to believe that the general thesis of causal determinism is true. If it were true, considerations of *divine* foreknowledge become irrelevant. Nevertheless, the understanding which we gathered as a result of criticizing Leibniz' distinctions can be usefully applied to the last problem our proposal faces.

Augustine On Freedom

Augustine's solution to the problem is put forward in Book III of *De Libero Arbitrio*.[1] He argues that God has genuine foreknowledge of actions and events but such foreknowledge does not have deterministic implications because it is foreknowledge of what human being *freely will choose* to do. He suggests that this divine prescience should be understood in the same manner as my knowing what someone else is going to do tomorrow. Since my knowing that Jones is going to mow his lawn tomorrow in no way determines that Jones must mow his lawn

---

We have also given indications of the criticism of this solution in our note on Helm (see above, Chapter 9, page 192.
[1] Augustine, *De Libero Arbitrio*, III, 2-3 (pp. 168-174).

tomorrow, my foreknowledge of such an event does not entail Jones' inability to do otherwise. That is to say, there seems to be no logical necessity, and there certainly is no causal necessity, that Jones could not do otherwise in spite of the fact that I know he will not. Foreknowledge understood in this way would certainly be theologically acceptable to the tradition for it places no restrictions upon human moral agency and still allows omniscience to include the widest range of possible facts. Moreover, it is not necessary to deny that God really has genuine *fore-*knowledge. And it seems to avoid the pitfalls of a two-logics systems. But it calls for revision of the infallibility premise and, as we shall see, that revision points out a telling objection.

Pike recognizes that there are crucial differences between the human and divine cases in Augustine's account. He suggests a case where Smith (a special human knower, e.g. a crystal-ball gazer) knows at t_1 that Jones will do A at t_2. He says that this means that Smith "correctly believes" at t_1 that Jones does A at t_2.

> It follows, of course, that Jones *does* A at T2. If he did not, we could not say that Smith knew (i.e., *correct y* believed) at T1 that Jones does A and T2. But now let's inquire about what Jones was *able to do* at T2. I see no reason to deny that it was within Jones's power at T2 to refrain from doing A— understanding this to be the power at T2 so to act that the belief held by Smith at T1 was false. If we suppose that Smith *knew* at T1 that Jones does A at T2 and, *as an additional contingent fact*, that the belief held by Smith at T1 was true. What appears to be a single contingency, *viz.*, the fact that Smith *knew* something at T1, really involves two contingencies, *viz.*, the fact that Smith held a certain belief at T1 and, secondly, that fact that that belief is true. When we

raise the question of what Jones is able to do at T2, we must
agree, of course, that it was not within Jones's power at T2 so
to act that Smith did not believe as he did at T1. But, as
regards the *second* contingency involved in Smith's
knowledge (i.e., the fact that the belief is true) there appears to
be no reason why we might not assign Jones the power at T2
to act in such a way that this second contingency fails.
Paradoxical though it may seem (and it seems paradoxical
only for a moment) Jones can be assigned the power at T1 so
to act that what was in fact knowledge at T1 was not
knowledge but false belief. This is simply to say that Jones
can be assigned the power at T2 so to act that the belief held
by Smith at T1 (which was in fact true) was (instead) false.
We are required only to add that since Smith's belief was, *in
fact*, true (i.e., was, *in fact*, knowledge) Jones did not, *in fact*,
exercise this power. If Smith believes at T1 that Jones does A
at T2, then as long as Jones does not exercise the power he has
at T2 to refrain from doing A, Smith may be described as
having *known* (correctly believed) at T1 that Jones does A at
T2.[1]

Pike claims that once these two contingencies are
distinguished, the essential difference between divine
foreknowledge and human foreknowledge is recognizable.
In his view, divine foreknowledge is not compatible with
the assertion that there is an additional contingent fact that
the belief held by God is true. Infallibility and essential
omniscience mean that if God believes that p then this
logically entails that p (that p must be the case follows
necessarily from God's belief). He concludes that
Augustine's proposal will be workable only if the idea of
infallibility is modified so that it will allow the production
of the same two independent contingencies present in the
case of human foreknowledge. But that means that the
strong sense of infallibility would have to be altered so that
it would be possible to suggest that God could hold a belief
which logically could be made false (that Jones has the

---

[1] Pike, *Timelessness*, pp. 79-80.

power so to act that the belief held by God would be false). Pike raises the question whether or not God would cease to be the individual that He is if He did in fact hold a false belief. He remarks that this modified view of infallibility is inconsistent with some crucial theological claims made by Augustine (in particular, the *via negativa* predicates). In Augustine's theology, considerations of other divine attributes make this solution untenable.

The Crystal-Ball Gazer

Removed from its traditional embellishments, the solution could be a powerful alternative to our proposal. Is the notion of contingent infallibility an answer to the foreknowledge problem? We must reconsider the crystal-ball gazer example in the light of footnote 28 of Chapter 4 of Pike's book. In that footnote, Pike proposes an extension of his critique of Prior. He claims that Prior's thesis that future contingent statements are not yet true nor yet false prior to the occurrence of the event referred to precludes human foreknowledge as well as divine and that this consequence represents a *reductio ad absurdum* for Prior. Pike says:

> Surely any adequate analysis of 'knowledge' and 'voluntary action' must allow that at least in some cases one can have knowledge of how another will voluntarily act in the future.[1]

Pike uses this claim as the basis of his crystal-ball gazer case. He clearly asserts that Smith *knows* what Jones will do and that this entails that Jones does what it is that Smith knows. But this entailment is not deterministic, according to Pike, because it is a contingent fact that Smith believes that Jones will do *A* and it is another independent contingent fact that Smith's belief is true. In relation to

---

[1] Pike, *Timelessness*, p. 86, fn. 28.

voluntary action, we can then assert that even though Jones could not act in such a way that Smith did not believe as he did, he *could* still act in such a way that Smith's belief was false. Pike concludes with the strange remark that "Jones can be assigned the power at T2 so to act that the belief held by Smith at T1 (which was in fact true) was (instead) false".[1] This is certainly a claim which requires further analysis.

What are the characteristics of Smith's knowledge in this case? We may say several things about the structure of Pike's example.

{1} Smith has some special and extra-ordinary means of knowing.
{2} Smith is never wrong in his knowledge claims
{3} To say that Smith know that p is to say that Smith correctly believes that p.
{4} If Smith correctly believes that p, then it follows that p.

There are also several important observations to be made about Jones' action in this example.

{5} Jones is not able so to act that Smith did not *believe* that p.
{6} But Jones is able so to act that Smith's belief that p is false.

Several of these assertions require elaboration and analysis. {1} seems acceptable as a framework for the example. Pike feels that it is necessary in order to make the example as closely parallel to a case of divine foreknowledge as possible and, for the moment, we can grant this possibility (although we may find that beginning with a presupposition of direct, intuitive knowledge of

---

[1] Pike, *Timelessness*, p. 79.

future actions eventually causes some problems on its own).   {2} introduces a claim of infallibility.   This is crucial for the production of a genuine foreknowledge case. Pike could hardly sustain a parallel to divine foreknowledge without this premise since without the premise, knowledge of future actions seems to fit our previous analysis of ordinary usage of the weak sense of 'know' (and, consequently, would be fallible, predictive knowledge).   On the other hand, introduction of an infallibility premise into the case of human foreknowledge has far-reaching effects which will only emerge after additional examination.   {3} and {4} are both derived from the infallibility premise.   If Smith is infallible in his cognitions, then his knows that p is equivalent to saying that his belief that p is always correct.   And if his belief that p is always correct, this must mean that p always occurs (where p is and event) or that p is always true (where p is a statement).   {2}, {3} and {4} imply the following: Smith's belief that p entails p.   The entailment may be a contingent one, but without this consequence, the claim of infallibility is nonsense.   If Smith's cognitions are never wrong, then it must be the case that the actions which he believes will occur never fail to occur.

But Pike's conclusions about the voluntary character of Jones' action are in conflict with the implication of this infallibility premise.   Pike says that the claim that Smith knew at t_1 that Jones does A at t_2 is equivalent to the claim that Smith believed at t_1 that 'Jones does A at t_2' and, "as *an additional contingent fact*", that Smith's belief is true.[1]   It is certainly true that saying that Smith knows at t_1 that p is equivalent to saying that Smith believes at t_1 that p (within the context of this example).[2]

---

[1] Cf. Lewis, "Paradoxes of Time Travel", pp. 151-152.
[2] Careful attention should be given to the shifts in tense in the quotation from Pike.   Notice especially the movement from 'knew' to 'having

But is it possible, given the infallibility premise, to separate Smith's belief that *p* from the truth that *p*? In ordinary cases of human knowing, such a separation would be entirely reasonable. But that is because there seems to be no reason for supposing that Smith does, in fact, *know* (under Pike's strong sense of 'know') that *p* where *p* expresses a proposition about a future human action not causally determined by Smith or anything else.[1] Pike has not considered fully both senses of 'know' in ordinary language. He is proposing a case where Smith is a special knower. And the unusual quality of Smith's knowledge lies in the fact that he knows *with certainty* that *p*.[2] The crucial difference between the case of Smith and the case of divine foreknowledge is not a question of infallibility but a question of how infallibility is to be understood. Pike holds that Smith is *contingently* infallible. Smith believes that *p* and it just so happens that *p*. But according to Pike, this is not possible for divine infallibility. Divine infallibility is *logically necessary* infallibility. Under this interpretation, he claims that divine foreknowledge entails determinism while human foreknowledge does not. But the question we must ask is this: Does contingent infallibility make sense in this sort of argument? That is, does the proposal of

---

known' and from 'was true' to 'is true'. These shifts show that Pike is committed to what we previously called *retroactive* assignment of truth-values. We will elaborate shortly.

[1] Cf. The distinction between *meaningful* and *true*, above Chapter 10, p. 238-240.

[2] Pike begins his example by stating that if we claim only that Smith believes that Jones does *A* at t_2 it is reasonable to say that Jones could refrain from doing *A* at t_2 . But this is a case of fallible knowledge. The logical conditions covering its usage are not straightforwardly applicable to the strong sense of 'know'. However, Pike wishes to move directly from the consequences of fallible knowledge for Jones' action to an application for infallible knowledge. In this respect, he tries to use both senses of 'know; at the same time.

contingent infallibility make any difference to the actual outcome of Jones' actions?

> If Smith is contingently infallible, then {2} must be elaborated as follows:

> {2ª} While it is logically possible that Smith could be wrong in his beliefs, it just happens to be the case that Smith never is wrong in his beliefs.

But this revision implies that the conditions which Pike wishes to attribute to Jones' action do not hold. If Smith knows that Jones does A at t_2, then it follows that Jones does A at t_2. It also follows that Jones *logically* could have done otherwise, i.e. some other state of affairs is conceivable without self-contradiction. But it does not follow that Jones *actually* could have done otherwise for, as a matter of fact, if Smith knows that Jones does A at t_2, then Jones, in fact, cannot fail to do A at t_2 (as Pike himself points out). Pike's restriction of the infallibility premise offers a way around the notion of logical determinism associated with his thesis (and the historical position) of essential omniscience, but it does not provide a solution to the problem of voluntary action. It makes no difference if infallible foreknowledge is a human or divine characteristic nor if the infallibility premise is contingent or necessary. It is still the case that Jones *actually* cannot act in any way other than acting so that Smith's belief is correct. It may be logically possible that Jones could act in such a way that Smith's belief could have been false, but if Jones *in fact* acted in such a way, then even the contingent notion of infallibility would have to be discarded. And if the infallibility premise (in either form) is discarded, the problem of foreknowledge and free will cannot be generated at all.

Let us look at this situation another way. Pike allows the logical possibility that Jones might act in such a way that the belief which Smith held could have been false. That is to say, we could *assign* a truth-value to Jones' possible action which would in fact entail that Smith's belief is false because we can make this assignment on the bare logical possibility that it is not self-contradictory. Since Smith's belief is merely a contingent one, it is always logically possible that it will not be the case. In a case of necessary infallibility, it would be contradictory to assert that God believes that Jones will do *A* but it is logically possible that Jones will not do *A*. Thus, Pike wishes to overcome the determinism of the foreknowledge problem by asserting a thesis of contingent infallibility.

But all of this is complicated by the fact that Smith is (contingently, to be sure) *never wrong* in his beliefs. This claim can be understood in two ways. We might mean that in every case in the past, whenever Smith believed that *p*, it was later true that *p*. Or we might understand this claim to assert that it is omnitemporally true of Smith's cognitions that whenever Smith believes that *p*, then *p*. On the first reading, it would still make sense to say that at t_1 Smith believes that *p* will occur at t_2 but it is logically possible that *p* will not occur at t_2 and that Smith is wrong. For no matter how accurate Smith's past beliefs had been, that would not guarantee his infallibility in the next instance. In addition, the past accuracy of Smith's beliefs is a case of retroactive assignment of truth-values to tensed propositions. In Pike's example, to say that Smith *knows* that *p* says more than that he guesses correctly, infers, etc..[1]

The second reading offers the necessary guarantee. For if Smith is omnitemporally infallible, he can never (for all time) be wrong. That guarantee might still be a

---

[1] Cf. Ryle, *Dilemmas*, p. 20.

contingent one (it might just happen to be the case that snow is always white), but it is nevertheless a restriction on what can actually take place (if snow is always white, then even though there is no *logical* contradiction in saying that we can conceive of snow being red, such a *logical* possibility can never actually be the case). And in the case of Smith's belief that 'Jones does *A* at t_2', this must mean that Jones actually could not have done anything other than *A* regardless of the fact that something other than *A* was logically possible. For something other than *A* might be coherently *conceivable*, but that does not entail that it is coherently *producible*.

On the first reading the infallibility premise is not sufficiently powerful to generate the argument. Infallibility in the past is no threat to future contingencies (one might even wonder if it is really "infallibility"). On the second reading, actual (as opposed to logical) guarantees of infallibility still destroy the hope of voluntary action for more is required for voluntary action than logical possibility and that is all that Pike gives us. Suddenly this analysis by Pike looks very much like the solution which he rejected in the mouth of Leibniz. For Smith to be only contingently infallible on the second reading is still enough to make Jones' action necessary—not logically necessary, of course, but nevertheless necessary in the sense germane to the issue of moral freedom. We must conclude that Pike's claim that any adequate analysis of human knowledge must include the foreknowledge of some human action is mistaken. Pike is trying to move from the weak sense of 'know' to the strong sense without entailing the required necessity. For the foreknowledge problem cannot be generated without the additional premise of infallibility and there is no reason to suppose that human knowledge requires such a premise in any form. The crystal-ball gazer example is not sufficiently clear or strong enough to provide genuine concern over the problem of foreknowledge and free will because it is not sufficiently clear that such claims could qualify as infallible knowledge.[1] By placing the proposition of Smith's belief into the past ('knew'), Pike's retroactive assignment of truth falls prey to the confusion created by treating future contingencies as though they had ontological diplomas in a realm of timeless certainty. Pears and Gale have shown that such mistakes lead to philosophical misery. Pike is in no better position than Swinburne when he asserts that an omniscient individual "believes all true propositions".[2] But in Pike's case, these ambiguities tend to increase with time until we arrive at a position which sounds as though God can believe that p and yet it not be true that p.[3]

Conclusions

In the final analysis, Pike's affirmation that the foreknowledge problem seems unavoidable is undoubtedly correct *if* theologians continue to maintain that God is infallible and that God knows with certainty all true propositions; past, present and future. We have seen that there are good reasons for rejecting this combination. The traditional solution of timeless omniscience fails to solve the problem without creating even more serious consequences. Augustine's proposal seems to violate several conditions of moral freedom and truth-value assignment. And Pike's proposal of contingent infallibility is a difference that makes no difference. But our revised formulation of temporal omniscience derived from the

---

[1] Cf. Helm, "Divine Foreknowledge and Facts", p. 314, fn. 3 where he remarks that Pike's examples do not qualify as knowledge at all.

[2] Pike, *Timelessness*, p. 54.

[3] Pike claims that "if 'Jones does A at T2' is true, then it must be known (infallibly believed) at T1 by an omniscient being. This is not to say that it is *true at T1*—it means only that it is believed (or known) *at T1*" (Pike, *Timelessness*, p. 71).

logical consequences of the doctrine of God's personhood and the logical restrictions placed upon any tensed understanding of knowledge offers a legitimate solution to the foreknowledge problem. More correctly, it is a *dissolution* of the problem since the definition of temporal omniscience shows that God cannot have knowledge of the outcome of free human actions in advance of their performance, and without this condition, the problem does not exist. What we have shown, then, is that temporal omniscience not only accounts for the range of all possible facts known as possibilities and all actual facts known as actualities, it also is compatible with the central affirmation of God's personhood and it eliminates traditional theological puzzles which result from expanded versions of omniscience. Furthermore, it is not demeaning to God that He should face such logical restrictions for those logical restrictions are ones God chose to embrace when He freely chose to create moral agents like Himself within the temporal arena.

We may conclude this chapter by noting that the dissolution of the problem of foreknowledge and free will offers further support to the belief that we have a correct analysis of the doctrine of omniscience...This support is contextual and derivative but nevertheless important. For we began with an attempt to make sense of the traditional elaborations of immutability, timelessness and omniscience and we found that these doctrines were related to each other in significant ways. The more we pressed those relationships, the more difficult it became to maintain other theological features of the idea of a Christian God. Moreover, the problem of foreknowledge and free will was the direct result of certain inescapable implications of the traditional doctrines of omniscience and immutability. After analysis, we have shown that timelessness as an understanding of eternity offers no help toward a resolution of the resulting theological difficulties. But once we were able to break free of the metaphysics surrounding the traditional theological system, we formulated independent accounts of omniscience, personhood and eternity which we found to be consistent with each other. And that consistency had the welcome effect of eliminating the problem of foreknowledge. If the truth about God follows any of the canons of rationality, it must certainly follow the canon of internal logical consistency. This result is important for it shows not only that resolution is impossible within the traditional categories but that development of temporal categories for a theology of God fits together so well that areas of related but independent concern are also brought into the fold.

CHAPTER 12

EPILOGUE

It is, perhaps, appropriate to make some remarks about the implications this study has for wider theological concerns. We have limited our present analysis to the examination of the impact of temporality on the doctrine of omniscience. We discovered that certain logical restrictions associated with temporal omniscience dissolve the foreknowledge problem. As long as God continues to allow the freedom of other agents, He cannot know the actual outcome of the future choices of those agents in advance. He could, of course, abrogate that freedom by divine fiat but that would only entail that the class of future events which cannot now be known with certainty would be reduced to the class of events which were the outcome of God's own choices. It would not entail that God would know all future contingencies as though they were now fixed in their causes. These logical restrictions place no limits on what God can fallibly know about the future (i.e. have good reason based on present evidence to believe probable). But such knowledge is subject to continual modification.

This re-evaluation of the doctrine of omniscience leads quite naturally to some related theological topics. One large area which we have already commented on and will not explore further is the logic of the divine attributes. If omniscience is to be interpreted within the context of temporality, several of the more important divine attributes will also have to follow suit. Exploration here reaches beyond the topic of this study. Suffice it to say that some of the direction for this re-interpretation has been given in the brief discussion of the alternative account of immutability. But we may make some tentative suggestions on three topics: the notion of providence, the problem of evil and the role of Jesus.

Voluntary Chaos

Limited omniscience introduces an important element into the structure of each of these three topics. It is predicated on the logical uncertainty of the future: any actions or reactions which God might intend will have to deal with a certain amount of unavoidable chance or indeterminacy. We might call this consequence *voluntary chaos*. It is chaotic in the sense that there is no accounting for it in terms of antecedent conditions and causal laws; it is impossible to predict with certainty. That does not mean that the introduction of chance into the scheme of history is an introduction of a completely random process. At any particular point of decision, most free agents will be able to give reasons why they chose to do *A* rather than *B*. But those reasons may include completely arbitrary factors, factors which may have no other bearing on the actual choice other than as individual idiosyncrasies. Moreover, free agency may even be compatible with the hypothesis that some human actions actually are completely random. Theologically, however, the introduction of a chance element is a voluntary one in at least two senses: first, God's initial and continuing decision not to abrogate human freedom is a voluntary choice which grounds the necessary conditions for the existence of the chaotic element in history; and second, actors within the human and divine drama each sustain their own conditions of chaos as long as they continue to act as free agents.

The Doctrine of Providence

Voluntary chaos poses a *prima facie* difficulty for the Christian doctrine of providence for it entails that to some extent God's creation is out of His own control. Insofar as God cannot know what is actually going to happen in the future, He appears to be unable to do things now which would *guarantee* that His purposes will come to pass. And the doctrine of providence certainly has the implication that God's purposes will ultimately and inevitably be realized. But this difficulty may not be insuperable for the chaotic element of the unknown future of human history depends upon God's choice to continue to grant the sustaining conditions and God holds the final trump card. Omnipotence always allows Him to curtail the existence of other free agents and reduce the number of unknown future events to those which are His and only His choices. Perhaps providence will have to be seen as a statement about this final trump card. On the other hand, if we are forced to give up the notion that God exercises providential care over His creation at every temporal moment in every possible way, we may have to relinquish a long-held belief but this might be offset by a substantial gain in understanding the interaction and shared responsibility between God and Man. For if the future history of the world depends in some real way upon the actual choices of men, then to that degree God is in fact cooperating with men to bring about His ends. And part of the responsibility of the future lies quite firmly on the shoulders of every individual man. Under these conditions, there is some truth in saying that God could not do it without us.

Yeshua ("Jesus")[1]

The concept of voluntary chaos could have its greatest impact when applied to the role of Yeshua. Its initial consequence seems to be the denial of the doctrine of *non posse peccare*. Since God cannot know for certain the future acts of free agents, it follows that He could not have known in advance that Yeshua would complete the soteriological task. This fact certainly underlines the fundamental risk which God took not only by creating other free agents but also by exposing the unity of the divine Being to the uncertainty of the human condition. One must ask what it must mean for our concept of God as personal to know that He was willing to sacrifice the triune nature of His Being in the possible failure of Jesus' mission. The theological paradox implied in the combination of the traditional idea of omniscience and Yeshua's sinlessness with the idea of Yeshua as a human free agent could be removed on these grounds. Under these conditions, it would be possible to understand Yeshua as an individual active agent working toward the reconciliation of God and His creation. None of his activities could be taken for granted as though they were fixed from all eternity in the mind of God. Understanding Yeshua in this way concentrates our attention on the prophetic character of God's deliberations. It is this element of the struggle with an unknown future that contributes to our final topic—the problem of evil.

Evil

One of the greatest embarrassments of Christian theology has been the apparent conflict between a God who is all-powerful and completely good and a creation which reveals unremitting evils. We may be able to make some

---

[1] Yeshua is the Hebrew name of the man Christians call Jesus

headway on this issue if we take seriously the suggestion that creation is out of control. Of course, as we previously noted, it is out of control because of certain voluntary choices. But it is, nevertheless, out of control. God's interaction with this creation must be based on anticipatory judgments, some of which will require alteration because they turn out not to be the case. Although I will not attempt to detail any more of the account here, I believe that it is possible to explain the existence of the evil world in spite of a good God as a function of chaos and prolepsis. Even if the account ultimately fails, the exercise would be well worth pursuing since it would reveal the necessary conditions for freedom in a world with an unknown, open and humanly uncontrollable future. We may discover a new approach that would account for the occurrence of evil without divine culpability.

Bibliography

Albritton, Rogers. "Present Truth and Future Contingency." Philosophical Review, LXVI (January, 1957), 29-46

Anselm of Canterbury, St. *Anselm of Canterbury*, Vol. One: *Monologion, Proslogion, Debate With Gaunilo and Meditation on Human Redemption*. Translated by Jasper Hopkins and Hebert Richardson. London: SCM Press, 1974.

_____. *St. Anselm's Proslogion: With A Reply On Behalf Of The Fool By Gaunilo And The Author' Reply To Gaunilo*. Translated by Mr. J. Charlesworth. Oxford: Oxford University Press, 1965.

Aquinas, St. Thomas. *Aristotle: On Interpretation: Commentary by St. Thomas Aquinas and Cajetan*. Translated by Jean T. Oesterle. Milwaukee, Wisconsin: Marquette University Press, 1962.

_____. *Basic Writings of Saint Thomas Aquinas*, Vol. One. Edited and Annotated by Anton C. Pegis. New York: Random House, 1945.

_____. *Commentary on Aristotle's Physics*. Translated by Richard J. Blackwell, Richard J. Spath and W. Edmund Thirlkel. London: Routledge & Kegan Paul, 1963.
322_____. *Summa Contra Gentiles*, Book I. London: Burns, Oats and Washbourne, 1924.

_____. *Summa Theologiae*, Vol. 2: "*Existence and Nature of God*" (Ia. 2-11), translated by Timothy McDermott. London: Blackfriars, 1964.

_____. *Summa Theologiae*, Vol. 3: "*Knowing and Naming God*" (Ia. 12-13), translated by Herbert McCabe. London: Blackfriars, 1964.

_____. *Summa Theologiae*, Vol. 4: "*Knowledge In God*" (Ia. 14-18), translated by Thomas Gornall. London: Blackfriars, 1964.

Aristotle. *On Interpretation*, in *The Organon*: *The Categories, On Interpretation, Prior Analytics*. Translated by Harold P. Cooke. Loeb Classical Library. Cambridge, Mass.: Harvard University Press, 1949.

_____. *Metaphysics*: *Books X-XIV*. Translated by Hugh Tredennick. Loeb Classical Library. London: William Heinemann, 1947.

_____. *Physica*. Vol. II of *The Works of Aristotle*. Edited by W. D. Ross. Translated by R. P. Hardie and R. K. Gaye. Oxford: Oxford University Press, 1930.

_____. *The Physics: Books 1-4*. Translated by Philip H. Wicksteed and Francis M. Cornford. Leob Classical Library. London: William Heinemann, 1963.

_____. *The Physics*: Books 5-8. Translated by Philip H. Wicksteed and Francis M. Cornford. Loeb Classical Library. London: William Heinemann, 1960.

Augustine, St. *City of God*: *Books VIII-XVI*. Translated by Gerald G. Walsh and Grace Monahan. Washington, D.C.: Catholic University of America Press, 1952.

_____. *Confessions*. Translated by Vernon J. Bourke. New York: Fathers of the Church, Inc., 1953.

_____. *De Libero Arbitrio (The Free Choice Of The Will)*, in *The Teacher, The Free Choice Of The Will, Grace And Free Will*. Translated by Robert P. Russell. Washington, D.C.: Catholic University of America Press, 1968.

_____. *De Morisbus Ecclesiae Catholicae Et De Moribus Manichaeorum (The Catholic And Manichaean Ways Of Life)*. Translated by Donald A. Gallagher and Idella J. Gallagher. Washington, D.C.: Catholic University of America Press, 1966.

_____. *De Trinitate (The Trinity)*. Translated by Stephen McKenna. Washington, D.C.: Catholic University of America Press, 1963.

_____. *De Utilitate Credendi (The Advantge of Believing)*. Translated by Luanne Meagher. New York: Fathers of the Curch, Inc., 1947.

_____. *The Happy Life*, in *The Writings of St. Augustine*, Vol. I. Translated by Ludwig Schopp. New York: CIMA Publishing Co., 1948.

Bar-Hillel, Yehoshua. "Indexical Expressions." *Mind*, LXII (July, 1954), 359-379

Barr, James. *Biblical Words for Time*. Revised Edition. Studies in Biblical Theology. First Series, No. 33. London: SCM Press, 1969.

Barrow, Isaac. *The Geometrical Lectures of Isaac Barrow*. Translated by J. M. Child (LaSalle, Ill.: Open Court Publishing Co.), 1916.

Benjamin, A. Cornelius. "Ideas of Time in the History of Philosophy." *The Voices of Time: A Cooperative Survey of Man's Views of Time As Expressed By The Sciences And By The Humanities*. Edited by J. T. Frazer. New York: George Braziller, 1966.

Boethius. *The Consolation of Philosophy*. Translated by S. J. Tester. Loeb Classical Library. Cambridge, Mass.: Harvard University Press, 1973.

_____. *The Theological Tractates: Including De Trinitate, De Fide Catholica and Quomodo Substantiae*. Translated by E. K. Rand, S. J. Tester and H. F. Stewart. Loeb Classical Library. Cambridge, Mass.: Harvard University Press, 1973.

Burkholder, Leslie. "Freedom And Omniscience." *Southern Journal of Philosophy*, 12 (Spring, 1974), 3-8.

Burnet, John. *Early Greek Philosophy*. 4th Edition. London: Adam & Charles Black, 1930.

Castañeda, Hector-Neri. "Omniscience and Indexical Reference." *Journal of Philosophy,* LXIV (April 13, 1967), 203-210.

Cherniss, H. F. "The Characteristics and Effects of Presocratic Philosophy." *Studies In Presocratic Philosophy,* Vol. I. Edited by David J. Furley and R. E. Allen. (London: Routledge & Kegan Paul) 1970.

Corburn, Robert. "Professor Malcolm on God." *Australasian Journal of Philosophy,* 41(1963), 143-162.

Cornford, Francis M. "The Invention Of Space." *The Concepts Of Space And Time: Their Structure and Their Development.* Edited by Milič Čapek. Boston Studies In The Philosophy Of Science, Vol. 22. Dordrecht, Holland: D. Reidel Publishing Co., 1956.

Cornford, Francis M. *Plato's Cosmology: The Timaeus of Plato translated with a running commentary.* London: Routledge & Kegan Paul, 1937.

Cullmann, Oscar. *Christ and Time: The Primitive Christian Conception Of Time And History.* Revised Edition. Translated by Floyd V. Filson (Philadelphia, Penn.:Westminister Press), 1964.

Danielson, Dennis. "Timelessness, Foreknowledge, and Free Will." *Mind,* LXXXVI (July, 1977), 403-432.

Dummett, Michael. "Bringing About The Past." *The Philosophy Of Time: A Collection of Essays.* Edited by Richard Gale. London: Macmillan, 1968.

Evans, C. O. *The Subject Of Consciousness* (London: George Allen & Unwin), 1970.

Findlay, J. N. "Time: A Treatment Of Some Puzzles." *The Philosophy Of Time: A Collection Of Essays.* Edited by Richard Gale (London: Macmillan), 1968.

Gale, Richard. "'Here' and 'Now'." *Basic Issues In The Philosophy Of Time*. Edited by Eugene Freeman and Wilfrid Sellars (LaSalle, Ill.: Open Court Publishing Co.), 1971.

_____. "'Is It Now Now?'." *Mind*, LXXIII (January, 1964), 97-105.

_____. *The Language of Time*. London: Routledge & Kegan Paul, 1968.

_____. "The Open Future: Introduction." *The Philosophy Of Time: A Collection of Essays*. Edited by Richard Gale. London: Macmillan, 1968.

_____. "A Reply To Oaklander." *Philosophy And Phenomenological Research*, 38 (December, 1977), 234-238.

_____. "What, Then, Is Time: Introduction." *The Philosophy Of Time: A Collection Of Essays*. Edited by Richard Gale. London: Macmillan, 1968.

Garson, James. "Here and Now." *Basic Issues In The Philosophy Of Time*. Edited by Eugene Freeman and Wilfrid Sellars. LaSalle, Ill.: Open Court Publishing Co., 1971.

Geach, Peter. *God and the Soul*. London: Routledge & Kegan Paul, 1969.

_____. *Mental Acts: Their Content And Their Objects*. London: Routledge & Kegen Paul, 1957.

Hampshire, Stuart. *The Age of Reason:* The Seventeenth Century Philosophers. New York: New American Library, 1956.

Heidel, W. A. "Qualitative Change In Pre-Socratic Philosophy." *The Pre-Socratics: A Collection Of Critical Essays*. Edited by Alexander P. D. Mourelatos (Garden City, New York: Doubleday Anchor), 1974.

Helm, Paul. "Divine Foreknowledge and Facts." *Canadian Journal of Philosophy*, 4 (December, 1974), 305-315.

_____. "Timelessness and Foreknowledge." *Mind,* LXXXIV (October, 1975), 516-527.

Hick, John. "Ontological Argument for the Existence of God." *Encyclopedia of Philosophy.* V, 538-542.

Jaeger, Werner. *Aristotle: Fundamentals of the History of His Development.* 2d. Edition. Translated by Richard Robinson. Oxford: Oxford University Pres, 1948.

_____. *The Theology of the Early Greek Philosophers.* Translated by Edward S. Robinson (Oxford: Oxford University Press), 1947.

Kahn, Charles H. "Anaximander's Fragment: The Universe Governed By Law." *The Presocratics: A Collection Of Critical Essays.* Edited by Alexander P. D. Mourelatos. Garden City, New York: Doubleday Anchor, 1974.

Kenny, Anthony. "Divine Foreknowledge And Human Freedom." *Aquinas: A Collection of Critical Essays.* Edited by Anthony Kenny. New York: Doubleday, 1969.

_____. *The Five Ways: St. Thomas Aquinas' Proofs of God's Existence.* London: Routledge & Kegen Paul, 1969.

Kerferd, G. B. "Aristotle." *Encyclopedia of Philosophy.* I, 151-162.

King-Farlow, John. "'Could God be Temporal?' A Devil's Advocacy." *Southern Journal of Philosophy,* 1 (Summer, 1963) 21-28.

Kirk, G. S. and J. E. Raven. *The Presocratic Philosophers: A Critical History With A Selection Of Texts.* Cambridge: Cambridge Univerisity Press, 1957.

Kneale, M. "Eternity and Sempiternity." *Proceedings of the Aristotelian Society,* LXIX (1968-1969), 223-238.

Kneale, William. "Time and Eternity in Theology." *Proceedings of the Aristotelian Society,* LXI (1960-1961), 87-108.

Kretzmann, Norman. "Omniscience and Immutability." *Journal of Philosophy*, LXIII (1966), 409-421.

Kuhn, Thomas S. *The Structure of Scientific Revolutions.* 2nd. Edition (Chicago: University of Chicago Press), 1970.

Leibniz, Gottfried Wilhelm von. *Discourse on Metaphysics.* Translated by Peter Luca and Leslie Grint. Manchester: University of Manchester Press, 1953.

_____. *Leibniz Selections.* Edited by Philip P. Wiener. New York: Charles Scribner's Sons, 1951.

_____. *Theodicy.* Translated by E. M. Hubbard. Indianapolis, Ind.: Bobbs-Merrill, 1966.

Leslie, John. "The Value of Time." *American Philosophical Quarterly*, 13 (April, 1976), 109-121.

Lewis, David. "The Paradoxes Of Time Travel." *American Philosophical Quarterly*, 13 (April, 1976), 145-152.

Lindley, R. C. and J. M. Shorter. *The Philosophy of Mind: A Bibliography: Part I: The Self.* Oxford: Sub-Faculty of Philosophy, 1977.

Lloyd, G. E. R. *Early Greek Science: Thales to Aristotle.* London: Chatto & Windus, 1970.

Lloyd, Genevieve. "Tense and Predication." *Mind,* LXXXVI (July, 1977), 433-438.

_____. "Time and Existence." *Philosophy*, LIII (April, 1978), 215-228.

Lucas, John R. *The Freedom Of The Will.* Oxford: Clarendon Press, 1970.

_____. *A Treatise on Time and Space.* London: Methuen & Co., 1973.

_____. "True." *Philosophy*, XXXXIV (July, 1969), 175-186.

MacKay, D. M. "On The Logical Indeterminacy Of A Free Choice." *Mind*, LXIX (January, 1960), 31-40.

McTaggart, J. M. E. "Time." *The Philosophy Of Time: A Collection Of Essays*. Edited by Richard Gale. London: Macmillan, 1968.

Mayo, Bernard. "Infinitive Verbs And Tensed Statements." *Philosophical Quarterly*, 13 (October, 1963), 289-297.

Merlan, Philip. "Neoplatonism." *Encyclopedia of Philosophy*. V, 351-359.

_____. "Plotinus." *Encyclopedia of Philosophy*. VI, 351-359.

Moen, Arthur J. "Paradigms, Language Games, and Religious Belief." *Christian Scholar's Review*, 9 (June, 1979)

Newton-Smith, William H. *The Structure of Time*.

Oaklander, L. Nathan. "The 'Timelessness' of Time." *Philosophy and Phenomenological Research,* 38 (December, 1977) 228-233.

Owen, G. E. L. "Plato And Parmenides On The Timeless Present." *The Pre-Socratics: A Collection Of Critical Essays*. Edited by Alexander P. D. Mourelatos. Garden City, New York: Doubleday Anchor, 1974.

Parkinson, George H. R. *Leibniz on Human Freedom*. Studia Leibnitiana, Sonderheft 2. (Wiesbaden, West Germany: Franz Steiner Verlag), 1970.

Pears, David F. "Time, Truth and Inference." *Proceedings of the Aristotelian Society*, LI (1950-1951), 1-24.

Penelhum, Terrence. "Divine Necessity." *Philosophy of Religion.* Edited by Basil Mitchell. Oxford: Oxford University Press, 1971.

Pike, Nelson. *God and Timelessness.* New York: Shocken Books, 1970.

Plato. Laws. Vol. IV of *The Dialogues of Plato.* Translated by B. Jowett. 4th Edition. (Oxford: Oxford University Press), 1953.

_____. *Timaeus.* Vol. III of *The Dialogues of Plato.* Translated by B. Jowett. 4th Edition. (Oxford: Oxford University Press), 1953.

Prior, Arthur. "The Formalities of Omniscience." *Papers on Time and Tense.* (Oxford: Oxford University Press), 1968.

Quinton, Anthony. *The Nature of Things.* London: Routledge & Kegen Paul, 1973.

_____. "Spaces and Times." *Philosophy,* XXXVII (April, 1962), 130-147.

Reichenbach, Hans. *Elements of Symbolic Logic.* New York: Macmillan, 1947.

Rescher, Nicholas. "On The Logic of Chronological Propositions." *Mind,* LXXV (January, 1966), 75-96.

_____. "Truth And Necessity In Temporal Perspective." *The Philosophy Of Time: A Collection Of Essays.* Edited by Richard Gale. London: Macmillan, 1968.

Russell, J. L. "Time in Christian Thought." *The Voices of Time: A Cooperative Survey of Man's Views of Time As Expressed By The Sciences And By The Humanities.* Edited by J. T. Frazer.

Ryle, Gilbert. *Dilemmas.* Cambridge: Cambridge University Press, 1969.

_____. "Plato." *Encyclopedia of Philosophy.* VI, 314-333.

Sayre, Kenneth and Frederick Crossen, eds. *The Modeling of Mind*. Notre Dame, Ind.: University of Notre Dame Press, 1963.

Schleiermacher, Friedrich. *The Christian Faith*. Translated By H. R. Mackintosh and J. S. Stewart. 2d. Edition. Edinburgh: T. & T. Clark, 1956.

Schlesinger, George. "The Reduction of *B*-Statements." *The Philosophical Quarterly*, 28. (April, 1978), 162-165.

Shoemaker, Sydney. "Time Without Change." *Journal of Philosophy*, LXVI (June 19, 1969), 363-381.

Smart, J. J. C. "Spatialising Time." *The Philosophy Of Time: A Collection Of Essays*. Edited by Richard Gale. London: Macmillan, 1968.

Swinburne, Richard. *The Coherence of Theism*. Oxford: Oxford University Press, 1977.

Talmage, Frank. "Gersonides." *Encyclopedia of Philosophy*. III, 317-318.

Taylor, Richard. "Fatalism." *The Philosophy Of Time: A Collection Of Essays*. Edited by Richard Gale. London: Macmillan, 1968.

_____. "The Problem of Future Contingencies." *Philosophical Review*, LXVI (January, 1957), 1-28.

van Fraassen, Bas. C. *An Introduction to the Philosophy of Time and Space*. New York: Random House, 1970.

Whitrow, G. J. "Time and the Universe." *The Voices of Time: A Cooperative Survey of Man's Views of Time As Expressed By The Sciences And By The Humanities*. Edited by J. T. Frazer. New York: George Braziller, 1966.

Williams, Donald C. "The Myth Of Passage." *The Philosophy of Time: A Collection Of Essays*. Edited by Richard Gale. London: Macmillian, 1968.

CPSIA information can be obtained at www.ICGtesting.com
Printed in the USA
LVOW070207140712

290066LV00008B/111/P